National Administrator Credential

For

Administrators, Managers, and Directors of Early Childhood Education & Care Centers

Fourth Edition

COPYRIGHT © 1994, 2000, 2007,
2023
The NECPA Commission, Inc.

All Rights Reserved

CONTENTS

Preface i
Introduction 1
Competency I
    History & Personal and Professional Development 3
Competency II
    An Effective Organization 20
Competency III
    Internal and External Systems 37
Competency IV
    Laws and Regulations 65
Competency V
    Staff Management and Human Resources 104
Competency VI
    Educational Programming 131
Competency VII
    Marketing, Advertising, and Public Relations 185
Competency VIII
    Financial Management 209
Competency IX
    Operational Planning and Evaluation 245
Competency X
    Leadership and Advocacy 269
Appendix 294
Abbreviations 305
Glossary 307
Sources 313
Contributors 321

Preface

The NECPA Commission, Inc. has a longstanding commitment to providing high quality early childhood education to the young children and families of America. The NECPA Commission, Inc. recognizes, and national studies have demonstrated, that one of the critical elements in this high standard of service is a professional, well-trained staff. Quality is especially dependent on the training and experience of center management. While professional credentials have existed for some time for classroom teachers, there has been no such national recognition for administrators of child care and other early learning programs.

The National Administrator Credential (NAC) course closely tracks the ten competencies (i.e., skills and abilities) covered by this text that are essential to master if one is to be a successful early childhood education administrator. This list of ten competencies was developed some years ago by Gwen Morgan of Wheelock College, and by Nancy Travis and Joe Pereault of Save the Children. Additional work on the competencies was done through a Professional Development and Training System Planning Grant from the state of Georgia.

The National Administrator Credential course has conceptual origins in Texas and came to full fruition under the leadership of the Georgia Child Care Leadership Forum. It was revised in 2004 and in 2009. The coursework incorporates the best ideas and knowledge of numerous professionals in many areas of expertise.

In rewriting the 2009 textbook, the NAC course has been organized to meet current administrative, leadership, management, and educational needs as well as best practices. Part of this redesign is the secondary option to complete the NAC on-line.

The NECPA Commission, Inc. is very proud to offer the only classroom-based national credential for administrators of child care and early childhood education programs. This course is one of the most valuable in which you will ever participate. We know you will be proud of your credential, as it will attest to your mastery of administration skills and will document your ability to perform in your profession.

Introduction

A major focus of the course is to assist administrators in understanding basic business practices and in developing a cooperative learning environment that encourages teamwork and practical optimism as a basis for the success of early childhood education centers in all areas of management and leadership. As such, this course is organized into ten broad sections encompassing the professional development competencies for administrators of early childhood education centers. The sections are designed to function as stand alones (though it is recommended that the instruction begin with the first competency).

Each section of this course is made up of related modules. Within the modules you will find the following components:

Topic – A broad description of the content contained within the module

Learning Objectives – The expected learning outcomes for the module

Guided Learning – A variety of instructional components and resources designed to guide the participant in obtaining the knowledge and skills necessary to complete the program

Self Assessment – At the end of each section you will be guided to a variety of activities to be completed prior to the next class meeting. These activities will always include reflective writing in the learning journal being kept throughout the course. Each module will direct you to the activities that should be completed in the *Course Competency Workbook* and the *Course Journal*.

Summary of Key Points – At the end of each section is a synopsis of the important points covered in that section. Use this to review.

Additional material can be found at the end of this course guide, including:

Sample Forms and Resources – A variety of relevant sample forms and resources are included for your use

Abbreviations – To assist you in more easily understanding the text

Glossary of Terms – At the end of the text is a glossary of terms for your reference.

> Because the use of dual-gender words (he or she, his or her) becomes cumbersome and difficult to read, the editors have chosen to use masculine pronouns in some places and feminine pronouns in others. The choice is strictly arbitrary and does not reflect the actual make-up of any particular group.

Competency I

History of Early Childhood Education, and Personal and Professional Development of the Child Care Professional

Competency I

History of Early Childhood Education, and Personal and Professional Development of the Child Care Professional

Learning Objectives:

- To understand the historical perspective, the milestones, and the key national organizations involved in early childhood education

- To be able to recognize the primary purposes of early childhood education in the United States

- To understand that political, social, and economic factors influence early childhood education

- To be able to list and describe the various types of early childhood care and education available to families in the community

- To reflect on, evaluate, and strengthen skills and career goals

Competency I: History & Personal and Professional Development

An Effective Administrator Knows the History and Key Milestones of the Early Childhood Education Industry. She Understands that She Works In a Dynamic and Evolving Profession that Serves Three Major Purposes of Society

Think about your history in the field of early childhood education. On a piece of paper, draw a line representing your time in the field. On the far left of the line write the year you first entered the field on the far right place today's date. Make brief notes on the line representing your personal milestones in the field – perhaps you were promoted, or completed a degree or credential.

Think about how much has changed since you entered the field. Each of us comes to this course with different experiences. Some of us have seen a lot of change, while others have just begun their careers. Would you like to learn from other's experiences, successes and errors? Would you like to be able to explain why we do things from an historical perspective? Learning about the history of early childhood education helps gain recognition of how far the field has come and such enhances our ability to be part of future change efforts.

Types of Programs

The term non-maternal care is used by some government agencies to describe care of children by anyone other than their mother. Perhaps you have heard many other terms to describe this type of care. Below are listed common terms associated with non-maternal care.

Child Care	Babysitting	Custodial Care
Day Care	After-school care/School Age Care	Reggio Inspired
Informal Care		Accredited Program
Nursery School	Laboratory Schools	Faith-based program
Pre-School	Kith and Kin Care	Learning Center
Pre-K	Montessori School	Registered Homes
Nanny Care	Head Start	Registered Centers
Family Day Care	Parent Cooperative	Learning Centers
Home Care	Mothers Morning Out	

Settings for Non-maternal Care in the United States

Each setting has particular characteristics as to sponsorship, program goals, profit status, curriculum, or organizational structure.

Private Homes	On-site Workplace (Shopping Centers, Y's, etc…)
Faith-based Programs (Churches, Synagogues)	Centers and Free Standing Facilities

Competency I: History & Personal and Professional Development

Effective Administrator Understands that Early Childhood Education Operates Within an Ever Changing Environment

The field of childhood care and education, like all other service related businesses, operates within an ever changing and often challenging environment. This environment is made up of external factors that influence how we operate and are also discussed in Competency X. Frequently we fail to realize that the political, economic, and social factors indicated in the trends of the twentieth and twenty-first centuries affect the everyday running of our centers.

Factors that An influence our operations are whether the economy is bustling, creating greater demand for early childhood education services and putting strains on our labor pool, or if the economy is in recession or a slow period lowering the demand for services. State polices affect reimbursement rates for children funded through the Child Care Development Block Grant, and, a state licensing or regulatory change regarding teachers' professional development may influence training budgets, who may be hired, and the number of staff needed if child–staff ratios are changed. All may ultimately affect tuition and fees.

The decision of school districts to offer free before and after school or extended-day care frequently has an impact on surplus income and free state preschool programs that exclude the private not-for-profit and for-profit sectors affect the number of children who may come to our programs.

There are numerous political, social, and economic factors that have the potential to influence not only the demand for childcare in the community, but also many other aspects of the operation of business. Therefore it is imperative for early childhood education administrators to keep up to date on the latest events that may affect their ability to offer high quality services.

Primary Purposes for Child Care in the United States

- Supporting employment outside the home
- Enhancing child development
- Intervening with economically disadvantaged and ethnic minority children to socialize them into the mainstream and provide needed services.

Historical Perspective

1800's

Day nurseries were established in Boston to care for children of working widows and working wives of seamen. The idea was to keep children safe and fed while the poor mother worked, education considered a secondary outcome.

> Margarethe Meyer opened the first known kindergarten in Watertown, Wisconsin in 1856. German was the language of instruction.

Elizabeth Peabody opened the first English language kindergarten in Boston in 1860. She opposed the teaching of academic subjects to the young children in her charge.

The proper learning environment and outcomes for young children were debated.

1900's

Early kindergartens and nursery schools focused on enhanced social development of middle to upper-class children with enriched environments and social experiences for a few hours a week.

World War II saw men leave their jobs to join the armed services; women become more prevalent in the workforce. As a result, child care centers became more prevalent, many were attached to plants and factories. Women remained in the workforce after WWII ended. In 2008, there were an estimated 71 million (59.3%) women over the age of 16 in the workforce.

During the 1960's educators and child development experts recognized the value of nursery schools for poor children. The Perry Preschool Project (High Scope Approach) examined the lives of 123 African-American children ages three and four who were born into poverty. Children were divided into two groups: Group One received a high quality pre-school program while Group Two received no pre-school. Over a period of time the study showed that participants in Group One:

- Experienced fewer arrests (21% verses 31%)
- Were more likely to be employed (43% verses 35%)
- Achieved higher levels of education (37% vs. 25%)
- Had a higher marriage commitment
- Gave birth to fewer out-of-wedlock children

Head Start

Head Start was conceptualized and implemented as part of the War on Poverty program in 1965 under the Johnson Administration. It began as a six weeks demonstration program for economically disadvantaged children. Designed to enhance learning opportunities of poor and minority children, it included family and health intervention components to serve children's developmental needs. As it was originally designed, it did not serve working mother's needs. Nor did it serve infants and toddlers.

Private Companies

Beginning in the 1970's, national and regional companies such as Children's World, Kinder Care, and La Petite Academy were founded.

Various Studies

Studies consistently made news headlines and worked to make the public and public policy makers aware of the importance or early childhood education.

The Abecedarian Project initiated as a controlled study of the potential benefits of early childhood education for economically disadvantaged children; study years were 1972–1977. The continued tracking of the control group demonstrated that long lasting benefits resulted from a quality early childhood program.

The Cost Quality Outcomes Study was published in 1995; it stated that most child care was mediocre.

The Quality 2000 Initiative was published; its purpose was to address the quality crisis in early childhood education. The study detailed eight areas for suggested improvements with recommendations.

Legislation

The 21st Century Learning Program (established by the Clinton Administration) was designed to create community learning centers to provide academic enrichment activities during non-school hours for children, particularly for students in areas of high poverty and lower-performing schools. Grant money flows from the federal department of education to state departments of education.

Welfare Reform (1996) established different criteria for receiving public assistance and emphasized the need for mothers and fathers to be in the workforce. The outcome was a greater demand for early care and education services for young children.

New Terms and Concepts

The term UPK (universal pre-kindergarten) was introduced and the concept promoted by many early care and education advocacy groups. The term VPK (voluntary universal pre-kindergarten) followed.

The concept of tiered reimbursement to pay for services provided by early care and education centers was introduced and executed in several states.

Trends of the 21st Century

- National early care and education companies are beginning to consolidate.

- No Child Left Behind, the educational program of the Bush administration, was implemented. Accountability was a key word.

- Tiered reimbursement is linked to state rating systems that judge the quality of center based care and financial reimbursement based on level of accomplishment.

- Discussions on the proper early childhood educational environment have become more polarized as public schools and public policy makers urge school readiness. Didactic teaching verses developmentally appropriate practices are issues in the discussions.

- States or special interest groups have proposed state solutions to poor quality child care. For example, in California Proposition 82 (or Preschool for All) urged a voluntary program that would provide preschool for all four year olds via various tax methods; it was defeated in 2006. And in Florida, the Gold Seal and Quality Care initiatives were introduced.

- In 2008, both major party presidential candidates issued policy statements regarding early childhood education.

Important National Early Childhood Education Associations Who Provide Support to Constituent Groups

- NANE, National Association for Nursery Education (founded 1926) became NAEYC, National Association for the Education of Young Children in 1964. NAEYC is an individual membership group that promotes excellence in education.

- National Head Start Association founded in 1973 to advocate for the Head Start program before Congress

- Children's Defense Fund founded in 1973 to be a voice for children and families

- NCCA (National Child Care Association was in 1987. A federation of state associations, regional and national companies, and individuals; it is the voice for the private licensed early care and education community.

- NBCDI (National Black Child Development Institute) is dedicated to improving the quality of life and opportunities for African-American children

- NCCIC (National Child Care Information Center) a national clearing house and technical assistance center linking parents, providers, policy-makers, researchers, and the public to early care and education information. NCCIC is funded by the Child Care Bureau

- NICHDT (National Institute of Child Health and Human Development) sponsored by the U.S. Department of Health and Human Services

- NACCP (National Association of Child Care Professionals) an association of individual members involved in early care and education

- NACCRRA (National Association of Child Care Resource and Referral Agencies) a membership organization composed of state resource and referral networks, staff of resource and referral agencies, non-profit and government agencies, corporations, individuals, child care providers, and students. (NACCRRA has a mission to ensure that families in every local community have access to high quality, affordable child-care.)

- Pre-K NOW (2002) an education and advocacy organization funded by the PEW Charitable Trust

Competency I: History & Personal and Professional Development

Important Terms and Acronyms

B & A: Before and After School Care

Block Grant, also known as the CCDBG or Child Care Development Block Grant: principle funding source for families who receive child care assistance. Has a percentage set aside for quality improvements. Requires parental choice. Once was called the CCDBF or Child Care Development Block Fund

CCP: Certified Child Care Professional

CDA: Child Development Associate

Child care

Child care and early education

Custodial care

DAP: Developmentally Appropriate Practice

Day care

Early childhood education

Faith-based programs

Family day care

Family home care

Head Start Home day

care Informal care

Laboratory schools

Montessori schools

Mothers' morning out

Nanny care

NCLB: No Child Left Behind – educational program of the George W. Bush Administration

Nursery school

Parent cooperatives

Pre-K or Pre kindergarten

Pre-school

R & R: Resource and Referral Agency

Reading readiness

Reggio-inspired schools

School-age child care

School readiness

TANF: Temporary Assistance to Needy Families – replaced the old ADC and AFDC at the time of welfare reform legislation

UPK: Universal pre-kindergarten

VPK: Voluntary pre-kindergarten

An Effective Administrator is Capable of Self Review and Assessment and Can Identify Stages of Development; Knowing Oneself Is a Necessary First Step Toward Developing Excellence and Quality

The Roles and Responsibilities of a Center Administrator

The director of a center fills a very complex role. They will have to know federal, state, and local laws and regulations that affect their center. The director will worry about child to staff ratios and will have monetary responsibilities. They will have to hire qualified staff and will have to know early childhood education principles. The director has to be a good leader and a good manager. These are just some of the functions of the job.

All directors come with different levels of experience, knowledge, and skills. Some are fairly new directors while others have been in the position for many years or have been directors of many centers or programs. It makes sense that the longer a director is in a position, the more confident they will grow in that role. Primary concerns and focuses will change, the need for support will be different, and even the approach to learning and self-development might shift as a director matures.

Paula Jorde-Bloom has described a number of director career development stages that seem to help explain these needs and differences in primary concern, focus, self-directedness, and approach to learning and development. The chart that follows reflects her descriptions. *Synthesized from:*

Bloom, P. (1991). *Blueprint for action: achieving center-based change through staff development.* Mt. Ranier, MD: Gryphon House.

Bloom, P. (1997, November). "Navigating the Rapids: Directors reflect on their careers and professional development." Washington, DC: NAEYC, *Young Children.*

Director's Stages of Development

Stage	Primary Concern and Focus	Self-Directedness	Training and Development Approach
Beginning (0–1 year)			
Competence Building	Realizing what they don't know Wanting to know more		On-site assistance Access to specialists Colleague advice

Competency I: History & Personal and Professional Development

Stage	Primary Concern and Focus	Self-Directedness	Training and Development Approach
Competent (1–4 years)			
Enthusiastic and Growing	Confident in role Constantly seeking new ways to enrich abilities Moves from struggling to juggling – "How can I do this better?" Realizes hard work often goes unrecognized Realizes director won't be liked by everyone	Shows an interest in learning how to do it better	Consultants Conferences Professional Associations Journals and Magazines Films Visits to demonstration projects Credential programs Being mentored
Career Frustration	Aware of what they don't know Balance between personal and professional obligations Balance between people and paper demands Balance between meeting needs of individual and needs of organization Is concerned about time and time management		

Competency I: History & Personal and Professional Development

Stage	Primary Concern and Focus	Self-Directedness	Training and Development Approach
Master (4 years and beyond) Reflective and Inspiring	Achieving the highest level of competence Is concerned about time management, but no longer stressed over it Can reflect on how they are doing, while they are doing Ability to work with neutrality and objectivity Comfortable and confident in leadership style Understands most issues are complex and should be viewed from multiple perspectives, not more quick fixes Sees connection between developmental concepts and instructional strategies used with children and one's work with adults Perceived as a leader by colleagues Mentor to other directors Task focused but has direct concerns about the impact of the program on the lives of children	Self-directed Sets own goals and standards Management approach: non-directive	Seminars Institutes Courses Degree programs Books Journals Conferences Instructing others Mentoring others Leadership roles in professional associations Advocacy roles
Career Wind-down	Preparing to leave the administrative role Looking forward to a career change or retirement		

Self Development Is a Continuous Process

A positive self-image and self-confidence are vital building blocks for a successful director.

An effective director is continually open to change and eager for growth, which means there is need to evaluate objectively one's own strengths and weaknesses, both personally and professionally. There is also a need to develop resources and opportunities for personal and professional growth.

Self Confidence and Professional Growth

Being an effective director requires a proper balance of self-confidence and professional growth and development. To lead adults you need to earn their confidence, and to manage an organization you need to act decisively. In both cases you need, first and foremost, confidence in your own skills and knowledge.

Your confidence can be sustained through professional development. You need to be aware that the environment in which you work is ever changing and your knowledge base needs to be ever expanding. In addition, periodically you should evaluate your performance and your attitudes.

Self-evaluation

Self-deception is an easy practice to substitute for self-evaluation. As a person in authority, it is difficult for you to get objective feedback about your performance. Yet it is vital that you have an accurate understanding of how you are doing. You can't improve your performance if you don't know what you are doing right and what you are doing wrong. Here are some approaches you can try in order to get the feedback you need.

Self-assessment

The easiest route is to assess yourself. Forms such as the "Self-Evaluation – Center Director" at the end of this section provide a useful format for looking at your own performance. The books by Crisp and Jorde Bloom listed in the bibliography also contain useful self-evaluation forms. This is a good place to start. Chances are, a person tends to be harder on oneself in a self-evaluation, you will find more than enough areas where you need to focus your attention. However, no matter how critical you are of yourself, your perceptions may well be skewed by the edited feedback you receive from staff.

Evaluation by Staff

Since the most important determinant of your success as a director will be your ability to lead staff, there is no substitute for understanding how staff perceive your leadership efforts. The best way to get objective feedback is to ask staff to evaluate your performance anonymously. The "Leadership Assessment Guide" at section F of Competency X is one tool for performing such an evaluation.

To achieve best results from using "The Leadership Assessment Guide," start by introducing it at a staff meeting where you can go over the terminology so that everyone is in agreement. Then complete one copy of the assessment yourself, and have each staff member complete it anonymously. Add up the teacher ratings for each element and calculate the average.

In reviewing the ratings look first for elements where both the staff and you gave yourself high ratings. These are areas where you should take pride. Next identify any areas where the staff rated you high and you rated yourself low. These may be elements where your expectations are much higher than those of the staff. If so, you will have to decide if you should lower your own expectations in order to focus energy on other more problematic areas.

The third pattern to look for is in areas where both the staff and you rated your performance low. These areas will certainly require improvement efforts. Finally see if there are any elements where you rated yourself high and your staff rated you low. Surprisingly and sadly, this is not an uncommon occurrence. Often this is the case in ratings on decision making and feedback. These areas will require more investigation to get to the heart of the matter.

The most difficult step is to share the ratings in a staff meeting. This tells the staff you are committed to bringing about change in the areas where your ratings were lowest and that you value their suggestions and comments. Where did you rate yourself higher than your staff rated you? After working to improve your performance, have your staff complete the Leadership Assessment Guide again.

Time Management

What is your time worth to the center you direct? If you work forty hours a week and let one hour each week fail to be productive is that so bad? Let's figure it out. If you make $25,000 per year that equates to $625 per year of wasted funds! What if you waste an hour a day? You, as director, set the model for the entire staff in wise use of time. What if everyone on staff wasted an hour a day? How much would that cost the company?

An efficient director plans to use her time well? It is not by chance that some are able to accomplish far more than others in the same amount of time.

Plan to Succeed

Weekly and daily written notes of what you *must* do and want to do will set the tone for getting the job done. Plus these notes will act as benchmarks for you to watch your own improvement and accomplishment in your job or personal life.

Prioritize Tasks

Once you have written down the critical activities you need to accomplish look over the list and number them in the order of importance in getting them done. Number one is the most important task you need to accomplish today. It must be done before all else. Whether is it a phone call, the bank deposit or evaluating a teacher do it first. Then check it off and move to of time.

Set Goals That Motivate You

If you want to succeed you must have goals. Without goals you lack focus and direction. Write a list of goals you have for yourself and your program. The key to success is writing specific goals you honestly want to achieve. Write down why you want to achieve each goal. Then make a plan with measurable timelines and objectives for accomplishing each goal. Refer to this when you start to doubt your ability to accomplish the goals you have defined. Give yourself monthly or weekly tasks to do that demonstrate progress toward goal achievement. Keep a copy of your goals posted in your office where you will see them often. Reward yourself for a job well done when you attain each goal.

Manage Distractions and Interruptions

Distractions keep us from focusing on the critical needs and goals of the day. These can be work related, self indulgent, fun for everyone or serve some other purpose. But at the wrong time they are robbing us of time to get our work done. Your job is to make the decision of what is most important at this moment. Then focus on moving forward with your daily plan. Of course there are interruptions that must be dealt with immediately. Handle the situation and then get back on course.

Delegate

Delegation helps you get everything done that is on your to do list. It also helps train staff for future management positions by giving them a chance to lead or individually accomplish goals. Remember delegation is not dumping. You are giving another member of staff a task you know they are capable of accomplishing and then mentoring them to the finish. Here are some rules to assure the delegated task is finished and the staff member feels rewarded for accepting the challenge:

- Assess the capability of the person(s) to whom you are delegating the task. Give additional training if needed.

- Explain the relevance and importance of the task, and explain why you selected them for the responsibility.

- State explicitly what you want achieved. Clarify specifically how you will measure success.

- Agree on what resources and time will be required to get the job done.

- Agree on when the job will be finished, what ongoing review dates will be required, and how this will be tracked.

- Support and communicate.

- Notice and congratulate on a job well done. Review and discuss any problems that arose along the way.

Don't Procrastinate

Efficiency experts tell us that if one does not take action within 48 hours of the time the idea generates, it probably will not happen. Everyone who has ever taken a shower has had an idea. It is the person who gets out of the shower, dries off, and does something about it, rather than procrastinate, who makes the difference.

Procrastination happens in many ways, but perhaps the most common form of procrastination is the "paper shuffle," in which papers are shuffled from one side of your desk to the other and the only thing you accomplish is shuffling paper. Efficiency experts tell us to handle paper only once. When a piece of paper comes into your office, decide if you are going to act on it or if you are going to ignore it. Pitch what you plan to ignore and act on the rest. Either act on it immediately or put it in a file separated by dates. File the paper behind the date you need to act on it. Then set aside a specific time each day to act on that date's papers - and do it.

The center director who builds a staff that functions as a team, who manages her time and that of her staff effectively, and who plans carefully for the future of the center will contribute significantly to the success of the center and its mission.

And a Few More Ideas

If you commute long distances or sit in heavy traffic, you are the victim of a lot of unproductive time. Time spent commuting on public transportation may be used to jot down notes or to return phone calls. If you are in a traffic jam use the time to relax to pleasant music, enjoy a book on tape, or just appreciate the quiet for a change.

Try to eliminate the non-essential activities in your life, both at work and at home. Delegate duties whenever possible. A good manager always delegates responsibilities. Doing so shows your respect for your employees, empowers them to be part of your team, and frees up time for you.

Carefully examine your to do list each day to see whether your tasks will contribute toward your goals. If not, eliminate them - or at least push them to the bottom of the list. Prioritize your list and work through it in order.

Make better use of the telephone. Practice a polite but businesslike phone manner that says, "I'm glad to talk to you, but my time is limited." Use the fax machine or your email for shorter, more to-the-point communication.

Try to make only essential calls. Return all necessary phone calls at the same time. One good time to place your calls is early in the morning when you are more likely to find the person ready to talk and in the office.

Self-analysis Activity

"To give meaning and direction to life," contends Hans Selye, author of *Stress Without Distress,* "we need a lofty long-range purpose." Selye further observes that this purpose must have two salient characteristics - "it must be something that requires hard work, and its fruits must be sufficiently permanent to accumulate as life goes by."

Typically, when directors enter the child care field, they enter with a profound sense of purpose – to craft an exemplary program, to make a difference in the lives of children, to build a successful business. Often, as years go by, and they become consumed with the endless hassles of keeping the center on its feet, they begin to lose sight of their original goal. Day-to-day survival becomes the overriding concern.

For that reason, it is important for you to periodically step back and reassess where you are headed. Be brutally honest with yourself in answering the following questions:

- What were your goals when you entered this profession?
- Are you still excited about these goals?
- If not, what are your long-range goals now?
- Is your current position moving you closer to the accomplishment of these goals?

You may find that you still believe in your original goals and that your current position is helping you achieve these goals. This should reassure you and motivate you to redouble your efforts.

Or, you may find that you have lost enthusiasm for your earlier goals, or that your current position has turned out to be an ineffective vehicle for achieving your goals. In either case, you need to re-evaluate your current position.

Walking through the steps of this job analysis can be a stimulating activity. But transferring your ideas into reality may be frustrating. For example, if one of your proposed actions is to limit the time you spend on repairs and maintenance, you may have a difficult time getting the toilets and your creaky, old air conditioners to cooperate with you. Or, you may not be able to find money in the budget to hire a part-time bookkeeper. Or, you may find that no one on your current staff is eager or able to take on some of the tasks that you want to delegate. To keep from getting too frustrated, view the project of shifting to the ideal use of your time as an ongoing challenge that may take you a year or so to achieve.

Another possibility is that you will find that no amount of restructuring your current position will work for you. If the problem is that the organization where you work simply has different priorities than you do, or has organizational problems that are insurmountable, looking for another directing job may be the answer.

More drastically, you may conclude that being a child care director is no longer what you should be doing. This is often an unpleasant conclusion to face. You probably came into the field with a high level of commitment to making a difference in the lives of children, teachers, and families. To leave the field may feel like an admission that you failed. But that is not the case. It is just a case of the match not being right. You can do far more good by starting a new career with vigor and commitment than by continuing half-heartedly in your current position.

Most likely, however, you will find that you can reinvigorate your career by taking time periodically for self-analysis. By regularly readjusting your own work priorities and shifting the work flow within your organization, you should be able to keep the organization working at its highest level while at the same time keeping your career stimulating and meaningful.

Summary

Showing competence in understanding the history of early childhood education, and the personal and professional development of the child care professional, an effective administrator:

- Understands that early childhood education operates within an ever changing environment

- Knows the history and key milestones of the early childhood education industry. She understands that she works in a dynamic and evolving profession that serves three major purposes of society.

- Is capable of self review and assessment and can identify stages of development. Knowing oneself is a necessary first step toward developing excellence and quality

If you feel you lack confidence in any of the skills listed above, please go back and review the appropriate section in this chapter.

Competency II

An Effective Organization

Competency II

An Effective Organization

Learning Objectives:

- To understand why an organization needs a mission statement
- To be able to write a clear and concise mission statement that supports organizational values and understanding of child care needs in the community (This includes a review and critique of organizational mission statements.)
- To understand how to define and write goals and objectives to accomplish the mission of your organization
- To be able to distinguish between the six types of legal structures that an organization can adopt
- To understand how to conduct a demographic study
- To understand how to conduct a needs assessment and competition study
- To be able to determine relative market share

> **An Effective Administrator Develops a Management Philosophy which Includes a Clear Mission Statement and Clear Objectives Based on the Values of the Program and Understanding of Child Care Needs in the Community Being Served**

Mission Statement

A mission statement is a clear and concise statement that simply describes what your organization exists to do. It is a description of the overall purpose of your business or organization, communicating its essence to stakeholders and the public. It should be short, preferably only one sentence long. Mission statements create clarity and unity of purpose, allowing decisions to be made according to deeper principles.

A good mission statement provides vision and direction for your center for at least 10 to 20 years. Your mission statement is a guiding set of ideas articulated, understood, and supported by the center's board, staff, volunteers, and clients. A good mission statement is easily understood, and can be transferred into individual action every day. It has measurable and tangible goals and should be firmly rooted in the environment in which the organization operates

Mission statements should include:

- What do you want your business to do? (The overall strategic objective)
- How do you want to do it? (Overview of your products and services)
- To whom do you want to do it? (Target publics, markets, clients)

Lewis Caroll summarizes the importance of mission statements eloquently through the words of the Cheshire cat in *Alice in Wonderland*, "If you don't know where you're going, it doesn't matter which way you go."

Often centers want to write more about who they are, what they do, and why. Adding descriptive information about a program is fine, but doing so should not be confused with having a clearly stated mission statement. Vision and guiding principles will be discussed after this section about mission statements.

The following three concepts are critical in defining the mission of your center:

The Purpose Statement

The purpose statement clearly states what your program seeks to accomplish: Why does your program exist? What is the ultimate result of your work?

An example of a purpose statement is to eliminate homelessness. In defining purpose, it is essential to focus on outcomes and results rather than methods: How is the world going to be different? What is going to change? Thus, the purpose of a mental health counseling agency would never be simply to provide counseling services, for that is describing a method rather than a result. Rather, the purpose might be to improve the quality of life for its clients.

The Business Statement

This statement outlines the business (e.g., early care and education, after school, Head Start…) your organization chooses in order to pursue its purpose. Specifically, you must answer, "What activity are we going to do to accomplish our purpose?" For example, there are many ways to work on the problem of homelessness. These include constructing housing for homeless individuals, educating the public and advocate for public policy changes, and providing job training to homeless individuals.

Each of these are different businesses, but they may be different means of achieving the same purpose.

A note of caution: Using adjectives such as quality is unclear and has multiple meanings to different cultures or families. Choose words that clearly paint a picture of what you do and why. Avoid industry jargon others might not understand.

Values

Values are beliefs the staff of your program hold in common and endeavor to put into practice. The values guide your staff in performing their work. Specifically, you should ask, "What are the basic beliefs that we share as a center?"

Examples of values include: a commitment to excellent services, innovation, diversity, creativity, honesty, integrity, and so on. Values may include beliefs such as: "Eating vegetables is more economically efficient and ecologically responsible than eating beef." (Vegetarian Association)

Marvin Weisbord writes in *Productive Workplaces* that values come alive only when people are involved in doing important tasks. Ideally, an individual's personal values will align with the spoken and unspoken values of the organization. By developing a written statement of the values of the organization, group members have a chance to contribute to the articulation of these values, as well as to evaluate how well their personal values and motivation match those of the organization.

One example of a mission statement is:

"At the ABC Development Center we develop, teach a curriculum [business] that fosters children's ethical, social, and intellectual development [purpose]. While nurturing children's capacity to think skillfully and critically, we also strive to deepen children's commitment to pro-social values such as kindness, helpfulness, personal responsibility, and respect for others - qualities we believe are essential to leading humane and productive lives in a democratic society [values]."

Another example of a mission statement which includes all three elements and is shorter:

The YMCA of San Francisco, based in Judeo-Christian heritage [values], seeks to enhance the lives of all people [purpose] through programs designed to develop spirit, mind and body [business].

One development approach is to use time at a staff meeting to discuss these questions and find out where the areas of consensus are and where there are differences. There is a process benefit to hashing over a center's mission statement as well. In the course of discussion and debate, new staff are introduced to nuances of the mission of the center and changes in the environment and old staff refresh their understanding of both. As a result, the group will have confidence that the mission statement which emerges (whether it is a new statement or a rededication to the old mission statement) is genuinely an articulation of commonly held ideas.

Note: Groups are good at many things, but writing is not one of them. Have group discussions about big ideas and concepts and then let one or two individuals draft and redraft the wording before submitting a reworked version for the group to respond to. It is important to circulate the draft mission statement a few times to board, staff, and other stakeholders. Some consultants advise organizations to also seek an outside opinion from someone unfamiliar with the organization to see how easily the mission statement can be understood.

Vision Statement

A vision statement is sometimes called a picture of your center in the future but it's so much more than that. Your vision statement is your inspiration, the framework for all your strategic planning.

A vision statement may apply to an entire center or to a single classroom or age group in the program. Whether for all or part of a program, the vision statement answers the question, Where do we want to go? What you are doing when creating a vision statement is articulating your dreams and hopes for your center. It reminds you of what you are trying to build.

While a vision statement doesn't tell you how you're going to get there, it does set the direction for your business planning. That's why it's important when crafting a vision statement to let your imagination go and dare to dream – and why it's important that a vision statement captures your passion.

Unlike the mission statement, a vision statement is for you and the other members of your center, not for your customers or clients. When writing a vision statement, your mission statement and your talents can be a valuable starting point for articulating your values.

Be sure when you're creating one not to fall into the trap of only thinking ahead a year or two. Once you have one, your vision statement will have a huge influence on decision making and the way you allocate resources.

Some of the positive outcomes that can result from establishing a vision statement are:

- Greatly improved business focus
- Everyone has the same program / center view of the future - no misunderstandings
- Enhances the professional perception of your program

- Fosters a team oriented environment
- Enhances employee morale
- Helps attract and retain the best people

Examples

To stand out as a region with passion for service professionally delighting our customers whom we see as the essence of our operations (Vision statement for utility provider.)

The classroom is one in which the potential for learning is open and free to every child.

Putting Your Mission and Vision Statements into Action

Your mission and vision statements are the beginning of effective strategic planning for the success of your early care and education program. It is the process that your center management team should use to think about how the center will be successful.

However good your mission is, it will fail if people don't understand it. They won't know where the center is going, or how to help you get there. Employees will probably get frustrated and confused; customers may feel dissatisfied; and other stakeholders may lose their faith in your center's ability to deliver.

So your center needs both effective strategic planning and good communication of strategy. Just as a map is usually more effective than a list of directions, so a graphical description of your strategy can often communicate your strategy more effectively than a weighty document.

One popular technique for communicating strategy graphically is called The Pyramid of Purpose. It is called this because it describes the elements of strategy graphically.

There are many ways of describing strategy. One approach, which also illustrates the hierarchical structure well, is to think of business strategy while answering the following questions.

- Why are we doing what we are doing? (mission and vision statements)
- What do we need to do to fulfill our intended purpose? (goals and objectives)
- How exactly are we going to do what needs to be done? (actions)
- Who (or what) is going to make sure it's done? (people)
- How exactly are we going to do what needs to be done? (actions)
- Who (or what) is going to make sure it's done? (people)

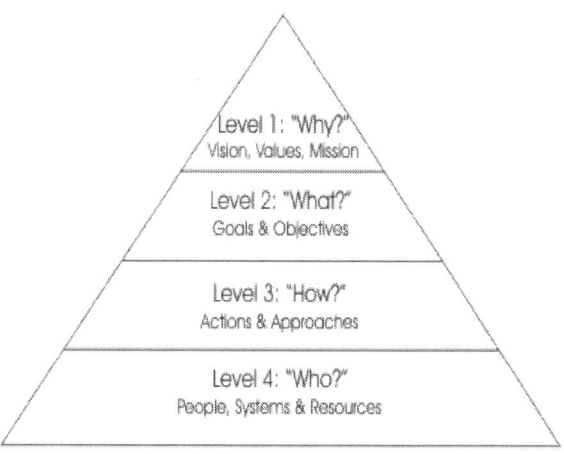

Figure 1: **The Pyramid of Purpose**

Moving from the top (mission statement) you must decide what the mission statement means in real life, day to day activities within the business. Generally it is a good rule of thumb to have no more than five goals and objectives. Some areas or general topics you might consider are:

- Products and services (program, curriculum, ages served, future planning, staffing)
- Marketing (promotion, pricing, market share, niche)
- Operational infrastructure (facility, equipment and supplies, vehicles, maintenance and repair, location)
- Management team (leadership style, experience, duties, hiring, training)
- Finances (budget, cash flow, grants)

From here you must design exactly how you are going to accomplish each of these goals. Level three of the pyramid gives action to the words. The actions specifically describe the details of how you are going to promote your center, write job descriptions, set up classrooms, and set criteria for hiring staff. These should be objective and measurable. Time frames should be included such as, prior to opening the center, in the first year, by the end of five years, by the end of the current year, once a week, daily, etc.

The fourth level of the pyramid is the people, systems, and resources you need to accomplish the entire plan. Define who is responsible for what (organizational chart), what specific programs or systems you will use, whether you will purchase commercial programs or create your own, and what community and industry resources you will use to help you along the way. Delegation plays a major role in finding success. Learn how to delegate tasks and responsibilities to staff to create a successful experience for all involved. After all the work to create levels one through three of the pyramid, it is imperative that this level of people, systems and resources be carefully planned and implemented. Notice that it is the people who are the foundation of the pyramid – without them the entire structure will collapse.

Goals and Objectives

Goals are the desired results you hope to accomplish through the mission of the center. Goals define what you are trying to achieve through your work. Goals may be short term like "increasing facility's curb appeal," or long-term, such as "children developing a sense of independence." Use actions words when writing goals.

Objectives are the things you need to accomplish in order to achieve your goals. They are usually thought of as being observable and measurable. When writing objectives, make sure they are measurable.

Sample Mission Statement

The mission of ABC Child Care Center is to offer a high-quality child care program at market rates that benefits the child, the family, the staff, and the community.

Sample Goals

ABC goals for children include:

- Building physical strength, coordination and motor skills
    - A sample objective for this goal is to asses the level of indoor physical activity equipment
- Establishing a foundation for good health, hygiene and safety habits
- Expressing ideas and feelings creatively through music, movement, dramatic play, art and language
- Developing a sense of self, and increasing independence
- Exploring concepts and developing intellectual curiosity
- Persevering in the face of difficulty

ABC goals for families include:

- Secure competent care for their young child in a developmentally appropriate environment while they pursue careers or other interests
- Meeting others concerned with the interests and needs of their young child
- Enhanced understanding and appreciation of child development and their own child
- Enhanced knowledge and skills in child rearing
- Enhanced linkages to community services that provide assistance and support to families of young children

ABC goals for staff include:

- Working with children in a developmentally appropriate setting

- Continued professional development
    - An objective for this goal would be 12 class hours of continuing education annually
- Earning a competitive wage
    - An example of an objective for this goal would be to review cost to provide care with 10% wage increase included in the costs

An Effective Administrator Understands the Legal Structure of Organizations and How This Structure Effects His Operations

Whether you are starting a center from scratch or managing a center that already existed when you joined the organization, it is important for a director to have a basic knowledge of the legal structure of the business. There are both advantages and disadvantages to the various legal forms one may choose to adopt when creating a business. In this section you will become acquainted with some of the terminology and considerations that are a part of selecting the legal form of a business.

Before we review the various possible legal structures, it is important to stress the need for any business, regardless of size or structure, to employ proper legal and accounting advisors to assist in the development and review of the business. Nothing in this section is intended to provide the reader with legal or accounting advice. Legal and accounting advice should only be provided by an experienced professional after thoroughly reviewing the particular needs of the client. An uninformed decision to operate the center in one legal form versus another can result in personal liability, increased personal and business taxes, difficulty in obtaining financing or grant monies, and serious difficulties in future efforts to expand or sell the business. Be sure to retain the services of an attorney and an accountant who can provide you with proper advice and counsel. Not only will they offer you the proper foundation for the center, they will serve as excellent resources over the years as the center evolves and as changes which challenge your management decisions occur.

Although there are variations to each form of legal structure of a center, there are six basic types of structures that you should be aware of:

Sole Proprietorship

This is the most common form of organization. A sole proprietorship is exactly what it sounds like - a business that is owned by a single person. The proprietor or owner employs individuals to work at the center and operates the center like any other business. In most cases, the proprietor will run the center under an assumed name - the "XYZ Child Care Center." In order to operate under this name, the proprietor may need to file a certificate to operate under an assumed name, or what is commonly called a D.B.A. (doing business as) certificate with the county, town, or state.

The sole proprietor is not paid a salary or wage as an employee is paid. The owner's income comes from the profits or surplus that the center generates. In addition, in a sole proprietorship, the proprietor is responsible for all taxes the center may generate from any profits, and these profits are reported on the personal income tax statements of the owner.

Self-employment taxes such as Federal, State, FICA, and Medicare are the responsibility of the proprietor. This is a positive feature of the sole proprietorship as the owner is not subject to separate business taxes, or additional income taxes in excess of the normal personal taxes.

One other important consideration in choosing the sole proprietorship form of business is the personal liability that the owner has for all debts of the center including personal liability for any damages, law suits, claims, or like obligations that the business may incur. For instance, should an employee or customer be injured at the center, the proprietor would be personally responsible for any costs which might exceed any insurance coverage that the center may carry. The sole proprietor may be sued personally and her personal assets (e.g., home, car, bank accounts) may be at risk.

Partnership

A very simple way to look at a partnership is to envision a center that operates like a sole proprietorship, but which is owned by two or more people, or partners. As in a sole proprietorship, the partners are individually responsible for the debts or obligations of the business, and the profits of the business are recorded on the partners' individual tax returns. The partners are also responsible for the same type of self-employment tax as described in the sole proprietorship. (However, the partnership must complete its own tax return which details the operation of the business and which is included in the partner's personal return.)

Similar to the sole proprietorship, the partners typically are not employees of the business. A partner would normally receive income from working in the center by receiving her portion of the profits. However, there are provisions for a type of wage payment to a partner, called a guaranteed payment. This guaranteed payment has certain restrictions which should be thoroughly discussed with your accountant prior to proceeding in this direction.

Partnerships also may operate their businesses under assumed names, or D.B.A.'s, as mentioned under sole proprietorships. Similar filing requirements would be required with each partner's name and address identified on the application to operate under the assumed name. Additionally, most states require that a certificate or an article of partnership be filed with the secretary of state.

Partners, like sole proprietors, are personally liable for all debts and claims against the business.

Corporation

The easiest way to understand the benefits and operating requirements of a corporation is to envision the corporation as a person. The corporation is the entity that employs the workers, pays the bills, files the tax returns, and has the liability should the corporation incur any debt or obligations.

There are two common types of corporations. The first is the C Corporation. Firms such as General Motors, Walt Disney, and Kodak are examples of this type of corporation. This firm may have an unlimited number of stockholders and must file separate income tax returns that are designed for corporations. Additionally, in most instances, the corporation will be responsible for income tax on the profits of the corporation, many times at tax rates that differ considerably from personal tax rates. A C corporation may be owned by one person.

An owner of a center that is a C Corporation (also known as a C-Corp) can be an employee of the corporation and receive a salary like any other employee. That owner/employee must pay individual income tax on this salary and will receive a W-2 form and be subject to income tax withholding requirements. Should the corporation have a great year and make substantial profits, the owner may gain additional revenue through dividends the corporation may pay. You can see that a disadvantage of the corporate form of business has is that the corporation must pay taxes on income while the owner-employee also pays personal taxes on any salary or dividends, resulting in two taxations on the same money.

In addition to the C-corporation, there is another form of corporation called an S Corporation. An S Corporation has the legal advantages of a C Corporation but the tax advantages of a partnership. The profits on an S Corporation are not taxed. Rather, they are passed to the stockholders as pro-rata shares and taxed as the shareholders' personal income. In this way the shareholders receive the tax advantage of the lower individual income tax rate. An S Corporation can have no more than 35 stockholders, and all must be individuals or certain trusts or estates. An S Corporation can have only one class of stock. And finally, all stockholders must elect for the corporation to become an S Corporation by signing IRS form 2553.

A significant benefit of any type of corporation is the protection that the corporation provides the individual owner from personal liability. This is sometimes referred to as the Corporate Shell. In a corporate structure, should a lawsuit occur against the business, in most cases the business would be responsible for the payment of any monies with the owner protected from personal liability.

Limited Liability Company (LLC)

Many states now offer a type of business structure that resembles a cross between a partnership and a corporation. Like a corporation, an LLC provides limited liability to its members; members of an LLC are generally not personally responsible for the obligations of the LLC. Like a partnership, an LLC is not subject to an entity (business) tax, but rather, each member reports his/her distributive share of the LLC's income, gain, loss, deduction and credit on his/her personal return.

Non-profit

Many child care centers, especially if they are associated with charitable organizations or churches, are established as non-profit organizations. Often these are legally structured as not-for-profit corporations. In this case, the organization is a legal entity and assumes all liability for the debts and obligations of the corporation. The non-profit organization may be eligible to be declared tax-exempt by the IRS which would exempt it from paying taxes and enable it to receive tax-deductible donations. This tax-exempt status is conferred by the IRS in part because it is assumed that there will be no personal gain from the operation of the program. Therefore, there are no assets which later can be sold by an owner, and taxes are not levied on the organization.

Offsetting this apparent advantage, the non-profit center cannot be sold as a business owner would sell a for-profit business. A person or group establishing a non-profit center does not build any assets in the center over the years.

Serious consideration should be given to the proper legal structure of a center at the time that the center is formed. In later years, depending on the structure that has been chosen, the center can modify its structure as its needs change. However, the business structure that is chosen can have a dramatic impact on the way that the center can do business.

If you are considering establishing of a center, you should ask the following questions:

- Why is the center being developed? (To provide a service; to build up a value in a business which can later be sold, etc.?)
- Will the center need to receive outside financing for the development or growth of the operation, either in the form of borrowing money or receiving grants?
- Who will be the owner(s) of the center?
- Is the potential for personal liability a concern to the owner(s)?
- Is the owner going to be an employee of the program?
- What type of structure will best meet the current and future needs of the center?

Now that we know our mission and the legal structure needed to sustain our mission we will proceed to doing a needs assessment to discuss locations suitable for achieving our goals.

An Effective Administrator Assesses the Supply and Demand Characteristics of the Area Served, and Positions the Program to Respond to Those Needs

In order to be successful in any type of business, you must understand the market that you are attempting to serve. This is especially true in the provision of early care and education services.

Although many newspaper and magazine stories seem to imply that there is an unmet demand for early care and education, and all a center needs to do is open its door and the children will flood into the center, this is rarely the case. Early care and education centers need to perform thorough market evaluations prior to opening in order to insure there is sufficient demand to allow the center to reach a level of occupancy that will sustain the operating costs of the program.

A director must thoroughly understand the market needs and the mission of the center in order to consistently insure the programs and services offered are meeting the needs of the desired customer base. Unless the director understands these critical issues, it is impossible to develop and maintain any specific business goals and objectives.

One of the most important predictors of the success of a center is the supply and demand characteristics of the area served by the center. The successful center will position its program to respond to those needs.

Learn about the Centers in Your Proposed Service Area (i.e. Study Your Competition)

After conducting a competition study, you will be able to distinguish the gaps in the competitors' delivery systems. For example, if there is a big demand for school-age care and you know no one in the child care community is providing for this age, could you provide an after-school program?

Other examples of service gaps or a unique marketing niche might be the following:

- Where is your competition located?
- Are there any geographical barriers in your competition's location? (e.g., is it less accessible than your center?)
- What is the visibility of your competition's center? (e.g., is it more visible than your center?)

The Service Specifics of Your Competition

What are the hours of operation, ages served, cost of service? Are there any added value services such as transportation, accreditation, summer day camp? What is special about the center? Answering these questions will give you a good idea of what you are up against.

The History of Your Competition

How many years have they been in business? What is the background of the administrator, owner? Are they affiliated with any other organization such as a university, community organization, or church (networking capabilities)? If you can answer these questions, you'll have a good start at understanding your own role in the community.

The Licensed Capacity of the Competitor's Center

Is the center filled? Is there a waiting list? Are there certain age levels they do not serve (supply and demand)? Are there certain age levels which have waiting lists (supply and demand)? Getting answers to these questions will give you an advantage in the marketplace.

Other Significant Considerations

There are possibly several characteristics of your center that can set it apart from your competition. For instance, perhaps:

- Your playground is the only one in a three mile radius accessible to disabled children

- You offer cooking experiences for the children; they grow vegetables in your center's backyard garden
- You offer foreign language experiences; several of your staff are bilingual
- Your center has a security monitoring system
- Ninety percent of your staff has been with your center for over five years
- Your center has a parent advisory board
- Your facility is new or recently remodeled
- You offer emergency care or holiday care for school age children
- You are open at 5:30 A.M. and you are open until 7:00 P.M.

After you have obtained a good grasp of the needs and interests of the marketplace, you should develop a specific list of service features intended to meet the needs of the marketplace. These features could be as simple as the hours of the center and as complex as the pricing level for certain age groups in order to meet the needs of the desired clientele. Regardless of the number of features you establish, it is important each one be continually tested against the specific mission and objectives of the center to insure that it is compatible.

Once you have determined your competitive advantages, develop a comparative checklist. In your comparative checklist, you would highlight your unique niches. Build your program around your specific advantages.

".... my way of fighting the competition is the positive approach. Stress your own strengths, emphasize quality, service, cleanliness and value, and the competition will wear itself out trying to keep up."
Ray Kroc, founder of McDonalds.

Market Supply and Demand

In considering the supply and demand characteristics of the market of the center, the following subjects need to be considered.

Who Your Customers Are

Defining your customer is, in essence, defining your target market. Once you have defined your client, many other important elements (e.g., facility location, revenues, and expenses) come into focus.

The Locale of the Community You Will Be Serving

You will want to determine which of these locales best describes the area surrounding your center.

- Urban – within a one mile radius
- Suburban – within a two to 5 mile radius
- Rural – generally more than 5 miles

- Resort – depends on customer base; if customer base are workers they may come from long distances; if the base are resort guests they are within a short distance

The Customer Base Segment of the Community Being Served

You will want to determine who is most likely to be your customer base.

- Employers only
- Individual parents only
- Employers and parents

The Ages of the Children Being Served

You will want to determine which age group will be served.

- Infants/toddlers/two's
- Preschoolers
- School age

The Demographic Study

Once you have determined your target market, a demographic study should be conducted. A demographic study is merely collecting a census of information. You can obtain this kind of information through United States Bureau of the Census, Department of the Workforce Development, Bureau of Labor Statistics, Business Research Centers or U.S. Bureau of Economic Analysis. Many state universities also have research centers which can be helpful.

They can provide you with vital demographics and community statistics required to make informed decisions. There are three areas that should be examined in a demographic study:

Target Market

Target market is a defined group of potential clients who are likely to use child care. Pay attention to the market's distance from the center when you are defining your target market. Since parents do not typically wish to travel more than five to ten minutes from their home for care, limit your target market to a three mile radius if you are a suburban provider. If you are a rural provider, you can extend your potential target market to five miles, and an urban provider should be reduced to a one-mile radius. Be aware of geographical boundaries such as rivers or limited access highways which might impact the radius and, therefore, the demographics.

Market Share

Are there enough children to support an early care and education center? Market share is the total amount of available client base that is a specified age in an identified radius.

Relative Market Share

Who is your competition and what is their market share? Relative market share is the comparison between the total number of licensed early care and education slots and the total number of licensed early care and education slots needed.

Competency II: An Effective Organization

To obtain the relative market share, for a proposed center, use the following formula.
Total Licensed Slots Available **plus** *Total Licensed Slots in Your Proposed Center* **divided by** *Total Slots Needed* **equals** *Relative Market Share.*
To obtain the relative market share for an existing center, use the following formula.
Total Licensed Slots Available **divided by** *Total Slots Needed* **equals** *Relative Market Share.*

Determining the Potential Child Care Base

Parents in Target Market

National statistics indicate that 64% of all preschoolers have working mothers. Industry statistics indicate that, out of all preschoolers who need early care and education (64% of preschool population), 28 % will be cared for in licensed early care and education centers. The potential child base is, therefore, the total number of preschoolers in a designated target area multiplied by .64 and multiplied again by .28.

Employers in Target Market

There are several types of employers who are more likely to consider care as a benefit or service for their employees. Some of these employers include the health care industry, legal and professional fields, computer and high tech fields, and government entities.

Example

There are 1000 children in my area age 0 – 6.
There are three licensed child care centers providing space for 300 children.
I am proposing to build a center in the area that will be licensed for 150 children.

```
        1000 children in my area
  X      .64  % who will need care
Total    640  number of children needing care
  X      .28 % of families choosing child care center for care
         179  children who will be potential clients for the area (market share)
```

Current licensed spaces   300 (b)
Proposed spaces   150 (c)
Total available space   450 (d)

Total available space (d)   450
Divided by market share (a)   179
Equals relative market share   2.5 slots per child

Would it be a sound decision to build the proposed center? Why?

Competency II: An Effective Organization

Summary

Showing competence in building an effective organization, an effective administrator:

- Develops a management philosophy which includes a clear mission statement and clear objectives based on the values of the program and understanding of child care needs in the community being served

- Understands the legal structure of organizations and how this structure effects his operations

- Assesses the supply and demand characteristics of the area served, and positions the program to respond to those needs

If you feel you lack confidence in any of the skills listed above, please go back and review the appropriate section in this chapter.

Competency III

Internal and External Systems

Competency III

Internal and External Systems

Learning Objectives:

- To be able to develop systems to ensure compliance with local, state, and national codes

- To master the development of staff and parent communication systems

- To be able to create business practices and communications to maintain financial stability

- To be able to develop and use management systems regarding maintenance and janitorial needs that ensure health and safety of the center

- To be able to create and manage an efficient and nutritious food service

- To understand the development of facility security and safety systems

- The grasp the essential elements of sharing space

An Effective Administrator Develops Systems to Keep the Center Running Smoothly and to Comply with Applicable Laws, Rules, and Regulations, and Keeps These Systems Up to Date to Ensure the Safety of Staff and Children

It is essential for an effective administrator to develop management systems for tracking changes in federal, state, and local laws and regulations that effect early childhood education facilities. Systems are the various components of center operations that function interdependently to assist us in achieving our purpose.

In this competency we note the need to have and to develop management systems that assist in gaining compliance with the many rules, regulations, and laws that impact centers, that facilitate and aide communication with parents and staff, that help carry out the mission, goals, and objectives of the organization, and that help us evaluate how well we are doing operationally, fiscally, and educationally.

System management and development requires the ability to write clearly and precisely, the ability to hold staff and parents accountable to policy and procedures, the ability to respond to social, economic, and political changes, and demands a clear understanding of the fundamentals of early childhood education and care.

Typical systems needed in an early childhood education center are: Staff policies and procedures including payroll, vacation and holiday information, dress code etc.; parent policies and procedures (parent handbook), parent enrollment packets, parent communication forms; food service such as menu planning forms and food inventory; curriculum planning forms; safety check lists, field trip forms, and etc.

In addition to these written systems, early childhood education administrators need to determine effective ways to track changes in state licensing rules and regulations, federal laws, and local or state laws that affect how the center operates. Most of the federal laws are discussed in Competency IV

An Effective Administrator Understands the Importance of Communication and Develops Communication Systems for Staff, Parents, and the Community

Early childhood education programs must communicate the strength of their mission to their management team, employees, and customers to build confidence in performance. The key is ensuring a systematic and comprehensive approach to the communications process at all levels. Effective communication is created by:

- Demonstrating leadership
- Earmarking resources
- Focusing on the company's mission

- Maintaining valuable relationships
- Disclosing pertinent information
- Listening
- Responding and providing feedback

The biggest challenge to effectively communicating with employees is the management of the communication process itself. Failure to get the right message out to your workforce in a timely manner can have serious financial repercussions. Misinformation can be costly and result in delays in achieving the objectives or goals of the center. Effective communications ensures the uniformity of the messages across the board and linkage of center communications among the interested stakeholders: clients, investors, employees and management.

Developing and maintaining effective employee communication systems and skills are challenging tasks and require constant attention. Management should base all communication efforts on a clear, well-defined communications strategy tied to achieving the business objectives of the center. Best results for a center are normally achieved when the communications program is developed proactively. This helps to ensure:

- A comprehensive process covering all special interest groups within the organization and
- That we avail ourselves to all avenues of communication within the organization as part of the implementation and ongoing maintenance process

Good communication is one of the most vital skills an early childhood education program administrator can develop. These skills facilitate staff, parent, and community understanding of the mission, goals, and objectives of the early care and education facility. The many facets of our daily duties indicate the need for honing these skills.

Two way communication is key. We, as administrators, must accept the need and value of having a two-way communication system. If we create our communication model as one including both a sender and a receiver we will assure the receiver not only hears the message but also provides feedback to confirm understanding and relay information back. Given early childhood centers have relatively few levels of management supervising the teaching staff, or basically a flat management structure, it is critically important for information to flow horizontally and vertically in order to be inclusive, timely and effective. That is, the director must be open and willing to get information, instruction, policies and procedures to staff and then allow staff to give feedback, suggestions and their feelings about the information.

Communication with Staff

Administrators committed to lowering staff turnover rates are finding their ability to achieve and sustain improvement is largely dependent upon improving their communication with the staff. Factors frequently cited as influencing positive employee communication outcomes include:

Employee Trust in Management

Just like the children we work with, our employees must feel safe in their job. You, as director, must build a professional bond with each employee giving the feeling of "my boss cares about me and the job I perform. She will stand up for me when needed and always make correct decisions." Your employees must have confidence in your ability to do your job and maintain company values.

Visibility of the Mission and Values in Day-to-Day Running of the Center

You must not just be able to recite the mission and values of your center, you must live them and show your staff you believe in them and expect others to do the same.

Management Engagement in the Formal Communication Process

How often do you have a formal sit down conversation with individual staff members? This means, planning in advance, setting a mutually agreeable time, having a purpose to the meeting, and practicing active listening and problem solving skills throughout the meeting. One- on-one and small group meetings are excellent times to investigate and fine tune the task of living the mission and values. Staff who know that you value their ideas and concerns are much more likely to work with you on common goals.

Employee Understanding of Business Strategy, Goals and Objectives

From the time of hire each staff person should be shown the company's organizational structure and understand where they fit into it. Your initial training should include your mission, goals and objectives indicating how you ultimately achieve your purpose. This should be given in a face to face training to assure the new person really understands and buys into these key elements of your program.

Combine with Employee Recognition and Reward Systems

Everyone enjoys being recognized for their achievements. From the beginning your center should have a clear path of recognition and reward. Aside from verbal praise (which is vital!) how do you let staff know they are doing a great job? Notes, awards, recognition at staff meeting, incentive programs and special privileges are just a few methods of melting communication and rewards into one very visible system.

Visibility of Employee Feedback Systems Throughout the Organization

Where ever possible invite staff feedback. If you send out a memo to staff ask for suggestions or comments about changes or help with upcoming events. Open memo boards by time cards, time clocks and sign-in sheets are locations where ideas, frustrations and suggestions can be posted; staff suggestion boxes with published results or open time in staff meeting for sharing of ideas and issues will let everyone know they are a valued member of the team and their ideas are welcome and their angst is shared.

Focus on Continuous Process Improvement in the Organization

No program is static. We are all in a business with internal and external factors influencing our day to day existence. If we are open to change and improvement we can count on our program flourishing. Consider how the new research on brain development the past five years has changed and improved your program. We must be vigilant to maintain an open mind and open door policy of looking for methods, information and even threats that will help us improve our organization. And remember improvement includes each member of the team! As we improve the knowledge base, communication skills and vision of each team member we improve the organization as a whole.

Use Technology in the Dissemination of Information

In the age of computers and internet we are able to send more information to more people in less time. Many centers have taken advantage of these time saving devices and send messages, reminders, newsletters and billings to parents via email. Computerized check in/out and billing frees staff time for other productive tasks. When parents are checking children in or out most computer programs have capability to leaving messages to everyone, by class or individually.

Employee Engagement in the Communication Process

Many employees are intimidated by management and are reticent to give ideas or feedback. The director's encouragement, acceptance and gratitude for each staff person's feedback and suggestions will foster further communication. It is human nature to be able to think creatively and problem solve better when feeling safe.

Integration of Customer Satisfaction Scores Into Staff Feedback Systems

Staff need to know how they are doing in their job in the eyes of the parents. Any time a customer evaluation is completed it must be shared with staff. This is a perfect time to give liberal praise for a job well done and brain storm together how improvements can be made.

Regular Staff Meetings

Staff meetings held at regular intervals provide opportunities for the staff to share with one another, discuss individual classroom problems, brainstorm solutions, and simultaneously receive information regarding center policy or operational requirements and changes. Staff meetings allow time for fellowship and bonding that is not available during the work day when children are present.

During times when a full scale staff meeting is not feasible, put in place an informal system of communication that is direct and gets the word out quickly. This can be accomplished through a staff bulletin board or teachers' mailboxes located in the teachers' lounge or work area. Staff memos, general work information, required notices, individual memos, vacation schedules, etc. should be posted on the staff bulletin board or in staff mailboxes.

Use these ideas to make meetings less time consuming and more productive:

- Distribute an agenda before the meeting for all attendees to review.
- Establish a time limit for each item on the agenda.
- Define the purpose and the goals of the meeting.
- Address each item on the agenda and assign follow-up responsibilities and actions.
- Include only essential staff at the meeting.
- Start and end the meeting on time.
- Arrange the meeting space for productive activity; provide pencils, pads of paper, and water.

Strategic Planning

Strategic planning sessions should be held at least twice a year to give staff time to establish goals and measure outcomes. The staff should help place children in classes and help develop the curriculum that is designed to achieve educational goals. Teachers should be an integral part of developing school newsletters and planning parent/teacher conferences. Teachers can plan suitable field trips and make all necessary arrangements to carry them out. In essence, an empowered staff can be delegated many of the responsibilities that would otherwise be left to you. Details on how to do a strategic plan are in Competency IX.

Things to Consider When Creating an Employee Communications Program

The Role of the Director/Administrator

The director/administrator is the role model for the management team. It is critical to maintain a high level of visibility and credibility. Employees need to see clear evidence of support for the organization's communications program by the Director in order for the program to be successful. Directors should participate in periodic employee meetings, state-of-the-company meetings and question-and-answer briefings with employees.

The Role of the Management Staff

The management staff serves as an extension of the director and a role model for the rest of the management team. Consistency, constancy of purpose, and accessibility are critical, and the lack of these factors is a serious drawback to a successful program.

Creating a Communications Strategy

A focused communications process ensures employees receive and understand the information they need within the time frame prescribed. The strategy and its communication must be obvious with the culture and purpose of the organization.

Use of Multiple Communication Methods

Get the messages to employees by a process including a variety of communication methods and tools. Examples include state-of-the-company meetings, department staff meetings, newsletters(printed or electronic), memoranda and letters, company intranets, open door policies, lunch with the owner/director and staff e-mails. A variety of methods should be used to reinforce the message(s) over time.

Offer Communications Training

Basic training in public speaking and writing fundamentals is a prerequisite for success. Training and education ensures a consistent understanding of the organization's communications philosophy, a common program language and clarification of roles and responsibilities in relation to the program.

Safeguard Credibility

If employees perceive a lack of consistency in what the organization does versus what it says, a credibility gap will occur which will affect employee morale and productivity. Once this happens, it is often difficult to recover. Management can safeguard organizational credibility by giving straight answers to difficult questions. This will require patience, diplomacy and effective communication skills. The best way to handle these situations is to be in a position to anticipate them by staying close to your employees.

Actively Listen

Listen first with the intention to understand; then listen with the intention to respond. Take time to listen with understanding. We will hear more, and we will find that our answers will generally hit home more often the first time around.

Seek Input

People want to talk about what they think, share how they feel and let us know their opinions on what should be done to resolve certain issues. Possible ways to collect information from interested employees include questionnaires, focus groups, attitude surveys and anecdotal feedback from other managers.

Provide Feedback

Questionnaires, surveys and audits can be designed to periodically measure program success. Key findings and program changes must then be shared with affected audiences as they are identified or as they occur to ensure feedback.

Revisit Communications Strategy

Periodically revisit overall communications strategy to assess where it is helping the organization meet its goals and objectives and where it is falling short. Take remedial action as necessary to improve the plan.

An Effective Administrator Communicates Both Formally and Informally with Parents Regarding Their Child's Development

Effective administrators support various strategies for communicating with parents. This is accomplished by:

- Supporting staff in communicating with parents
- Providing a means for accommodating parents with diverse backgrounds and parenting expectations
- Educating parents about child development and behavioral expectations of children in group settings
- Providing information and support to assist parents in their roles as parents
- Providing information on community resources related to all aspects of family life

Why is it important to communicate with parents? The society we live in today has more working mothers than ever before. The 1950's and 1960's concept of the traditional family has been replaced by two working parents, single parents, and many combinations of blended families with children receiving care outside the home. The one element not changed is the parent's responsibility for what happens to his child. Family values and traditions are generated from the home. Early care and education centers, private sitters, churches and public/private schools must work together with these various family units. The developed partnership and communication between all concerned parties in a child's life serves as a critical link for the child's benefit. Parents want to know what is happening to their children and they want to be included in the decision-making process. It is imperative the early care and education center provide an array of exemplary written communication and train staff to communicate clearly and effectively. Parents can be personally included in the center mainstream via informal chats, telephone calls, short written notes from teachers, and invitations to visit in the classroom.

Train your staff to impart all communication in a positive manner. Communication channels will shut down if the parent receives nothing but criticism from center staff. The objective is to gain parental support and involvement, not alienation. A daily goal of each member of staff should be to relay a positive thought to every family member of the children being served. Pick up and drop off times are vital for staff communication with parents or other persons involved. A parent's impression of the center's program and their child's experience is primarily determined by what they see and hear when they are in the center. That means if a parent and child are greeted warmly by name, sees a clean, inviting and safe atmosphere, and receives some positive personalized information about their child the parent will likely have a positive impression of the program. And parents will tell others about their impressions of your program whether they be positive or negative.

If a communication breakdown does occur between a staff member and a parent, you must step in as a mediator to restore the relationship. Being a good communicator starts with being a good listener. You cannot become inflexible or insensitive to the concerns of a parent, and very often you will discover problems at the center are reflected at home. Work with the parent and the teacher to resolve misunderstandings and guide them in discovering what is best for the child.

Formal Communication Systems

Center Policies and Procedures

These include any written information given in the form of handouts or handbooks to the parents. Your policies and procedures should give parents information about the program's mission statement, philosophy and curriculum goals; policy concerning discipline; policy about children who bite; policy about sick children; policy about who may pick up children; state center hours of operation, emergency procedures, tuition schedules, and when miscellaneous fees; list holidays the center is closed; give daily classroom schedules for each age group; arrival and dismissal instructions; personal items to be supplied by parents; information on food service provided at the center, including times meals/snacks are served; transportation information; instructions for dispensing medicine; and circumstances for which parents will receive notification, such as medical emergencies, adverse reaction to medication and exposure to a communicable disease and enrollment forms to be completed. Complete policies can become quite lengthy and costly to print. Use a short synopsis of policies in your parent handbook with and invitation to read and/or receive a copy of the full policy.

Daily Schedule

A daily schedule indicates activities at given intervals throughout each day in each classroom of the center. The schedule should list activity times, snack times, lunch, nap time and outdoor times in sequential order. Schedules should be individualized by the organized groupings in your center.

Tuition/Fee Schedule

This schedule outlines tuition breakdowns for various ages of children and where applicable discounts for additional children in a single family, if any. It also indicates payment due date, registration fees, late payment charges, return check charges, vacation fees, field trip charges, and any other miscellaneous fees that might be incurred. Thoroughly discuss the fee schedule with new parents to clarify any questions. Advise parents of the center policy regarding non-payment of fees.

Student Evaluations /Assessments

These tools are used to notify parents of formal student evaluations which will be conducted and asks permission for their child to be included. Once evaluation results are tabulated, give parents a copy of the assessment and information on how to interpret the results. Make the purpose of the assessment process and how the results will be used clear to each child's parents. The use of any assessment tool means parents and teachers must be thoroughly trained and aware in interpreting and using the results. Guide and train parents and teachers in utilizing assessment findings effectively. It is important to remind parents how children develop at different rates and should not be compared to their peers at this or any level. Parents can reinforce and build a child's skills by providing learning opportunities at home and by keeping learning fun. If a child's developmental level is remarkably different from his peer group, encourage the parents to seek a more in-depth evaluation to screen for developmental delays or learning disabilities. Such an evaluation should be conducted by an outside professional who can recommend alternative remediation options for the child.

Speech, language, vision, and hearing screening may be done annually at the center by any number of local professionals. If all children are not screened, the classroom teachers may recommend screening for those children who do not fall in the range of normal speech patterns for the age group. Caution teachers not to make untrained assessments/diagnosis to parents, but rather report suspicions to the director who can then follow up with the parents.

Parent Newsletter

A parent newsletter keeps parents abreast of center happenings. This might include such information about the center programs, staff news, curriculum highlights, planned field trips, parenting tips, developmental expectations, center wide meetings, parents' conferences, center picture dates, and any other general information helpful to parents.

A formal communication link between the center and the parents serves to strengthen the relationship between the center and home. Daily work schedules do not always allow parents enough time to chat with teachers or get answers to questions they may have. A regularly published newsletter keeps communication open and flowing with parents and draws them into the mainstream of what is happening with their children.

Weekly/Daily Classroom Activity Notes

A weekly/daily classroom activities listings posted in parent information areas of each classroom stating the major activity taking place helps parents keep up with weekly themes and activities and reinforce topics at home. Teachers may use this to solicit parent participation in activities or provide enrichment materials.

Daily Classroom Activity Schedule

Posting a specific and detailed daily schedule for each class helps inform parents about what happens in their child's class each day.

Parent Bulletin Board

When placed in the vicinity of high traffic areas, a bulleting board will encourage parents to check for important center information. The parent bulletin board should contain pertinent information as required by state licensing or quality rating systems, such as:

A copy of the state license for the center

A copy of or location of current state rules

A statement advising parents of their right to review a copy of the center's most recent licensing inspection

A current communicable disease chart

A statement allowing parental access to any care area of the center upon notifying the staff of their presence in the building

A listing of people responsible for administration of the center in the director's absence

The current weekly menu

Emergency plans including severe weather	A statement requiring visitors to check in with the staff when entering the center
	A non-discrimination policy statement

Menu

A menu should be posted weekly indicating what will be served for breakfast, snacks, and lunch each day of the week the center is open. Date each menu to reflect the week of service and note any substitutions.

Parent/Teacher Conferences

These conferences should be scheduled as required by your policy and as set by the licensing, accreditation or quality rating system for your center. A conference allows parents and teachers to get better acquainted, share information about the child, ask questions, and discuss curriculum objectives for the class. A conference allows follow-up on goals and individual child performance. It also allows parents and teachers to jointly determine a child's readiness to move on to the next level of the program. An informal parent conference should be scheduled any time the director and staff feel a child is having problems or difficulties requiring parent input to resolve.

Open House

Invite parents to come and visit the classrooms, chat with staff, and view the children's work as a warm and special way to bond families with the center. An open house gathering should be a fun and festive occasion possibly geared to a particular time of year, such as fall, winter, or spring holidays. A sample agenda for this event may be a tour of the classrooms, refreshments, and a presentation by a group of the children. It is not a time to discuss problems or have spontaneous parent/teacher conferences. Parents should be encouraged to make an appointment for mutually-convenient time for conference.

Child Development/Parenting Classes

Regularly schedule classes with topics of parent interest or concern. Such classes could be offered to the parents in your program as well as others in the community. You might offer workshops on child development, discipline, stress management, nutrition, etc. If financially able you might encourage parent attendance by providing free child care. Draw on local pediatricians, adult education groups and family counselors to be presenters at these workshops. Before going to all the work of arranging for a class, poll the parents to see if there is sufficient interest to warrant the class.

Community Resource List

A list should be kept containing local doctors and their specialties, the location, phone number, and the services offered at the local health department, and contact information for reporting child abuse. The list should also include phone numbers for United Way or other organizations that help families in distress, a listing of local churches, listing and location of area public schools, and what, if any, extracurricular resources are available for children. This information may be gathered via the

Yellow Pages in the local phone book, the internet, calling the local health department, calling the area council of churches, checking with the local Chamber of Commerce, checking with the local Resource and Referral Office, department of education and recreation department, and by asking parents to provide feedback or suggestions regarding community resources.

Parent Advisory Group

This will give parents an opportunity to be a sounding board and give feedback to proposed goals and objectives. This parent resource group can be invaluable in recruiting parent volunteers, organizing and implementing fund raisers, and serving as a public relations team between the center and the community. Remember, the more involved the parent, the more likely the child is to perform well.

Informal Communications

Community Activity News

Community flyers concerning parenting classes, personal development classes, kids' fairs, community gatherings, etc., should be placed in a central location for parent examination and pick-up if desired.

Parent Library

Provide a parent library of books, magazines and videos in a convenient, central location to encourage browsing and checking out materials. Free parent help books are available at www.edpub.gov. You might order these to give to parents for their own reference library.

An Effective Administrator Establishes and Maintains Security Practices

Center security is of primary concern because of the enormous responsibility we have in caring for young children. It is unfortunate that life today is full of danger for adults and children alike. We must protect those in our care from dangerous situations that did not exist in years past.

You are ultimately responsible for the protection of the staff and children in the center. Basic safety measures keep children safe and parents reassured. Different centers employ different security features depending on their location, size, budgets, and needs. These include:

Releasing Children

You must be certain children are released only to persons authorized to take them. Make sure your systems keeps staff informed of all persons who may pick up children. Keep all legal papers provided to you regarding the release of children in a secure place with necessary information available to staff checking children in and out.

Incident Reports

You, as the director, need a formal communication system between your office and your staff so you know what problems occur in the classroom each day. Regardless of whether the problems are major or minor, you must stay informed. The use of an incident report to state what occurred, when, who was supervising, and what remedial measures were taken is an informal method of keeping track of daily happenings. Most parent complaints stem from minor incidents, so it is imperative you know about the bites and the scratches as well as the major falls and bumps.

Disaster Procedures

You must be prepared for fire, storm, and other natural disasters. Most states require all programs conduct fire and/or disaster drills monthly. Take these drills seriously. Practice using different exits, at different times of the day. New staff should be trained on these procedures from the first day they work. At least annually conduct a disaster drill with multiple components (no electricity, some rooms unusable, use emergency stored water, evacuate the property, etc.) giving all staff a better perspective. After any drill or even an actual incident the director should debrief with the staff to adjust procedures for future use.

Medications

Early care and education centers are frequently called upon to dispense prescription medication to young children. Not only do you need medication permission forms signed by parents, but written policies and procedures for staff to follow if and when they dispense medications of any kind. Include in your procedures a medication dispensing form that notes the day, time, and name of the staff person who has given the medication. Medicine should be dispensed according to the directions. Your policies should indicate that no child should receive any medication without written authorization from the parent or physician.

Fencing

Fencing is effective in the playground area, because it prevents children from wandering away from the center. It is less effective in keeping unwanted persons out. There are times when keeping children from harm from unwanted persons entering outdoor play areas conflict with local fire regulations about the safe evacuation route from the facility. The procedures you adopt should comply with all regulatory standards used in your area.

Electronic Monitoring

Many centers use video cameras to cover doors and parking areas. These are effective if someone is watching the monitor. Some centers use electric eyes or other methods of alerting you to someone entering the building. Even then, you would not want to confront an intruder. There are many security programs available to help monitor and control who enters your facility. Provide extra security by designing your policies so you or a staff person monitors the entry. All visitors must sign in and out of your center.

Emergency Procedures

The most valuable security tool we have today is the ability to call 911 for assistance - for police, fire, or ambulance. Some programs have telephones located in all rooms making calling for emergency responders even easier. In an emergency our brain might be unable to recall even basic information. Post emergency phone numbers and your address on each telephone for easy reference in an emergency.

Security Systems

Alarm systems are also good protective measures for both safety and fire. It alerts you to forced entry, the presence of fire or smoke, and some automatically phone the police or fire department. Some have a panic button discreetly hidden behind the desk to send a silent signal to the police department for help. Outdoor lighting is another added protection of the building after hours.

To assure children are properly treated in the center, you will want to:

- Carefully screen job applicants
- Observe teachers frequently throughout the day
- Be vigilant in selecting qualified substitute teachers
- Prevent children from coming in contact with repairmen, janitors, or other outsiders who may come into the center on an occasional basis

Many centers are designed with an open floor plan, enabling the teachers to see one another. Other centers employ viewing windows and surveillance cameras as a means of observing classrooms.

Most state regulations require centers have evacuation plans in case of fire or severe weather. Be sure every staff member reads and understands these plans. Hold regular drills to practice and refine your response. Plans for relocation to an emergency shelter away from the center should be part of the plan. Multiple methods of contacting parents (such as work and cell phone, signs, radio station announcements) in an emergency should be part of the plan and should be part of your drill process at least annually.

Planning ahead for potential disasters can minimize the impact on you, your staff and the families you serve.

An Effective Administrator Manages the Program Efficiently Using an Organized System Which May Include the Use of Computers Combined with a Paper System

A smooth, efficient center operation depends on having an organized record keeping system. Records must be kept on every facet of center operations, and some of these records must be maintained for long periods of time. An adequate storage system is necessary to house records and have them available for easy access. You will need a combination of paper based and software based systems to efficiently and effectively respond to all the required record keeping.

Keep formal records in the following center operational categories

Registration Form

This form should contain:

- The child's name
- Date of birth
- Sex
- Address
- Living arrangement
- School attending, if applicable
- Names and addresses of both parents
- Work addresses of parents
- Home, cell, and work telephone numbers
- E-mail addresses
- Names and addresses of person(s) to whom the child may be released accompanied by court documentation as necessary.
- Names and telephone numbers of emergency contacts when the parents cannot be reached
- A signed agreement between the center and parents regarding services and meals to be provided
- Authorization to obtain emergency medical care for the child if the parent is not available
- The child's physician or clinic and phone number
- A statement from the child's parents regarding the child's health, noting any allergies and physical, mental or developmental conditions which would require special attention, as well as any special needs the child may have and what agreement has been reached with the center to provide special services.
- The application form should be written as an agreement for you to provide services and should be signed by the enrolling parent or parents and dated.

Child Care Immunization Certificate

State rules vary on the length of time you may allow parents to provide you with proof of current immunizations for their children. Certainly this should be no longer than thirty days from the date of enrollment. You will want to note when the next immunization is due for each child and keep a tickler file on those dates so, at the first of each month, you can send a reminder to each child's parents of an immunization shot needed along with an updated certificate or proof of immunization. Once a new certificate is turned in to the center, the old certificate may be discarded. Certificates for school-age children may be unnecessary if your state requires each child to be fully immunized to enter school.

Keep the immunization certificate files updated. An easy way to be sure a certificate has come in on each child is to keep an extra copy of the master roll for highlighting the names of all children with a current certificate on file. It should be updated monthly, and it will show at a glance which children have not turned in a certificate. This allows you to follow up on new enrollments who must present a certificate within thirty days of enrolling. Many software packages designed for child care programs have a feature allowing you to quickly see which children are in need of immunizations.

Attendance Rosters

Each individual classroom should have a copy of the master roll sheet listing the children in the class. As children enroll or withdraw, their names should be added or deleted from the correct classroom roster. At the beginning of each month distribute new classroom rolls produced from the center's master copy. Attendance should be taken at least once daily, but more often if you feel it is necessary to get an accurate accounting of children attending. At the end of the month the completed attendance rosters should be turned in to the office and then kept on file.

Medication Administration

Many states have licensing requirements regarding the administration of medication. Some states require that the person or persons designated to give medication complete approved medication administration training and have current first aid and universal precautions training prior to administering medication. Some states require centers have a licensed health consultant to observe and document the competency of each staff member involved in medication administration. These consultants are usually licensed registered nurses with knowledge and experience in maternal and child health. The required consultations must be specific to the needs of the facility and include some of the following topics: training, delegation and supervision of medication administration and special health procedures, health care, hygiene, disease prevention, equipment safety, nutrition, interaction between children and adult caregivers, and normal growth and development.

As part of your procedures, parents should authorize the dispensing of medication on a center medicine form. The form should state the date, child's full name, name of medication, prescription number (if any), dosage, dates medication is to be given, times of day medication is to be dispensed, and the parent's signature. The medicine form should contain blanks for staff documentation to indicate who gave the medication and at what time. The medicine form must also contain a statement advising the parents that they will be notified of any adverse reaction the child may have to the medication. When the medicine form expires, it should be turned in to the office and kept on file.

Non-prescription medication should have the child's full name written on the container. Medicine should be stored in a separate container in the center's refrigerator away from foodstuffs, or if not required to be refrigerated, in a container away from the children in the classroom. (Most states have sample forms to meet state requirements and require written permission from a doctor for the administering of these non-prescription medications).

Field Trip Permission Forms

If a child is to participate in a scheduled field trip, you must obtain written permission from the child's parents. Children who do not have signed permission may not participate. The field trip form should cover the following information.

- The name and address of the trip destination

Competency III: Internal and External Systems

- The date of the trip
- The time of departure and the estimated time of returning to the center
- Parent approval must include field trip destination, signature and date of approval

Take a roster of children participating in the field trip and an emergency card on each child with you on the trip. Also leave a copy of the field trip roster at the center in case of an emergency. Make sure the children participating in the field trip are wearing identifying information stating the child's name, center's name, address, and telephone number.

Transportation Agreement

Anytime the center agrees to transport a child a parental authorization is required. This authorization should specify:

- Routine pick up location and time
- Routine delivery location and time
- Action to be taken if child is not at routine delivery location
- Safety rules to be enforced while transporting children

Each child who attends a center's after-school program falls in this category if you offer transportation from the child's school. Children who are transported to extracurricular activities outside the center must also have transportation authorization.

Transportation Checklist

Develop a transportation checklist to ensure children using transportation provided by the center are accounted for in all situations. Staff involved in transportation should check a roster of children's names every time a child gets on or off the vehicle. The person conducting the check should sign the checklist and turn it in to the person in charge immediately upon the arrival of the children at the center. Transportation checklists should be kept on file.

Major Accident Report Forms

If you are required to report to state authorities the occurrence of a major accident requiring medical treatment beyond standard first aid provided at the center, you should create a major accident report form used to send information to the state and the insurance company if a claim is to be filed. The form should contain the following information.

- Center name and address
- Name, age and sex of injured person
- Indicate if injured is enrolled child, staff, or visitor
- Date and time of accident and who witnessed the accident
- Place of accident.
- Nature of injury
- Medical attention given

- Cause of accident
- Describe activity engaged at time of the accident
- Remedial steps taken and recommendation to prevent recurrence
- A statement that the parent was notified and at what time
- A diagram indicating where on the body the injury occurred
- A notation of the time when the parent arrived to pick up the child
- The director's signature and date

Minor Incident

This form is a mechanism providing the director information regarding minor incidents or behavioral problems occurring in the classrooms from time to time throughout the day. The report should include the child's name, age, date, time of the incident, the name of the reporting staff member, the type of complaint, the treatment that was given, and an indication if and when the parent was called to report the incident.

Infant Feeding Schedules

Parents enrolling an infant should complete an infant feeding plan to be used by center personnel. The feeding plan should contain the following information.

- The child's feeding schedule
- The amount of formula/food to be given
- Instructions for the introduction of solid foods
- A notation of any type of commercial, premixed formula which may not be used in an emergency because of food allergies

The parents must sign the plan and update it regularly as the infant's dietary needs change.

Enrollment Files

Individual files should be maintained on each child in the program containing all the prescribed information pertaining to the child. As information changes, the enrollment form should be updated or replaced and old information retained according to your record and retention schedule.

Enrollee Evaluations

If the center employs any formal assessment tools, copies of the individual results should be placed in the children's files. If parents do not receive a copy, they should have access to the information in the center's file.

Diaper Changing Charts

This record is helpful for center personnel and it provides parents with information at the end of each day. It should include when a child's diaper was checked and/or changed, whether the child was wet or had a bowel movement, and how many times a child was changed in a given day. The staff person caring for the child should mark the chart appropriately and sign/initial the chart when finished with each change.

Sign In/Sign Out Record

Record daily attendance, arrival and departure as required by your program and your state licensing agency.

An Effective Administrator Provides a Nutritious, Sanitary, Cost Effective Food Service That Is Responsive To the Scheduling Needs of the Center

The first step in planning the food service program is to decide whether the food will be prepared in house or catered by an outside vendor. The majority of early care centers choose to prepare food in house, but if catering is the service of choice, food must be prepared in a facility with a current food service permit and maintained at a safe temperature (41 degrees or below for refrigerated foods or 140 degrees for food requiring heating before serving). The vendor must be able to provide the food at the time prescribed by the center. The cost of the meals would be included in the parent fee schedule as an included or additional cost.

Food prepared in house must be handled in accordance with state regulations governing food service. Safe practices include a designated kitchen that contains a safe food storage area, non-porous counter tops, ventilation system or windows that opens, a three compartment sink and commercial-grade dishwasher, a commercial refrigerator, and shielded kitchen lights. The water supply and sewage disposal system should be approved by local health officials if they are not part of the community water/disposal system. Many state or local health departments are now requiring commercial appliances including a fire suppressant system over the stove.

Food products not in original containers should be stored in sealed food service containers labeled with contents and date. All food containers should be stored above the floor on pallets or shelves. The kitchen should also have a large, suitable garbage can with a lid.

Select only good quality, USDA-inspected food. Eggs, pork, pork products, poultry, and fish must be thoroughly cooked to avoid the possibility of food poisoning. Keep hot foods at 140 degrees except during serving and cold foods or perishable items refrigerated at 41 degrees or below. Freezer temperatures must be zero degrees Fahrenheit or below. Wash all raw fruits and vegetables thoroughly before cooking or serving to remove any potentially harmful pesticides.

Menu Planning

As you plan for food service at the early care and education center, consider the daily food needs of the children. Vary the combination of meals and snacks according to the ages of the children, the time they arrive at the center, and the number of hours they spend at the center. Carefully plan the timing of meals so children don't become hungry and irritable between meals.

Research tells us that good nutrition is important for children; studies have demonstrated that good nutrition has a long term impact on brain development and cognition.

Children should not be served or have access to certain foods or drinks. Do not make soft drink machines or food vending machines available to children. For choking reasons it is suggested not serving peanuts, hot dogs, raw carrots, fish with bones or grapes to children under three years of age. When served these foods should be cut into small pieces for young children. Foods with little or no nutritional value and foods that do not meet USDA nutritional requirements should be avoided; these foods include sweets, cookies, and non-fruit based juices.

Be creative and imaginative as you plan appealing, economical and practical menus. Plan menus at least two to four weeks ahead to allow for food purchase and preparation scheduling. You will find it helpful to plan cycle menus that rotate systematically every four to five weeks. It is a way to provide variety and to control costs.

Vary the food being served. Variety is accomplished by the form of food (raw and cooked), size and shape of the food (round, cubed, sticks, etc.), color of the food, texture of the food (crisp, soft), and the flavor of the food (strong, mild, sweet, sour).

In planning meals consider the facilities and equipment available. Consider oven and surface-cooking capacity as well as refrigerator and freezer space. How many serving pieces do you need? How many children are you feeding in what time frame? Determine the serving size you will need and calculate the amount of food you needed for the total number of meals to be served. USDA Food Guidelines should be consulted to see menu choices are acceptably nutritious.

As menu planning occurs, consider the population being fed. Take into consideration regional food preferences, cultural sensitivities (are certain foods prohibited because of religious teachings) and ethnicity. Offer a variety of foods to appeal to diverse ethnic backgrounds such as Mexican, Chinese, Italian, Asian, Middle Eastern, etc.

Dietary Restrictions

Another concern in menu planning is focused on children with special diets who cannot eat from the standard menu. If the exception is for medical reasons, a doctor's statement should be kept in the child's file. If the exception is for religious reasons or personal preference, the parent should write a statement to be kept in the child's file. Staff members need to be advised of a child's diet restrictions, and the child should only be served foods that comply with the restriction. The modified menu must still meet the USDA Food Guideline nutrition requirements. If for some reason the center is unable to supply the special dietary needs of a child with diet restrictions, the director must advise the parents and arrange for the parents to provide meals for the child. Some centers are specializing in vegetarian menus or serving only organic foods to meet the wishes of families in their area.

Post dated menus weekly on a designated parent bulletin board near the office or lobby of the center. Note any substitutions made in the menu, and keep the menus on file after use. Review your menus on a regular basis to compare food selection with food waste, food item availability, and seasonal changes.

Competency III: Internal and External Systems

Purchasing

Most early care and education centers operate on a limited food budget, and the director has the responsibility of planning menus that stay within the budgetary limit. Therefore, comparison shopping becomes necessary to determine where to get quality for the best price. Compare prices and availability with local grocery stores and commercial food vendors. Buy only federally inspected food. Calculate the quantities you need based on the number of meals you will serve and buy according to your preplanned menu. Consider center storage facilities so you do not over buy. Perishable items should be used within two days of purchase while canned goods and staples can be purchased in greater quantities and stored longer. Check the use by date for shelf life.

Keep an accurate record of all food expenditures to determine the actual food costs per menu. You may be able to significantly adjust food cost by preparing the menu item from a recipe rather than buying it already prepared or vice versa. Check food prices frequently with food vendors and inquire about the availability of new food items.

Early care and education programs participating in the Child and Adult Care Food Program must serve nutritious food to both preschool and school-aged children in their programs. Centers participating in this program must comply with USDA Child and Adult Care Food Program nutrition requirements. These programs are eligible for assistance in planning and implementing their food service operations and receive monetary reimbursement for meals served.

Assistance with Food Service

When you have reached the end of your creative ability to enhance the weekly menu, turn to community resource people for fresh ideas. Local home economists, school food service coordinators, and the local cooperative extension service can provide a wealth of information and ideas about menu planning. Request literature or ask one of these professionals to visit your center to view the food service area and make suggestions. Food service seminars are generally available around the state.

Sanitation

Sanitation is one of the most important components of good food service. It is important to prepare nutritious meals, but it is equally important that the food be germ free and the food preparation area be clean. Keep all equipment and utensils clean and free of dust, dirt, food particles, and grease deposits. Examine food for spoilage and carefully wash food that is to be served raw. Store food properly and throw away portions served but not eaten. Take particular care handling meats to prevent cross contamination with other foods. Be sure food service workers wash their hands thoroughly with soap and water before handling food. People with colds, sores, or communicable diseases should not prepare food.

The person in charge of food service must be familiar with large-quantity food preparation and have knowledge of portion requirements by age groups. This person will be responsible for following menu requirements and preparing meals within the time frame allotted. She is also responsible for keeping the kitchen organized, clean and caring for food according to regulations.

Food Service

If children are served meals in their classrooms teachers should be trained to serve meals properly. Meals should be delivered in bulk at a regular meal time each day. Teachers may either serve all plates before bringing the children to the table or have the children take their seats and serve the food family style. Portions should be small but commensurate with the age of the child. Second and third servings should be available upon request. Serve the USDA recommended amount of milk at each meal, but give children small quantities at first to avoid spills and then refill to meet the requirement. All unused food, dirty dishes and silverware should be returned to the kitchen immediately after the food service. Place discarded food in a sealed garbage container. Wash and sanitize the tables and sweep and mop the floor to remove food particles and spills. Serve snacks both mid-morning and mid-afternoon. Place finger foods on napkins or paper plates, not directly on the table top.

Teachers should:

- Encourage children to try new foods and practice good table manners
- Role model good table manners by eating with the children and talking about good eating habits
- Encourage older children to help clean up after meals by stacking plates or wiping off tables

An Effective Administrator Oversees Janitorial and Maintenance Needs of the Building, Grounds, and Vehicles to Ensure Safety and Proper Repair

You do not have to know how to repair everything in the center. You just need to know when equipment needs repair and who to call to get it repaired.

Maintenance Request Forms

A good way to keep on top of maintenance needs is to ask your teachers to complete maintenance request forms weekly. The teacher will take an inventory of classroom and playground equipment each week and note on the form any broken items (including location of all parts) and anything in need of replacement or repair.

Someone should be designated to inspect the vehicles and the food service staff should perform inspection duties for the food service areas. The office, parking lot and entry will probably be your responsibility or you might delegate these areas to another member of management. The maintenance request forms should be turned in to you on a designated day of the week. You will then look at the request and determine what action to take. By performing these weekly checks, you will prevent greater damage occurring to equipment, limit liability, spread maintenance costs over a longer period of time, and keep the center in good repair on an on-going basis.

Competency III: Internal and External Systems

Calendaring Repairs

Since there are a number of maintenance chores to be performed at regular intervals, it is helpful to create a calendar for this purpose. You might include items such as: changing the furnace filters, changing the vehicle oil, rotating tires, carpet cleaning, etc.

Basic Tool Kit

Keep a basic tool kit available in the center for those minor repairs you and your staff *can* do - tightening a screw, snipping off a sharp edge, hammering in a nail. The key to preventing major repairs is to address maintenance needs as soon as you notice them. When a table wobbles, tighten the screws. When a sink runs slowly, plunge it. Check and tighten the bolts on play equipment, both indoor and outdoor, regularly. If you have the basic tools and regularly maintain your equipment, you will ultimately save a lot of money and provide a safer and more pleasant environment for the children and staff.

Suggestions for your basic tool kit are listed below.

- Claw hammer
- 1 Phillips head screwdriver
- 1 regular screwdriver
- Assorted nuts and bolts
- Brads, tacks, and nails
- Spray lubricant
- Wire cutters
- Scissors
- Heavy duty carpenters glue
- Steel retractable measuring tape
- Toilet plunger
- Assorted sand paper
- Assortment of wrenches
- Plier

Checklists

The director may wish to develop a checklist for each classroom, for the kitchen, playground, office and entry areas so staff will not overlook any equipment when making their inspections. For example, the checklist for a classroom might include such items as toys, cots, flannel boards, easels, etc.

In addition to equipment maintenance, the director is responsible for managing the maintenance of the building and grounds. As staff inspects equipment in their areas of responsibility, they should also bring to your attention any building maintenance or repair that is needed. You should certainly develop a checklist for your janitorial staff so no cleaning tasks are overlooked. The checklist can include daily, weekly, and monthly routine tasks. A checklist is also helpful for listing tasks that must be done on the grounds - mowing, edging, pruning, spraying, etc.

Perhaps your teaching staff will be responsible for some daily chores themselves such as keeping their supplies in order, wiping off the children's tables, cleaning up art project messes, etc. Be sure to clearly communicate your expectations to your staff in this regard. Demonstrate your expectation for specific cleaning and organizing tasks.

Expert List

Keep a list of maintenance and repair experts to call when needed. Ask other business persons for suggestions of companies and individuals whose work they have found satisfactory. Prepare your list before you need help. When you're desperate, you can't be choosy.

Keeping your building and grounds in top condition lessens the need for expensive major repairs, makes your center appealing from the street and from within, and says a lot about your professionalism. Just as important, it teaches children respect for their property and for the property of others.

An Effective Administrator Has Knowledge of Community Services, Is Able to Refer Families and Staff to Social Services, to Health Services and Education, and to Training Appropriate to Their Individual Needs

As part of your role as a liaison between parents and community, you are responsible for connecting parents with appropriate social service agencies such as the health department, local doctors, the local family and children service agency, family counselors, and developmental therapists. You work not only with children but with families as well. Because of your close daily contact with parents and children, you may get to know families quite well. When family dynamics dictate help or intervention, you must respond accordingly. You may provide a list of local and state social service agencies for parents to pursue, or make specific recommendations for services to address particular problems or needs.

Do you know where to refer parents or staff for any of the following?

Autism	Avoiding burn-out	Disinfecting equipment	Curriculum development
Child abuse and neglect	Childhood diabetes	Program quality improvement	Developing a business plan
Eligibility for subsidized care	Coaching and mentoring	Strategic planning	Literacy resources
Poisonous Plants	Licensing standards	Surface treatments for the playground	Menu planning
Setting tuition rates	Math activities for three year olds	Teacher credentials	Staff training/development
Writing a grant proposal	Overtime pay		Toddler classroom Arrangement

An Effective Administrator Manages Shared Space by Negotiating and Maintaining a Positive Relationship with the Host and Any Other Users

Sharing classroom space with another group may be difficult for everyone, especially the teacher. Often she never feels free to rearrange the room, lacks the space to store supplies, and often finds equipment moved, lost, or broken.

One common situation involving shared space in early care and education programs is in a church. Five days a week the classroom is used for preschool and child care, but on Sunday the room is used for church school. The church school teacher is a volunteer who may not know which materials she may use or what liberties she may take with room arrangement. The preschool teacher arrives on Monday and can be very frustrated as nothing is where it was on Friday!

It is the role of the director to negotiate an agreement between the two entities using the space - an agreement that will best meet the needs of both and infringe the least on either.

As director you will need to sit down with the person in charge of the other program and discuss your respective needs and how the common space can best be shared. Each program should have a locked area to keep supplies. Both parties should agree on:

- Wall space for children's artwork
- Furniture arrangement
- Use of audio/visual equipment, books, and toys
- How cleaning chores will be divided
- Who will be responsible for breakage and wear-and-tear
- What, if any, food will be permitted in the classroom
- What art media may be used
- The precise days and hours each program will have use of the space

After an initial discussion, both program directors should take their ideas to their staff for further input, discussion and ideas. A second meeting of the directors might include a teacher representative from each program. Here both groups should be able to reach a final agreement acceptable to all parties. One of the most important terms of the agreement should be regular meetings between the two program heads to assess how the agreement is working and to modify it if necessary. This on-going dialogue is critical so frustration will not build up and misunderstandings stand in the way of mutual success. The agreement doesn't need to be a formal contract, but minutes of the meetings where agreements are reached will help both groups recall exactly was agreed.

You and staff should accept that shared space will likely be a less-than-perfect arrangement. Try to have a sense of humor when problems are minor and deal with major problems immediately so they don't become insurmountable. Be understanding when your staff has difficulty in sharing their classrooms with others. Help them to deal graciously with the teachers who share their rooms, and be their advocate when needed.

Summary

In order to show competency in internal and external systems, an effective administrator:

- Develops systems to keep the center running smoothly and to comply with applicable laws, rules, and regulations, and keeps these systems up to date to ensure the safety of staff and children

- Understands the importance of communication and develops communication systems for staff, parents, and the community

- Communicates both formally and informally with parents regarding their child's development

- Establishes and maintains security practices

- Manages the program efficiently using an organized system which may include the use of computers combined with a paper system

- Provides a nutritious, sanitary, cost effective food service that is responsive to the scheduling needs of the center

- Oversees janitorial and maintenance needs of the building, grounds, and vehicles to ensure safety and proper repair

- Manages shared space by negotiating and maintaining a positive relationship with the host and any other users

If you feel you lack confidence in any of the skills listed above, please go back and review the appropriate section in this chapter.

Competency IV

Laws and Regulations

Competency IV Laws and Regulations

Learning Objectives:

- To identify local, state, and federal rules and regulations that effect early education programs

- To understand important legal information regarding child abuse and neglect, confidentiality, labor laws, health occupational safety laws, contracts, and anti-discrimination laws

- To be able to adhere to state licensing rules and regulations, and to local fire and health standards

An Effective Administrator Understands and Complies with Applicable Federal, State, and Local Regulations

In order to develop and maintain an effective organization, it is necessary for the center director to have a basic understanding of government and regulatory agencies effecting early childhood education programs.

Regulation from government comes in many forms. We know state, county, or local licensing agencies enforce program rules. One of the first steps for a new director is to become thoroughly familiar with state rules and regulations for early care and education programs. Without this working knowledge, she will not be able to assure compliance with the rules or work effectively with the licensing officials.

In addition to licensing rules, you need a good understanding of fire, building, zoning, and health code requirements. Criminal background checks and abuse or neglect registries are also a form of government regulation. Your center is subject to unemployment insurance requirements along with workers compensation. If you are proprietary, various forms of taxes are part of your relationships with government and, if your program is not-for-profit, you must negotiate the requirements established by government for those operations.

Below are listed the laws and regulations that govern you.

Federal

OSHA

The Occupational Safety and Health Administration develops rules employers must follow to prevent injuries to employees in the work place. The general duty of the employer is to ". . . furnish employees a place of employment free from recognized hazards likely to cause death or serious physical harm to the employees."

ADA

The Americans with Disabilities Act requires employers to reasonably accommodate employees and customers who have disabilities so these individuals can use the center and its program in the same way those without disabilities.

EPA

The Environmental Protection Agency has authority to regulate air pollution, water pollution, toxic substances, and solid waste. If your center is located in an area where local water, sewer, and garbage disposal services are unavailable, you would need to meet EPA requirements regarding water and waste disposal.

NLRB

The National Labor Relations Board enforces the National Labor Relations Act which gives employees the right to organize, prohibits unfair labor practices, and regulates the process of collective bargaining.

FLSA

The Fair Labor Standards Act requires employers to keep payroll records on all employees, pay men and women equal pay for equal work, pay at least the minimum wage to all covered employees, pay employees one and one half times their regular pay for time worked in excess of 40 hours in one week, and prohibits employers from oppressively employing child labor.

Federal Civil Rights Laws

These laws prohibit discrimination in employment on the basis of race, color, religion, national origin, age, or sex.

FTC

The Federal Trade Commission regulates competition, prohibiting monopolies and price fixing.

Immigration Laws

Requires all people furnish proof of their right to work in the United States.

State

Laws and regulations differ from one state to another. Your state department of education, department of human services, department of social services or department of health may impact your program through educational and licensing requirements or through the administration of the Child and Adult Care Food Program. Fire codes may originate at a state or local level. Your state department of transportation may have regulations for your vehicles and drivers.

Each state has its own rules and regulations governing early care and education programs. Generally these rules are developed by ad hoc committees composed of licensors, child development experts, community advisors and providers. The administrative procedure for promulgating regulations is typically prescribed by law and includes a public comment period. You must stay abreast of changes in your state's regulations and contribute to the development of new rules by serving on the committee that reviews the rules, by providing input to the state association representing providers, or by taking advantage of the public comment period to express your views in writing.

Various states have different laws regarding which programs must be licensed. Some states do not license family child care homes. Others do not license religious-based programs, part-day programs, Mother's Morning Out programs, or public school programs.

In most states failure to comply with the regulations results in penalties or revocation of license. The rules and/regulations should clearly state what the penalties are and what grievance/appeal procedure exists. You need to know your rights as well as your responsibilities. Are you permitted to dispute a finding of your licensing representative? What is the correct procedure? Must you sign a form with which you disagree? When may you contact your licensing representative's superior? Knowing your rights and exercising them in a firm but pleasant manner will foster a good working relationship with your licensing representative.

Your state may also have a law requiring a criminal records check for anyone working with children in an early care and education program. The law will specify the following.

- Who is responsible for obtaining the criminal records check - you or the employee?
- What constitutes a crime prohibiting a person from working in an early care and education program?
- Whether the background check must be completed or just initiated when the employee begins work and what restrictions, if any, must be placed on the employee while awaiting the results of the check
- Whether the check must be made of state criminal records, FBI records or both
- Your responsibility should an employee be found to have a criminal record

Local

Most local county, parish, or city entities have their own zoning codes, building codes, and building inspectors who regulate new construction and renovation. Local fire officials may also have jurisdiction over buildings open to the public. This may also be true of environmental health regulations and rules governing food service, drinking water, waste disposal, etc. Zoning codes are generally local matters as well.

You need a working knowledge of these laws and regulations and a system for documenting compliance with them.

An Effective Administrator Works with Legal Counsel and Demonstrates General Knowledge of Legal Issues Concerning Child Care

Custody Issues that Matter to Early Childhood Education Centers

"To whom may I release children?" The answer to this question in normal situations is probably the child's parents or someone designated by the parents. The normal situation is not the one that gives you headaches or threatens you with legal liability.

Married Parents

Both parents have equal custody rights to the child. There should be no trouble releasing the child to either parent or their designee, unless there are court documents stating otherwise.

Unmarried Parents

When a child is born out of wedlock, and the parents have not subsequently married or gone to court to have the child declared the legitimate child of the biological father, the biological father is said to be the putative father. Putative fathers have no custody rights under most state laws.

Divorcing Parents

When parents file a divorce action in which custody is an issue, the court hearing the case will schedule a temporary hearing. The purpose of the hearing includes determining which parent has temporary custody of the child. Initially, and for a short period after the complaint for divorce is filed, both parents will have equal custody as in the normal situation above. After the temporary hearing, one parent may have sole temporary custody, or both may have joint custody.

In many divorce cases this is not a problem for the early care and education director. Even if one parent is given temporary custody, the other parent likely will have visitation rights established in the temporary order and may, as a result of that visitation or other arrangement with the custodial parent, pick up or drop off the child. It is wise to have an original copy of the court's order and to ask the custodial parent for instructions. Note that court orders have expirations dates. The parent/guardian should provide a new court order which then becomes the document you will work with.

Where the early care and education director has problems is when divorcing parents have gone to war with one another. Custody is frequently a burning issue. If you believe one of the parents is trying to take the child when not authorized to do so, call the police. The police may not be any better able to handle the situation than you are, but at least you will avoid a great deal of liability for negligence and avoid a confrontational and perhaps dangerous incident. Again, it is wise to have an original copy of the court orders on file.

Divorced Parents

Where parents are divorced, a court will have given one of the parents permanent custody or both parents joint custody. Be aware of which parent is the legal custodian and ask for instructions from that parent regarding the other's access to the child. A copy of the original court document should be part of the paperwork provided to you by the enrolling parent.

Child Has Been Found Deprived by Juvenile Court

Occasionally you might have a child who is declared a ward of the juvenile court. The court will give someone (such as a relative or foster parent) temporary custody of the child. Ask for an original copy of the order and for instructions from the temporary custodian as to who may have access to the child. Do not be afraid to call your juvenile court to ask who the child's custodian is. It would be prudent to avoid becoming involved in a confrontation; call the police if it appears that there will be one.

Guardianships

Guardianship is established by the court. Should a child be enrolled in your center by a guardian, ask for an original copy of the guardianship order to keep in your file.

If someone (perhaps a parent) who does not have custody, or does not have permission from the custodian to take the child comes to the center, demands the child and insists on taking the child before the police can arrive, what should you do? There is no easy answer. You should resist access to the child as long as you can without incurring harm to yourself or others. Remember whether you or your center has any liability in such a situation largely depends on what a jury determines a reasonable person in like circumstances would have done. On one end of the spectrum you shouldn't give in the moment the person raises his voice, but you aren't required to get yourself killed to stop the person either. Call the police and stall as long as you can. If the person does leave with the child, get a physical description of the person, the child, and their car.

Releasing Children

Registration contracts should give authorization for specific individuals to pick up the child from your program. All persons picking up a child should be listed on the contract as authorized to pick up, and have picture ID. The parent or guardian should be notified immediately if anyone not authorized to pick up attempts to pick up.

For purposes of this discussion, there are five types of family situations.

- Married parents (normal relationship)
- Unmarried parents (father has not legitimated child)
- Divorcing parents
- Divorced parents
- Child has been found deprived by juvenile court guardianships

Child Abuse and Neglect Laws and Mandated Reporting

Most states have laws defining child abuse and neglect. These may include definitions of deprivation, molestation, cruelty to children, and reckless abandonment. It is important to be familiar with these definitions and with symptoms of child abuse.

Mandated Reporting

Many states include early care and education providers in the laws specifying persons required to report suspected child abuse. Usually these mandated reporters include physicians and other health care providers, teachers, and social workers as well. You need to know whether you are a mandated reporter and, if so, to whom you must report suspected abuse. You also need to know whether your state law requires your teachers to report directly or whether they are to report suspected abuse to you first and then you report it to the authorities.

Most state laws will spell out the penalties for not reporting suspected abuse and will also require the agency to keep the identity of the reporter confidential.

Competency IV: Laws and Regulations

Suspected Child Abuse

When a report of an abused child surfaces, virtually everyone involved starts asking who did it. No one wants to be suspected and everyone starts pointing fingers at anyone else in the picture. You and your center are not immune from finger pointing. In order to combat this sort of witch hunt, some center's staff are required to or choose to establish the practice of inspecting each child when he arrives at the center each morning, recording any visible injuries, and reporting any suspicions they might have.

What if you or someone on your staff is accused of child abuse? What are your rights? Generally, an investigation of child abuse will be conducted by, or in conjunction with, the police. Should a police officer wish to question one of your employees, you do not have a right to be present. The officer may allow you to be present, but you have no right to be there. These allegations are very serious as we have seen in past well-publicized cases. It is important to consult your attorney or your employee's attorney immediately.

Confidentiality Laws Regarding Children

If your organization has an arrangement whereby it receives federal funds administered by the U.S. Secretary of Education, it is subject to the confidentiality provisions of the *Family Education Right to Privacy Act* and resulting rules in the Code of Federal Regulations. Fortunately, for students under the age of eighteen, the applicable part of the rules provide the center shall "...give full rights under the Act to either parent, unless the agency or institution has been provided with evidence that there is a court order, State statute, or legally binding document relating to such matters as divorce, separation, or custody that specifically revoked these rights." The rules further require each institution have in effect a policy describing how the institution meets the requirements of the act.

Children's Files

You should have a statement in your parent policies notifying parents that they may have access to any written records concerning their child at any time they request it. Your policy should also state how the parent or legal guardian should go about requesting the information and who else, if anyone, has access to these records. You might also want to include assurance that a child's records are considered confidential and will not be shared with anyone other than those identified as needing the information.

Confidentiality of Records

Generally it is not a good practice to share information about your customers or staff without a good faith reason to do so. You should be especially careful about any information concerning:

- Health (generally)
- Legitimacy
- Any other information you would consider personal if it applied to you

You may not inform those within your own organization of any HIV/AIDS infection without the consent of the parent or guardian of the child. The director may not even know an enrolled child is HIV positive. If the parent or guardian agrees, the director and primary caregiver may be told. To protect yourself ask the parents to sign a release of information form indicating exactly who is authorized to know the information.

Labor Laws Regarding Children and Employees

Employment of Minors

Most state rules for early care and education programs specify minimum age requirements for various positions. Typically, persons in charge of a group of children must be at least 18 years of age. If your state regulations do not specify minimum ages, the following federal laws apply.

- Minors under 16 may not work between 9:00 P.M. and 6:00 A.M.
- No minor under 16 may work during school hours unless excused by the appropriate school system.
- If you employ a minor under 18, you must obtain an employment certificate from his school system.

Fair Labor Standards Act of 1938 (FLSA)

This federal law requires employers to pay a minimum hourly wage that is set by law. Currently the federal minimum wage is $7.25 per hour. States, cities, and municipalities may set a higher minimum wage.

This act also requires employers to pay employees one and one-half their hourly rate for any hours worked in excess of 40 hours per week. In determining whether an employee should be paid overtime pay, you may not average the hours for two or more weeks. You do not have to pay an employee for hours in excess of eight in one day unless those hours cause the total number of hours worked in a week to exceed 40.

These wage provisions do not apply to certain younger workers who may be paid at a lower rate for up to 180 days in a year, or independent contractors, volunteers, and certain executive, professional, or administrative employees who are salaried.

Equal Pay Act of 1963

This part of the FLSA requires equal pay for male and female employees working under similar conditions and requiring equal skill, effort, and responsibility.

The Fair Labor Standards Act (FLSA) and Early Childhood Education Industry Problems

A significant problem for early childhood education is the lack of understanding of wage and hour laws and the interpretation of time worked. The following scenarios require that staff be paid for time worked.

- Supervising or eating with children during meal times
- Parent teacher conferences
- After hour staff meetings

Competency IV: Laws and Regulations

- Lesson planning at home
- Running errands outside of work hours
- Reporting early or staying late and being paid a flat fee for extra time, not the required rate of time and one half
- Classifying incorrectly exempt and non-exempt employees
- Paying overtime after an 80 hour two week period instead of after 40 hours each week

More information about this act may be found in *US Department of Labor publication WH 1312, reprinted December 1986, Regulations Part 785.*

Daycare Centers and Preschools as Identified Under FLSA

Early childhood care and education centers and preschools are called day care centers in the language of the FLSA as they are defined as providing custodial, educational, or developmental services to preschool age children to prepare them to enter elementary school grades.

This includes nursery schools, kindergartens, head start programs, and any similar facility primarily engaged in the care and protection of preschool age children.

Individuals who care for children in their home are not considered daycare centers unless they have employees to assist them with the care of the children.

FLSA Statutory Requirements

Overtime

The Fair Labor Standards Act (FLSA) requires payment of overtime premium after 40 hours in a workweek. The premium must be at the rate of 1 1/2 times the employee's actual hourly rate. Periodic bonuses must be included in determining hourly rate.

Minimum Wage

The FLSA requires that all employees be paid at least federal minimum wage; the federal minimum wage is $7.25 per hour. States, cities, and municipalities may set a higher minimum wage.

Records

Accurate time records must be maintained of employees' hours of work each day. The records must accurately reflect when an employee reports to work and when the employee leaves and any work done outside the center. It is strongly recommended unpaid lunch time also be documented.

Exempt and Non-exempt Employees

The Department of Labor divides employees into two categories called exempt and non-exempt from minimum wage and overtime laws. On August 23, 2004 new rules addressing exempt and non-exempt employees went into effect.

Exempt employees are not paid overtime by meeting certain criteria related to Executive, Administrative, or Professional work. For example: The employee must be paid a fixed salary of at least $455 per week which is $23,600 per year and meet one or more of the regulatory tests for exemption. The employee's primary duty must be the performance of office or non-manual work directly related to the management or general business operations of the employer or the employer's customers. Primary duty refers to the use of discretion and independent judgment.

An exempt executive must be able to hire and fire or to make recommendations regarding hiring and firing. The professional exemption requires that the employee be a learned professional. In both cases the salary base of $455 per week or $23,600 per year applies.

Are teachers learned professionals? Teachers are exempt if their primary duty is instruction, lecturing in the activity of importing knowledge and if they are employed and engaged in this activity as a teacher in an educational establishment (s). This exemption contemplates an employee with a high level of education and specialized training as distinguished from a general academic education. The interpretation of the law acknowledges that preschools may engage in some educational activities, but employees whose primary duty is to care for the physical needs of the children do not ordinarily meet these criteria.

Employees who are paid more than $100,000 per year and who perform non-manual work will be considered exempt if they customarily perform any identifiable executive, administrative, or professional duty described in the standard duties tests.

Any employee who owns at least 20% equity interest in the enterprise in which he or she is employed and who is actively engaged in management is an exempt executive. The salary basis test does not have to be met for this exemption.

Exempt Classifications

Professional Exemption

A professional is one whose position typically requires at least a Baccalaureate degree and the duties include the regular exercise of discretion (e.g. teacher, center director).

Executive Exemption

An executive is one who supervises two or more employees, the position requires the exercise of discretion, or the individual is in charge of a stand-alone operation.

Administrative Exemption

An administrative person is one who exercises discretion and independent judgment in the formulation and implementation of corporate policy.

Center & Preschool Teachers

If classified as exempt, teachers do not have to receive overtime compensation; however, in many cases they do not meet the exempt requirements.

The professional exemption as applied to teachers contemplates an employee with a high level of education and specialized training as distinguished from a general academic education.

Work that can be performed by employees with education and training below the college level will not be considered work of a bona fide professional level under the regulations defining the exemption for bona fide professional teachers.

Preschools and Day Care Centers may engage in some educational activities. Employees whose primary duty is to care for the physical needs of the facility's children would ordinarily not meet all of the requirements for exemption as teachers under the applicable regulations.

Structural Requirements for Exemption

In addition to the education and/or type of work performed by the individual for whom an exemption is sought, there are certain structural requirements. The individual must be paid on a salaried basis. The individual's salary may not be reduced for partial day absences. The employer must maintain a paid sick leave policy allowing the employee a specified number of paid days of absence for personal illness. After the paid sick days are exhausted, the employee's salary may be reduced for full day absences.

The employee must be compensated on a salary basis of at least $455.00 per week. More information on this topic may be obtained in *WH Publication 1281, revised August 23, 2004, Regulations Part 541*.

FLSA as it Relates to Rest and Meal Periods

Short breaks or rest periods must count as hours worked. Short usually means 20 minutes or less. Meal periods are considered 30 minutes or more and generally need not be compensated as time worked. An employee is not considered relieved of their work if required to perform any duties whether active or inactive while eating.

Bona fide meal periods (typically 30 minutes or more) generally need not be compensated as work time as long as the employee is completely relieved from duty for the entire meal period for the purpose of eating a regular meal.

The employee is not relieved from duty if required to perform any duties, whether active or inactive, while eating. Thus, an employee is not considered relieved if required to continue to watch over children while they and the employee eat their meal.

FLSA and Compensated Work Time

On-site Work

Time an employee is required or permitted to be at the work site must be compensated. Time that an employee is permitted to be on premises solely for the employee's convenience need not be compensated, if no productive work is performed (i.e. waiting for a ride, arriving early due to the convenience of transportation). Time spent at Center for parties and activities is generally compensable.

Off-site Work

Any time spent by an employee on work-related matters is compensable. Compensable time includes shopping for school supplies, attending school recruitment fairs or children's parties, preparing class plans or materials for student activities at home.

Lectures, Meetings, and Training Time

Time spent in training, whether on or off site and whether or not sponsored by the employer, is compensable unless certain requirements are met.

Test to Exclude Training Time from Compensation

Attendance is Voluntary

Employee is not required or encouraged to attend.

Attendance is Outside Employee's Regular Working Hours

The training session must be held at other than the employee's regularly scheduled work time.

Course Material is Not Directly Related to Employee's Job

If the substance of the training is uniquely related to the Center's policies or issues, the training is compensable. However, if the information is generic to the child care industry, and would assist an employee working at any child care center such as the employee attending an independent school or college on his/her own initiative outside work hours, the employee does not have to be paid.

Employee Does Not Perform Productive Work

The in-service cannot include the employee performing any work that is of direct benefit to the employer.

State-Required Training

If the State imposes the training requirement as a condition of the employee maintaining his/her certification or license, the time is not generally compensable. If the State imposes the training requirement on the employer as a condition of maintaining its license, the training is generally compensable.

Travel Time

Travel time that is associated with compensable training is also compensable if it occurs during normal working hours. Travel time outside regular working hours is not compensable. Travel between job sites is compensable. Travel to and from home to work is generally not compensable, unless the employer requires the employee to travel to a distant site other than the location at which the employee is regularly assigned.

Typical Problems

Employers not recording all hours of work ,for instance asking the employee to clock out for lunch even though the employee is asked to be with the children in the nap room or to run an errand for the employer

Employees reporting early or staying late who are paid a flat fee for this extra time, instead of paying proper overtime if such is applicable

Classifying employees who do not meet all the tests for exemptions, as exempt teachers and not paying such non-exempt staff appropriate overtime compensation

Paying overtime compensation after 80 hours worked over a two week period of time instead of the required overtime payment after 40 hours worked in each week

Compensatory Time

The most recent interpretation of rules does not allow private sector employees to accumulate compensatory time in lieu of cash payment – this includes overtime. Employees must be paid in cash; employees may flex their hours within a given week and time paid is based on the hours worked.

Inclusion of Bonuses in Overtime Calculations

Employees that receive bonuses for attendance, length of service, productivity, or generally any other factor are entitled to inclusion of that payment in determining their base hourly rate for purposes of calculating overtime. At the end of each year, the base hourly rate of the employee must be recalculated, including bonuses received, and any overtime hours worked during the year compensated with overtime premium based on the bonus. "The only type of bonus excluded from this requirement is a purely discretionary bonus, such as a small Christmas or Thanksgiving check" (From Baker and Daniels, 2008).

National Acts Important to Business Organizations

National Labor Relations Act (NLRA)

This act gives employees the right to organize in unions and to bargain collectively. It also gives them the right to contest wages, hours, or conditions of employment provided the protest is lawful. You should know what type of organizing is protected by law and what your rights as an employer are. There is a concerted effort today from existing unions to organize child care employees.

Generally speaking, without a collective bargaining agreement or employment contract, employers may discharge employees for any reason. This is what is known as employment at will. Some state courts, however, have ruled that an employer may only discharge an employee for good cause. Some states have held that the personnel handbook represents a contract with the employee, though some of these states have also allowed a disclaimer in the handbook stating that it is not intended as a contract. You should contact your state labor department for information about when an employee can be fired. Don't wait until you need to fire someone. Get accurate information on your rights and responsibilities now.

Consolidated Omnibus Budget Reconciliation Act (COBRA)

If you have 20 or more employees and provide them with group health insurance, this act requires you to provide your employees and their families with the opportunity to continue their coverage at the group rate for 18 - 36 months after:

- Termination or lay-off
- The death of an employee
- Retirement or a disability that entitles the employee to Medicare
- An employee's dependent becomes ineligible for dependent coverage

You must notify the employee of the opportunity for continued coverage using a prescribed form and your must allow him/her 60 days to elect such coverage.

Even if you employ fewer than 20 employees, your state may have enacted additional laws that would require you to offer this coverage.

Fair Credit Reporting Act

If you request a credit report on a prospective employee who has applied for a specific position, you must tell the employee in writing that you have done so. Likewise, if you fail to hire or promote an individual based on a credit report, you must tell the person and give him the name of the credit reporting agency and its address. You may request a credit report on an employee that you are considering for a promotion without notifying the employee provided he has not applied for the position.

Family and Medical Leave Act (FMLA)

This federal law applies to any employer of 50 or more employees (including all employees within a 75-mile radius). If you own two or more centers within 75 miles of each other, you would have to count your employees at all of the centers.

The Act requires the employer to grant up to 12 weeks unpaid leave in any 12-month period for an employee to care for:

- A newborn or newly-adopted child
- A newly-placed foster child
- A spouse, child, or parent who is seriously ill
- The employee himself when unable to work due to injury or illness

To qualify, the employee must have been employed at least 12 months and must have worked at least 1250 hours in the 12-month period immediately preceding the leave. If the leave can be predicted, you may require the employee to give you at least 30 days notice. You may also require certification from a health care provider that the leave is required.

The leave does not have to be taken all at once. It can be spread throughout the year, but the employee must tell you that he is requesting leave based on the FMLA.

You must continue his health insurance coverage during the leave and you must reinstate him either in his original position or a comparable position with no reduction in pay or benefits after the leave.

Immigration Reform and Control Act of 1986

This law requires all employers, regardless of the number of employees, to verify every individual's identity and authorization to work in the U.S. by having him complete the I-9 form and keeping documentation of verification on file. There are significant monetary penalties for failure to comply with this law. The form has been changed over the years and it is important to check annually and use the latest form. As of this printing the latest form was to expire on June 30, 2009. Consult the immigration service for the new form.

After a person has filled out the I-9, it is important to take time and review the form for errors. Make sure every item is completed.

- Section 1 – Every item in this section must be completed by the employee.
- The employee must check one of three boxes that show status to work in the United States.
- The employee must use a street address and not a post office box.
- The employee must sign below the employee's signature line, not above it.
- The employee must place the date of signing in the correct box.
- The employer must review each of the original documents provided by the employee. The most common document for List A is the U.S. passport. The most common document for List B is the driver's license issued by a state agency. It is acceptable to use an expired driver's license, but be sure the photo on the driver's licenses matches with your new employee. The most common document used for List C is the Social Security card. Refer to the handbook for the list of acceptable documents from List A, or for List B and List C.
- Hospital-issued birth certificates are not acceptable.
- The employer or his representative must view the original documents and sign the employer's certification and print or type your name. Do not sign unless you have personally viewed the documents.
- Do not omit the business name and address in the employer's certification block.

- The form I-9 must be dated on the day it is completed. Ideally it is completed on the first day of employment or day of orientation. It must be completed within three days of hire.
- A new hire has 90 days to complete any missing documentation, such as a lost Social Security Card.

If you have been unaware of this form, start using it immediately. Document how you learned about needing it and date your forms according to the date they are signed and verified. This does not eliminate your past responsibilities, but you at least are showing good faith in initiating use based on when you learned about the law. Service industries are typical targets for audits. The I-9 form is included in Department of Labor audits too.

There are severe fines for not complying with this law. Even paperwork errors can cost a fine of nearly $500 per I-9 form. It is required that employers keep I-9 records in their own files; keep forms on past employees for three years; shred the forms when you dispose of them.

Federal Posting Requirements

Various federal laws and regulations require that certain information be posted where all employees can readily see it. The law varies according to the number of employees, whether or not you offer certain benefits, etc. The following chart should help you know what to post and where to get most of it: Additional help is available at www.dol.gov

Federal Posting Requirements

Subject	Regulation	Posting	Obtain From
Safety	OSHA	Job Safety & Health Protection OSHA 2203	OSHA
Safety	OSHA	Annual summary of job injuries Post by Feb 1	OSHA
Minimum Wage, etc.	Fair Labor Standards Act of 1938	Wage-Hour Poster 1088	Dept. of Labor
Age Discrimination	Age Discrimination Notice		Dept. of Labor
Equal Employment Opportunity	Civil Rights Act of 1964		Local EEOC office
Disability	Rehabilitation Act of 1973 ADA Act of 1990		Local EEOC office

Subject	Regulation	Posting	Obtain From
Medical Leave	Family & Medical Leave Act of 1993	FMLA Provision	Dept. of Labor
Selection/ Discrimination	Employee Polygraph Protection Act	Pre-employment Screening	Local Dept. of Labor

State Labor Laws Important to Business Organizations

Some states such as Colorado (The Colorado Affirmation Form) have adopted additional laws and require you comply with their eligibility to work form as well. Check with your state department of labor concerning additional laws.

Sexual Harassment/Hostile Work Environment

Sexual harassment exists when an employee is subjected to unwelcome sexual advances or any conduct of a sexual nature and the employee's response becomes a basis for an employment decision or when the conduct or sexual advance interferes with the employee's work or makes his work environment intimidating, offensive, or hostile. You should have a policy prohibiting sexual harassment and a clear course of action for any employee to complain of sexual harassment. You should take these complaints seriously and act on them immediately. You are required to train your staff concerning sexual harassment issues and how to report it to a member of management.

Garnishment

Most states have garnishment laws requiring employers to withhold portions of an employees' pay when so ordered by the court. The IRS can also garnish an employee's wages. You may not discharge an employee because of a garnishment. If you refuse or neglect to comply with a garnishment order, you may be liable for the full amount of the claim yourself.

Unemployment Insurance

You, as an employer, are required to pay unemployment taxes to the state. The state in turn passes these taxes on to the federal government where they are kept until claims are made by eligible individuals. To be eligible an employee must have lost his job for other than good cause, be currently unemployed but able to work, and have earned a certain amount of wages over a specified period of time. The employee cannot voluntarily resign from his job without good cause and receive unemployment insurance payments. Document the reason you terminated an employee's employment or why they leave. Have employees leaving your program sign a letter of resignation stating in their writing why they are leaving. If you are firing an employee, give him/her a letter stating why he/she is being terminated. Have the employee sign your copy with space for comments. Keep this information in the employee's file for reference.

Workers' Compensation

To eliminate law suits brought by employees who have been injured or developed illnesses as a result of their work or work environment, the government developed Workers' Compensation. This is the only recourse for an employee. These payments to eligible individuals cover lost wages and medical costs associated with the illness or injury. Various states have different pay scales for Workers' Compensation.

Drug Testing, Alcohol Testing, and Polygraphs

As a general rule, private employers may test employees for drugs and alcohol; however some states have restrictions on the use of drug and alcohol tests. Some employers are required to establish a drug-free policy and to routinely test employees. Most businesses whose employees are unionized are not permitted to test for drugs unless they first have union approval.

Except in rare instances, federal law prohibits polygraph tests to screen job applicants or to test employees.

Potential Liability Issues

Negligence Generally

Negligence is said to exist in the law when three things are present. They are:

- Existence of a duty
- Failure to exercise ordinary and reasonable care
- Resulting injury

Clearly the duty involved in operating a child care center is to provide safe care for children. State regulations are very specific about how that is to be done. However, you should be aware that just following the rules may not be enough. The problem is what constitutes ordinary and reasonable care varies from situation to situation. For example, what is ordinary and reasonable care for most children may not suffice at all for a child who has a disability. Ordinary and reasonable care inside the center may be totally inadequate outside by a swimming pool.

You must always be alert for potential danger, not only to the children in your care, but also for employees. Both may have a negligence claim against you or your center if hurt. Be aware that your state regulations establish a duty, a standard against which your conduct may be measured. In the context of the general safety of both children and employees, you should consider the regulations, as they pertain to safety, to be the minimum standard.

Some (but certainly not all) potential trouble areas are:

- Screening of personnel
- Maintenance and operation of motor vehicles
- Administering medicine
- Playground equipment

Negligence Per Se

With the knowledge of what ordinary negligence is, you should also know about a concept of *negligence per se*. An act or omission which is negligence per se is deemed to be actionable without resort to the three factors above. In other words, the three criteria listed above do not have to be present for one to be guilty of negligence per se. Most state law holds that violation of a statute constitutes negligence per se. In other words, if a violation of a statute is the cause of an injury, the person who violated the statute is liable for whatever damages a judge or jury decides the violation caused. Therefore, if you violate a rule or regulation, and someone is injured on your property as a result, you could be found guilty of negligence by the court. It is in your best interest to be sure that you fully comply with the rules and laws of your state.

Health and Occupational Safety Rules

Occupational Safety and Health Act of 1970 (OSHA)

The Occupational Safety and Health Administration is a federal agency with authority over any business employing at least one person. It has developed standards for health and safety in the workplace and has the authority to inspect the business premises and issue citations for non-compliance. Employers have the right to appeal these citations before the Occupational Safety and Health Review Commission. Among the many standards developed by OSHA are record keeping and reporting requirements and requirements for blood borne pathogen exposure control plans.

You must keep records of any accidents that occur in your center. You must also keep medical records on each employee. These records must be housed in a separate location from the employee's personnel records and must be kept confidential. The employee, however, must have access to his own medical file. Under the standard for blood borne pathogens, these files must contain:

- The employee's name and social security number
- The employee's hepatitis B vaccination status including vaccination dates and any medical records related to the employee's ability to receive vaccinations
- Results of examinations, medical testing, and post-exposure evaluation and follow up procedures
- The health care professional's written opinion
- A copy of the information provided to the health care professional
- Training dates
- Content or a summary of the training
- Names and qualifications of trainers
- Names and job titles of trainees

You are required to develop a written exposure control plan and to review and update your plan annually. OSHA has specific requirements for the content of the plan. Contact the The NECPA Commission, Inc. for a sample plan that will meet the OSHA requirement.

You are also required to provide employees with training on occupational exposure free of charge at the time of hiring and at least once a year thereafter.

Basics of Contracts

A thorough discussion of contracts could, and has in a number of cases, filled several volumes. It is not our purpose to go into the subject in detail, only to make you aware of the general requirements for a legally-effective contract. You should not hesitate to contact your lawyer about contract matters.

You may enter into contracts from two perspectives.

- With your customers for whom you provide services
- With others who provide services or goods to you

The vast majority of the time these will be two-party contracts which are expressed either verbally or in writing. It is this type of contract which we will consider here. For two (or more) parties to enter into a legally-enforceable contract there must be five things present. They are:

Parties Able to Contract

This includes individuals capable of entering into a contract and understanding its provisions - they must be adults and cannot be impaired by alcohol, drugs or be mentally impaired.

Agreement between the Parties

This agreement is a mutual understanding of what is to be done or not done by each of the parties in accordance with an offer and acceptance of that offer.

Consideration

There must be valid, valuable consideration - something each receives in return for abiding by the contract. Consideration is valuable if the parties bargained for it. Consideration may also be forbearance; if you do not exercise some legal right that may be consideration. For example, if I agree not to eat desserts for a month, you will give me a free membership to a health club. Consideration, however, is most often money.

Subject

There must be a subject or subjects upon which the contract operates. It is surprising how many times people write out a document they call a contract and forget to identify a subject. The subject matter in your contracts will, perhaps, be something like child care services or cleaning services for your center.

Legality

The subject matter (service to be performed, goods to be provided) must be legal. A contract to help someone rob a bank and then receive a percentage of the loot is not legal.

There are a great many exceptions and variations to the above rules. If you are negotiating any contract, you should consult your lawyer. If you are writing a standard contract for child care services, have a lawyer check it. You may have many occasions in your business to use contracts such as employment agreements, building contracts, termite bonds, advertising contracts, etc. An attorney can write these contracts to say exactly what you mean to say and so they will be accepted by the courts should there be a later dispute.

Anti-discrimination Laws, Including Disability Laws Regarding Children and Employees

Civil Rights Act of 1964

This law applies to employers with 15 or more employees and prohibits discrimination in hiring, discharging, or terms of employment against any person because of race, color, religion, sex, pregnancy, or national origin. The statute further makes it unlawful to discriminate against any individual for making a charge, testifying, or assisting or participating in the enforcement of this act.

Some states have added their own protected classes such as sexual preference, AIDS, or marital status. Check your own state's laws to be sure you are following them.

Civil Rights Act of 1991

This act gave persons who sue for mistreatment under the Civil Rights Act of 1964 the right to sue for both compensatory and punitive damages and have their case heard by a jury. If the employee wins the suit, he can collect back pay, reinstatement and attorneys' fees.

Age Discrimination in Employment Act (ADEA)

If you have more than 20 employees you may not discriminate in the hiring or employment of persons who are 40 years old or older. You may not force employees to retire because of age. Age can only be a condition of employment when it affects the bona fide occupational qualification necessary for safe and efficient operation of the business.

Some states have enacted even stronger age discrimination laws. Some have eliminated the 20-employee stipulation. Others prohibit age discrimination for any age.

Military Service

Employers are not permitted to discriminate in hiring or employment practices against anyone because of service in the U.S. military, either active or reserve duty. The employer must allow the employee time off for military service and reinstate the employee in the same position when he returns with no reduction in accrued seniority-based benefits. The employer does not have to pay the employee during the leave.

The Americans with Disabilities Act (ADA)

History and Purpose

The ADA was passed by Congress and signed into law by President George H. Bush on July 26, 1990.

The purpose of the ADA is to assure persons with disabilities the same civil rights under the law as every other citizen receives. Because of ADA we cannot discriminate against a person with a disability just as we cannot discriminate against anyone based on race, sex, age, color, national origin, or religion.

Who Enforces the ADA?

The ADA is a federal law administered by several federal agencies: The U.S. Department of Justice, the Equal Employment Opportunity Commission, the Department of Transportation, the Architectural and Transportation Barriers Compliance Board, and the Federal Communications Commission. Although the law itself was passed in 1990, regulation development is continuing will certainly be court cases that will further define the language in the law. Employers, business owners, state and local governments must act in good faith to follow the law and use their best judgment and the advice of their attorneys in determining their actions even in the absence of clear interpretation.

Learn all you can about the law, particularly as more rulings are made to clarify its provisions so that you will be prepared to serve the needs of disabled persons while maintaining the character of your program. If you are faced with providing accommodation which you question, you should certainly contact your attorney or the Department of Justice for guidance.

Who Must Adhere to the ADA?

Every government agency or service (federal, state and local governments) is required to adhere to the Americans with Disabilities Act. Federally-funded entities have been required to comply with Section 504 of the Rehabilitation Act prohibiting discrimination against disabled persons since its passage. Now they must also comply with ADA. Their compliance is more immediate than of private organizations, because no expense to comply with ADA provisions is assumed to be too great for a government agency.

Every business that is open to the public also falls under the Americans with Disabilities Act. There are very few exceptions: private clubs that have very selective membership criteria and religious groups are two exceptions.

What about church-based child care programs? If the program is operated in the church building by the church itself, it does not fall under the ADA. If, however, the church contracts with another entity to provide the program in the church building, the program is covered by ADA. In order to be exempt, the church must actually make decisions about the policies of the program and actually hire the staff.

What is a Disability?

The Americans with Disabilities Act defines a disability as:

- A physical or mental impairment that substantially limits one or more of the major life activities of an individual (such as breathing, seeing, hearing, speaking, walking, or learning)
- A record of having such an impairment (such as cancer which is in remission)
- Being regarded as having such an impairment (such as severe scarring)

Temporary impairments, such as a broken bone, which are expected to heal in a short time, are not considered disabilities under the ADA. However, if an injury is long lasting, the person may be considered disabled for the period of time it takes to heal if his injury substantially limits one or more major life activities. Conditions not considered disabilities include pyromania, compulsive gambling, kleptomania, any sort of sexual disorder, or psychoactive substance use disorders resulting from current use of an illegal drug.

Let's look again at the first definition above. What does substantially limit actually mean? If a child has a limp, does that substantially limit any of his major life activities? What further information do you need in order to answer this question?

Every case is different and must be assessed individually. A five-year-old with a severe limp that prevents him from running distances might be considered disabled if participating in your kindergarten class' daily lap around the high school track. On the other hand, a three-year-old with a light limp might not win the playground relay race but could certainly participate. The child need not excel at the activity, just be able to participate as an average child would.

Sometimes chronic diseases can substantially limit a person's major life activities. For example, a child with severe asthma may be unable to participate in the regular school program during an asthma attack. This child may require special attention at this time or may even need certain allergens removed from the environment in order to prevent asthma attacks. Likewise, a child with diabetes may suffer from periods when his blood sugar is low. This child may become lethargic, incoherent, or even unconscious. Such episodes would certainly limit his major life activities.

Even some behavioral disorders can be considered disabilities that substantially limit major life activities. For example, Attention Deficit Disorder (ADD) can prevent a child from learning.

A child who cannot do some major life activity that other children his age can generally do would be considered to be substantially limited.

ADA Impact on Early Care and Education Programs

Early care and education programs, like many businesses, are affected by ADA in two important ways.

- In serving children and parents with disabilities
- In meeting the needs of employees with disabilities

Serving Children and Parents with Disabilities

The excellent program you have always offered children and families should be accessible to all children and families. Under the ADA you cannot exclude a child from full participation in your program because of a disability if there is a way to reasonably accommodate that child. Similarly, you cannot exclude a parent who is disabled from participating in the activities in which other parents take part.

When a parent comes to your center to enroll his child, you must not consider the child's or parent's disability in determining whether to accept the child for enrollment. Perhaps you may exclude the child for some other reason but the disability cannot be the reason. For example, if a child with a disability is 18 months old and you only accept three and four-year-olds, you can legitimately not accept the child, provided that you adhere to this policy under all circumstances. If the parent uses a wheel chair and other parents in your program must climb several steps to enter the building to pick up their children, you cannot let this parent's disability prevent you from accepting the child. You will have to accommodate this parent in some way so that he can come into the building just as other parents do. The point is to make every activity and service the same for persons with disabilities as it is for everyone else who uses you services.

The service you offer to persons with disabilities cannot be different from that offered non-disabled persons, nor can it be separate unless that is the only way to deliver the service as effectively as you do for other individuals. And finally, the law requires you to offer your service to persons with disabilities "in the most integrated setting appropriate to the needs of the individual."

This may require you to make a number of changes in your policies or procedures, but you do not have to make changes that will fundamentally alter the nature of your program. If your program is located in a homeless shelter and is specifically for children who are homeless, providing them with social services and medical attention in addition to early education and care, then you do not have to accept a child who is disabled if that child is not homeless as well. Doing so would fundamentally alter the purpose of your program. If, on the other hand, you operate a program for after-school age children five to twelve and you are asked to enroll a seven-year-old child who wears leg braces, you cannot refuse this child even though he may be unable to participate in all the outdoor physical activities the other children enjoy.

In some cases a person's disability can make others uncomfortable. For example, a person with a disability may be unable to eat without spilling food on himself. This can be unpleasant for those around him. You cannot, however, refuse to accept a child into your program because his disability makes others uncomfortable. This person falls under the protection of ADA and must be admitted if he meets all other qualifications for enrollment.

What if the disability makes the child a threat to other children? If the child is a direct threat to other children or to staff, you may refuse service. You do have an obligation to provide a safe environment for all children and staff. A two-year-old who bites other children does not have a disability, because biting is not atypical of two-year-old children. He is not, therefore, covered by ADA. A six-year-old with a behavioral disorder which causes him to bite does have a disability and is covered by ADA. However, if you are unable to control the biting and it is a danger to other children and to your staff, you may ask the parent to remove the child from your program.

Before asking a parent to remove a child from your program because you have determined that he is a danger to others, think carefully about the situation and whether there are any steps you might take to prevent the child's being a danger. In the case of the biter, consider what might prompt the child to bite another. Can you alter the child's activities or environment to make biting less likely? Can you bring in an extra staff person during the times that the child is most prone to biting to help prevent an injury from occurring? Keep a log to record when the child bites, what the circumstances were when the child bit, what precautions you are taking to prevent him from biting, and what actions are taken when he bites. This will enable you and your staff to determine whether there are any further steps you can take to prevent this behavior and will also document your sincere attempts to accommodate the child should you have to ask the parents to remove him.

Always discuss the child's disability with the parent before giving up. The parent deals with the child's disability on a daily basis and probably has developed strategies for handling special situations. The parent can be the best source for ideas for effective methods of accommodation. Don't hesitate to involve others (with the parent's permission) in the community knowledgeable in accommodation.

Behavioral disabilities may be some of the most difficult to deal with and to accommodate. Be sure to put in writing what type of behavior is acceptable in your program and what the consequences are for unacceptable behavior. This is the behavior expected of all children and should be enforced uniformly. Try to work with parents of children with behavioral disorders to assure consistency between school and home and to lessen confusion. Read about developmental and behavior disorders and take workshops on this topic to learn ways to deal with these children. Ask your state's Child Care Administrator if his department has "quality" dollars for training for your staff in managing children with behavioral disabilities. Document your experiences with these children, noting what steps you have taken when the child's behavior is unacceptable and whether your actions were effective. If you see that a child will require more staff, specialized care, or some service you do not offer, you must assess the impact on your program of providing this accommodation and determine whether it seems reasonable.

The Americans with Disabilities Act states that you must make reasonable modification for persons with disabilities. But what is a reasonable modification? Undoubtedly this term will ultimately be defined by the courts over a period of years. Businesses are being sued by disabled persons who believe they have been discriminated against because of their disabilities. The business owners may believe they are unable to accommodate the disabled persons without modifications that they consider unreasonable. The courts decide which party is right. This scenario is likely because the law itself does not clearly define reasonable modification.

In fact, this has already happened in cases involving child care centers. A parent who has a young child with diabetes enrolled him in a child care center and asked that the staff regularly test the child's blood glucose levels in order to determine whether the levels were too high or too low - either situation being dangerous to his health. The test requires the staff to prick the child's finger and draw blood. The blood droplet is placed on a specially treated chemical strip and read by a machine. The center's corporate policy was to refuse to do this procedure. Many center owners and directors would be concerned about the liability of contact with blood and disposal of the lancets used to prick the finger and the blood itself. While the courts did not actually rule on this case, the Justice Department did rule that the procedure requested by the parent is in fact a reasonable modification of policy in this case. Similar rulings in the future will shed more light on what is reasonable and what is not.

You should contact the US Department of Justice and request guidance pieces on topics you are concerned with. The DOJ publishes these as a means of giving you more information on how the Department is likely to rule in a given situation. Contact information can be found in this chapter.

Another area of confusion lies in the question of what physical modifications must be made to buildings and facilities to meet the requirements of the ADA. The Architectural and Transportation Barriers Compliance Board (ACCESS Board) sets standards for making facilities accessible to disabled persons. These standards include lighting requirements, width of hallways and doors, bathroom modifications, water cooler heights, playgrounds, etc. Existing buildings are not required to comply with all requirements that have been developed for new construction.

Readily Achievable

Existing programs must meet those requirements that are readily achievable and must have a written plan for future compliance. What does readily achievable mean? Again we are faced with a vague term that the law does not clearly define. In determining whether a modification in your facility is readily achievable, you should assess:

How Difficult It Will Be to Accomplish

Will it require construction that will disrupt the program for a day or more? In making the change, will other areas of the building be adversely affected? For example, if you must widen the hall, will you lose valuable classroom space, reducing the number of children who can use your program?

How much it will Cost

Study the cost of the modification as it relates to your total budget. Will it prevent you from carrying out other aspects of your program that will benefit the children? Will it cause you to increase your fees and, if so, how will that impact the families who use your program? All programs are different, so the cost impact must be assessed individually. What is financially readily achievable for one program may not be so for another program.

When determining whether the cost of a modification is reasonable, the courts will look at the size of your program and the net profit generated from your program and how the expense will affect the rest of the services you offer. Just being a part of a large chain of centers does not mean that you must automatically institute any modification regardless of cost. The courts found the cost to one large early education company of providing a staff person to work one-on-one with a child was unreasonable because the cost of the employee would exceed the tuition paid by the child's parents. Even though the net income of the parent company of the center in one quarter exceeded $2.4 million, the court noted the center operated on what the court deemed a shoestring budget. Additionally, the court found the center was in the business of offering group care and to offer one-on-one care would fundamentally alter the purpose of the program. You are not required to make any accommodation or modification that will fundamentally alter your program.

But remember, you must be sure that parents as well as children have full access to your building. Any part of your facility designated for parents' use must be accessible to all parents. Therefore, if parents sometimes come to the playground to pick up their children, the playground will need to be accessible for all parents. That may require a ramp out of one door to the playground for a person who uses a wheel chair or better lighting in the hallway for a visually impaired parent.

The US Architectural and Transportation Barriers Compliance (ACCESS) Board has developed standards for playgrounds which include requirements for play equipment, access to the equipment, and for surfaces. These standards affect any new playgrounds and any playgrounds which have been reworked or modified after October 18, 2000.

If you provide transportation for children, it must also be accessible for children with disabilities. That does not mean that you must have lifts installed on your vehicles, because the law specifically excludes that. As the law defines discrimination, it states discrimination includes "a failure to remove . . . transportation barriers in existing vehicles . . . used by an establishment for transporting individuals (not including barriers that can only be removed through the retrofitting of vehicles ... by the installation of a hydraulic or other lift), where such removal is readily achievable."

If you purchase a new vehicle, be sure it can accommodate persons with all types of disabilities. In the meantime, you might contract with a transportation company with specially equipped vehicles or even rent a vehicle if an occasional field trip is the only time you might face such a problem.

<u>Your</u> Written Compliance Plan

Even if you currently serve no children or parents with disabilities, your business comes under the requirements of the Americans with Disabilities Act (ADA) and you must begin planning ways to make your facility and playground accessible to persons with all types of disabilities. Often these modifications will be simple and inexpensive such as rearranging furniture and equipment to provide more space for the turning radius of a wheel chair or installing smoke detectors with flashing lights as well as audible alarms for the hearing impaired. Every center should have a five-year compliance plan in writing. The plan can be based in part on your plans for expansion or modification of the facility. When modifications are carried out, accessibility improvements can be made. Make all of the modifications you can now and write down your future plans for compliance with ADA and give a time frame for these modifications to be made.

Also bear in mind that modifications requiring a substantial monetary outlay may increase the value of your facility and make it more marketable should you decide to sell. These modifications will certainly create goodwill that cannot always be measured. Furthermore, these modifications making your facility more accessible to persons with disabilities are tax deductible up to $15,000. Modifications qualifying for this deduction include items such as barrier removal (widening doorways, halls, building ramps, etc.), providing books on tape, or sign interpreters. New construction and remodeling do not qualify.

Some early education businesses can take a tax credit in addition to the tax deduction. You must have fewer than 30 employees and your annual gross receipts must be less than $1 million to qualify for this tax credit. The credit applies to 50% of the cost of barrier removal above $250 and below $10,250.

Use the table below as a guide for assessing the accessibility of your facility:

Accessibility to Building
1. In the parking lot, is there at least one parking space that is accessible for a disabled person for every 25 spaces? An accessible space should be at least eight feet wide with a five-foot access aisle marked with striped paint. This space should be as close to the accessible entrance as possible and should be marked so that disabled persons can easily see it and those without disabilities will not use it. Use the international symbol for accessibility for your sign.
2. Are there curb cuts in the parking lot so that a person using a wheel chair/assistive devise could get up on the curb?
3. Are the surfaces in the parking lot and walkways to the entrance of the building made of materials that will enable a person using a wheel chair/assistive devise to roll it easily?
4. If parents or children arrive at your center before daylight or after dark, are the parking lot, the walkways, and signs well lit?
5. Are all walkways free of protrusions and tripping hazards and bush or tree limbs?
6. Are walkways at least 36 inches wide?
7. Do ramps rise no more than one inch per foot? Are long ramps (six feet or more) protected with railings on either side?
8. Is the accessible entrance to your building at least 32 inches wide?
9. If there is a threshold at the entrance, it should be no more than 1/4" in height or 1/2" if it is beveled.
10. The door knob should be the lever type that can be opened with a closed fist and should be low enough for a person using a wheel chair to operate.

Within the Building
11. Is there a counter in the reception area that would present a barrier to a disabled parent? All parents should be able to see the person who is stationed at the front entrance and be able to read any bulletin boards or literature available, use the phone if it is available to parents in general, get a drink of water, and write a check easily.
12. Are the halls, walkways, etc. at least 36" wide?
13. Is the movement space between pieces of equipment or furniture at least 36" wide?

Accessibility Within the Building
14. Is the floor surface material easy to roll a wheel chair on? It should be a tightly-woven carpet with no pile or a hard, smooth surface.
15. Are permanent signs designed with raised letters or also in Braille? Are the signs low enough to be read by someone in a wheel chair?
16. Is there sufficient space for a disabled person to turn a wheel chair around (at least five feet) in any activity area?
17. Can children in wheel chairs reach toys, books, and materials that are available to other children?
18. Can children in wheel chairs get up to the tables to work with other children? If there is a sink or water fountain in the classroom, can they use this equipment?
19. Are there things you can do in the classroom to assist a visually-impaired child? For example, can you change the texture of the floor covering to delineate various areas of the room, can you provide books on tape in the reading area, can you give these children lots of art experiences that involve touch rather than sight such as modeling clay rather than sight such as modeling clay rather than crayons.

The Bathroom

20. Are there signs for the bathrooms that all children can read? They should clearly identify the sexes in words (Girls, Boys), in international symbols, and in Braille or raised letters.

21. Is there at least one bathroom that is accessible for disabled persons?

22. Can a disabled person in a wheel chair get into the toilet stall?

23. Can a disabled person in a wheel chair get onto the toilet?

24. Are there grab bars behind and beside the toilet?

25. Can a disabled person in a wheel chair get up to use the sink? Are the pipes under the sink insulated so that a child using a wheel chair will not burn himself?

26. Can faucets be easily turned on and off with a closed fist?

Other Rooms in Your Child Care Facility

27. If you have a separate cafeteria, gymnasium, or media center, can a disabled child get there by himself?

28. Can the disabled child sit at the lunch table with others?

29. If children are asked to help with the clean up, can children with disabilities help in this way too? Think of ways you can help children on crutches, in wheel chairs, and those who are visually impaired carry their dishes or wipe off the tables.

Playground and Other Outside Recreation Areas

30. Can disabled parents and children easily move from inside the building to the playground?

31. If there are ramps, is the rise no more than 1" per foot?

Playground and Other Outside Recreation Areas
32. If ramps are six feet long or longer, are there handrails on either side?
33. Can a person in a wheel chair or using an assistive device easily cross the playground surface to the equipment?
34. Is there a way for visually impaired persons to recognize play areas that might pose a threat such as swings or other moving equipment?
35. Is the play equipment designed so that a child using an assistive device can climb and slide and participate in the same experiences that other children enjoy?

Accessibility to Building
36. In the parking lot, is there at least one parking space that is accessible for a disabled person for every 25 spaces? An accessible space should be at least eight feet wide with a five-foot access aisle marked with striped paint. This space should be as close to the accessible entrance as possible and should be marked so that disabled persons can easily see it and those without disabilities will not use it. Use the international symbol for accessibility for your sign.
37. Are there curb cuts in the parking lot so that a person using a wheel chair/assistive devise could get up on the curb?
38. Are the surfaces in the parking lot and walkways to the entrance of the building made of materials that will enable a person using a wheel chair/assistive devise to roll it easily?
39. If parents or children arrive at your center before daylight or after dark, are the parking lot, the walkways, and signs well lit?
40. Are all walkways free of protrusions and tripping hazards and bush or tree limbs?
41. Are walkways at least 36 inches wide?
42. Do ramps rise no more than one inch per foot? Are long ramps (six feet or more) protected with railings on either side?
43. Is the accessible entrance to your building at least 32 inches wide?

Competency IV: Laws and Regulations

Accessibility to Building

44. If there is a threshold at the entrance, it should be no more than 1/4" in height or 1/2" if it is beveled.

45. The door knob should be the lever type that can be opened with a closed fist and should be low enough for a person using a wheel chair to operate.

Within the Building

46. Is there a counter in the reception area that would present a barrier to a disabled parent? All parents should be able to see the person who is stationed at the front entrance and be able to read any bulletin boards or literature available, use the phone if it is available to parents in general, get a drink of water, and write a check easily.

47. Are the halls, walkways, etc. at least 36" wide?

48. Is the movement space between pieces of equipment or furniture at least 36" wide?

Accessibility Within the Building

49. Is the floor surface material easy to roll a wheel chair on? It should be a tightly-woven carpet with no pile or a hard, smooth surface.

50. Are permanent signs designed with raised letters or also in Braille? Are the signs low enough to be read by someone in a wheel chair?

51. Is there sufficient space for a disabled person to turn a wheel chair around (at least five feet) in any activity area?

52. Can children in wheel chairs reach toys, books, and materials that are available to other children?

53. Can children in wheel chairs get up to the tables to work with other children? If there is a sink or water fountain in the classroom, can they use this equipment?

Accessibility Within the Building

54. Are there things you can do in the classroom to assist a visually-impaired child? For example, can you change the texture of the floor covering to delineate various areas of the room, can you provide books on tape in the reading area, can you give these children lots of art experiences that involve touch rather than sight such as modeling clay rather than sight such as modeling clay rather than crayons.

The Bathroom

55. Are there signs for the bathrooms that all children can read? They should clearly identify the sexes in words (Girls, Boys), in international symbols, and in Braille or raised letters.

56. Is there at least one bathroom that is accessible for disabled persons?

57. Can a disabled person in a wheel chair get into the toilet stall?

58. Can a disabled person in a wheel chair get onto the toilet?

59. Are there grab bars behind and beside the toilet?

60. Can a disabled person in a wheel chair get up to use the sink? Are the pipes under the sink insulated so that a child using a wheel chair will not burn himself?

61. Can faucets be easily turned on and off with a closed fist?

Other Rooms in Your Child Care Facility

62. If you have a separate cafeteria, gymnasium, or media center, can a disabled child get there by himself?

63. Can the disabled child sit at the lunch table with others?

Competency IV: Laws and Regulations

Other Rooms in Your Child Care Facility
64. If children are asked to help with the clean up, can children with disabilities help in this way too? Think of ways you can help children on crutches, in wheel chairs, and those who are visually impaired carry their dishes or wipe off the tables.

Playground and Other Outside Recreation Areas
65. Can disabled parents and children easily move from inside the building to the playground?
66. If there are ramps, is the rise no more than 1" per foot?
67. If ramps are six feet long or longer, are there handrails on either side?
68. Can a person in a wheel chair or using an assistive device easily cross the playground surface to the equipment?
69. Is there a way for visually impaired persons to recognize play areas that might pose a threat such as swings or other moving equipment?
70. Is the play equipment designed so that a child using an assistive device can climb and slide and participate in the same experiences that other children enjoy?

Meeting the Needs of Disabled Employees

If you have fewer than 15 employees for each working day for at least 20 weeks during the year, you are not subject to this section of the ADA. Other exemptions are the federal government and corporations wholly owned by the U.S. government, Native American Indian tribes, and private membership clubs that are tax exempt under 501 (c).

The law states, "No covered entity shall discriminate against a qualified individual with a disability because of the disability of such individual in regard to job application procedures, the hiring, advancement, or discharge of employees, employee compensation, job training, and other terms, conditions, and privileges of employment."

The covered entity is whoever is responsible for your program - you, your corporation, the government, etc. A qualified individual can be a prospective employee or one of your current employees. A qualified individual is "an individual with a disability who, with or without reasonable accommodation, can perform the essential functions of the employment position that such individual holds or desires."

The law goes on to state that, if you have a written job description for a position prepared before it was advertised, that will be considered evidence of the essential functions of the job. Therefore, it is a good idea to develop written job descriptions for each position so that you will be able to assess a potential employee's ability to perform that job with or without accommodation.

Some would recommend the opposite approach. If you have no job description for a position, there is no precedent for determining the job responsibilities. However, this is contrary to the spirit of the law which is to determine the necessary abilities an employee needs to perform a particular job, and then to hire the best person for that position irrespective of his disabilities.

When you develop job descriptions, be sure to be complete but to list only the essential functions of the job. The essential functions are those tasks necessary for the job to be performed satisfactorily. When designing your written job descriptions, do not mention any functions that would tend to screen out persons with disabilities unless there is no other reasonable way to accomplish these tasks. When determining whether a function of a job is essential, think about whether there are alternative ways of accomplishing it, how many staff persons are available, whether all employees in that same position are required to perform this function, and whether the job would exist if the function were not performed, etc.

One good way to begin is to have the person currently holding the position write down every task he does over a period of days. When all the tasks are listed, analyze them to determine which are essential to the proper performance of the job, then word the job description in terms of the goals and tasks which must be performed. For example, in describing the duties of the infant teacher, rather than saying the person must be able to lift 20 pounds several times a day, you could state the teacher must be able to take care of the physical needs of the young children including diapering, feeding, and moving them.

This job description will be your blueprint when hiring an employee for this position. Show each applicant the description of essential functions and ask him if he is able to perform these functions with or without accommodation. He is not obligated to tell you he has any disability. However, if he tells you he is unable to perform one of these functions, due to a qualified disability you will need to determine whether you can reasonably accommodate the employee applicant in a manner that enables him to do the job. Ask the applicant how you might be able to assist him so he can accomplish the required tasks. Often the person with a disability will have a simple, easy-to-accomplish solution.

What is reasonable accommodation? The ADA states a reasonable accommodation may include making your building and equipment accessible to persons with disabilities; restructuring a job so the employee who becomes disabled can continue to do it (this might mean reducing the hours); reassigning an employee who becomes disabled to a vacant position; acquiring some equipment that enabling an employee with a disability to perform a particular task or modifying training materials so an employee who is disabled could participate just as other employees participate. Remember an employee who is not disabled when hired may become disabled. Also an employee who has a disability may have never told you of the disability because he has been able to perform all job tasks without accommodation. If the job requirements change, he may need accommodation and may request it. For example, an employee with multiple sclerosis may have been able to perform all his job functions during an eight-hour day. You have decided to change schedules and put everyone on ten-hour days. This will not allow him enough rest, so he may request you allow him to remain on the old schedule.

You are not required to make any accommodation that would place an undue hardship on your business. Obviously the next question is what is an undue hardship? The law lists the factors to be considered in determining whether an accommodation poses an undue hardship. These are:

- The nature and cost of the accommodation needed
- The overall financial resources of the facility; the number of persons employed at the facility; the effect on expenses and resources or the impact otherwise of such accommodation upon the operation of the facility
- The overall financial resources of the covered entity; the overall size of the business of a covered entity with respect to the number of its employees; the number, type, and location of its facilities
- The type of operation or operations of the covered entity, including the composition, structure, and functions of the workforce of such entity; the geographic separateness, administrative, or fiscal relationship of the facility in question to the covered entity

You may need to revise your job applications and your interviewing techniques to be sure nothing you do will tend to screen out a person with a qualified disability. You do not want to ask any questions that would require the applicant to reveal a disability. The point is to make your hiring decisions without taking any disability into consideration. Therefore, you must not ask whether the person has a disability or any question about his medical history.

Before the interviewing process begins you should describe what it entails and ask if the applicant needs any accommodation in completing the application and interview process. This can be done through a statement on the application itself. If the applicant has a disability that would interfere with the application/interviewing process, you may need to provide some accommodation that would enable him to complete this process on the same footing as any other applicant. An example might be an individual who has a learning disability making reading difficult. You might have someone read the questions on the job application to the applicant and write his answers on the application.

During the interview process for all employees you should give the applicant a tour of the facilities. This will enable an applicant who is disabled to assess any barriers to his disability and think of possible accommodations that might be made to allow him to perform the essential duties of the job.

After the application and interview process is completed, you may make a job offer contingent on your being able to reasonably accommodate the applicant's disabilities if any and/or contingent on satisfactory completion of a medical examination. Since you have already made a job offer, you may now ask if the applicant needs any accommodation. If so, you may ask for suggestions as to what accommodation you might make to enable the person to perform the job. You are not obligated to accommodate the person in the manner he suggests. You may think of another way in which to accommodate this person. Any questions you ask at this point must directly relate to the applicant's ability to perform the job. You cannot ask questions about the medical nature of the disability.

If you require a medical examination, you must require it of all job applicants. This is probably the only way you can determine whether a person has an infectious disease that would pose a direct threat to others in your program. Testing for the human immunodeficiency virus (HIV) is not permitted in the medical examination. You may not withhold a job offer because a person is HIV positive. You must instead use universal precautions that will prevent the spread of HIV. Drug testing may be permissible in some states both in a pre-employment physical examination and in regular follow-up tests to determine whether employees or applicants are currently using controlled substances. Those persons are not covered under ADA.

You may ask the medical professional performing the examination whether the potential employee poses a direct threat to the health and safety of himself or to other persons in your program. You may also ask whether any inability to perform a job task is disability related and whether, with accommodation, the person will be capable of performing the job tasks. Other than these questions, you cannot ask anything else of the physician without the permission of the job applicant.

Any medical information you receive from a physician or the applicant or employee himself must be kept strictly confidential. Supervisory personnel may be told of the restrictions you are placing on the disabled person's work and any accommodations you are making so the employee can perform his job if they have a need to know. But beyond that only the employee should reveal any information about himself. Keep employee medical records in files separate from their other records and under lock and key.

If the job applicant has disclosed, either voluntarily or after an initial job offer, that he has a disability, you may ask him to demonstrate how he would perform the essential job functions. In fact, it is a good idea to require this of every applicant. Some child care program directors ask applicants who have been given tentative job offers to come into the center and work with pay for a half day or full day to see whether they like the work and can do the work satisfactorily. If the applicant is unable to perform one or more of the essential functions of the job, you must try to make some sort of reasonable accommodation to enable him to do the job. For example, if an applicant can do everything for the three-year-olds except getting the cots out of the storage room, you might have the applicant switch duties with someone else just while the cots are being readied. If, however, you discover that the applicant cannot perform the essential functions for the position and that accommodating this person would necessitate an undue burden, you do not have to hire this person even if their other qualifications are suitable.

Remember, as long as you are not taking into consideration a job applicant's disability in making a hiring decision, you can hire the most qualified applicant. Once you have determined you can reasonably accommodate an applicant's disability, that person should be considered equally with any other applicants. No preference must be given to disabled persons.

> **When you have questions regarding employment policies and the Americans with Disabilities Act, contact the Equal Employment Opportunity Commission (EEOC). This government agency also publishes *Guidance Pieces* which will help you understand your responsibilities and rights.**

Summary

Showing competency in laws and regulations, an effective administrator:

- Understands and complies with applicable federal, state, and local regulations
- Works with legal counsel and demonstrates general knowledge of legal issues concerning child care

If you feel you lack confidence in any of the skills listed above, please go back and review the appropriate section in this chapter.

Competency V

Staff Management and Human Resources

Competency V

Staff Management and Human Resources

Learning Objectives:

- To be able to create effective personnel policies and job descriptions
- To understand how to safeguard and maintain staff records
- To know how to recruit, hire, provide incentives, and keep good employees
- To be able to conduct an effective interview process for prospective employees
- To understand how to ensure that your staff continues to develop professionally
- To be able to develop a formal staff evaluation procedure
- To know how to use staff evaluations to promote high quality early childhood education
- To gain confidence in providing your staff with guidance and leadership in order to encourage personal and professional growth

Competency V: Management and Human Resources

An Effective Administrator Provides a Mechanism that Defines Tasks, Job Roles, the Distribution of Authority, Quality Standards, and Concepts of Teamwork and Decision Making Within the Program

As an administrator you most likely will establish the personnel structure of the organization. Personnel management is another component of system management and includes recruiting, maintaining, and training staff. It is important to develop a list all job classifications within the center and to have a complete job description for each. You are responsible for hiring personnel for each position, training staff, and leading staff in the decision-making process.

Job Descriptions: An Overview

Many employers document the content of the jobs with the company. Some of the common methods of job documentation are checklists, standards of performance lists (SOPs), and job descriptions. Many employers choose to use the written job description.

Job descriptions document the major functions or duties of a job along with the responsibilities and other critical features, such as skill, effort, and working conditions. Job descriptions may be specific and detailed or generic and general. Job descriptions tell:

- Who (usually the incumbent or the supervisor)
- Does what work (including review of the work of others).
- Where
- When (or how often)
- Why (purpose or impact)
- How (it is accomplished)

The Law

Generally, federal law does not require employers to have job descriptions, but there are some exceptions such as jobs where employees handle or dispose of hazardous waste.

Federal regulations and guidance governing the Americans with Disabilities Act (ADA) do not require employers to have job descriptions. Employers choosing to have job descriptions must focus on essential functions and ensure that all essential functions are covered.

Another requirement of the ADA is that essential functions be distinguished from non-essential ones if the employer chooses to describe non-essential functions. There are several practical approaches to meeting this requirement. Employers may: indicate time spent, identify with an asterisk, list under separate heading.

Non Prejudicial Language

It is also important to use language that effectively establishes the nature and importance of essential functions without being prejudicial to persons with disabilities. Examples are:

Frequently (frequency) lifts, carries or otherwise moves and positions (non-prejudicial language) objects weighing up to 25 pounds (intensity) when stocking supply room and setting up equipment (operational linkage).

Typically (non-prejudicial language) bends, stoops and crouches on a regular basis (frequency) to adjust settings on machinery (operational linkage).

Constantly (frequency) moves about (generic action verb) to coordinate work (operational linkage).

Keeping Job Descriptions Current

Job descriptions (and other forms of job documentation) have the potential to become the subject of contention, including grievances or litigation.

It is critical that accuracy be maintained. The employer should designate one party responsible for keeping them current and reviewed regularly.

A plan of this type should reflect the personnel resources available to do the review and the character of the job content.

Use of Disclaimers

Disclaimers remind readers that job descriptions are not meant to be all-inclusive and/or the job itself is subject to change.

Nothing in this job description restricts management's right to assign or reassign duties and responsibilities to this job at any time.

This job description reflects management's assignment of essential functions, it does not prescribe or restrict the tasks that may be assigned.

Critical features of this job are described under the headings below. They may be subject to change at any time due to reasonable accommodation or other reasons.

Summary

Job descriptions can be very useful to employers, employees and job applicants. However, there are pitfalls. To avoid them, the employer must:

Carefully consider the format and degree of detail to be used (generic/general v. specific/detailed, disclaimer(s), etc.).

Ensure that the descriptions are prepared with care (clear, accurate and sufficient for the intended purpose(s), using non-prejudicial language).

Keep them current.

Basic Organizational Structure of an Early Care and Education Center

The organizational structure of an early care and education program is based on the number and types of positions needed to serve the number of children enrolled. The number of staff positions needed is directly proportional to the size of the program. A basic structure would include:

- A center director
- An Assistant director
- Van driver
- Cook
- Lead teachers or group leaders
- Assistant teachers
- Janitor/maintenance person (optional)
- Volunteers (optional)

Once basic staffing requirements have been met, more staff should be added as enrollment increases. Once a basic staffing structure has been adopted, provide written job descriptions for each classification. A job description states clearly what is expected of the employee and protects the center from legal liability if questions arise concerning job expectation and performance. Each job classification should have a written description that covers the following information.

Director

The person holding this position is responsible for managing the total operation of the early care and education center. This includes planning, developing, organizing, and maintaining all programs essential for ensuring quality child care. Specific responsibilities may be listed in the areas of:

- Curriculum planning and implementation
- Hiring teaching staff, administrative support staff, and operational support staff
- Financial management
- Hiring substitute staff
- Food management
- Enrollment and retention
- Marketing
- Developing and maintaining an effective organization
- Communication systems
- Community relations
- Legal knowledge in the areas of center management and operation

Assistant Director

This person is responsible for supporting the director. This person should have knowledge and expertise in the same areas as the director, since he actually functions as the director when the director is absent.

Lead Teacher

This person is charged with nurturing the children in his care as well as supervising their activities to ensure a safe environment. His responsibilities include:

- Implementing the curriculum provided by the program through planned activities that respect the physical, emotional, social, and cognitive needs of each child
- Maintaining an orderly, attractive, classroom that appeals to children
- Supervising and training assistant teaching staff
- Observing, recording, and reporting any significant individual or group behavior
- Assisting and supervising children in accomplishing daily routines, i.e. naps, meals, bathroom, and dressing
- Planning weekly lessons consistent with curriculum outline, goals and objectives
- Using positive discipline techniques prescribed by center policy
- Attending all staff meetings and training sessions
- Displaying knowledge of emergency procedures to be followed for accidents or bad weather
- Having knowledge of historical and release information on each child
- Complying with center infection control guidelines and procedures
- Performing any reasonable duties requested by the director

Assistant Teacher

This person is charged with supporting the lead teacher in all aspects of the day-to-day activities. His responsibilities include, but are not limited to:

- Assisting the lead teacher in performing all duties and responsibilities assigned to the lead teacher
- Nurturing and supervising the children in his care
- Attending all required training sessions
- Being familiar with all company policies and procedures

- Complying with infection guidelines and procedures
- Being able to follow directions and make good judgments
- Having knowledge of emergency procedures and being able to respond to emergency situations.

Cook/Janitor/Support Personnel

People who hold these positions are responsible for completing specified duties in their assigned job areas that serve as support for the overall function of the early care and education center. Specific tasks for each position should be delineated, but the scope and breadth of these tasks may vary from program to program. Employees in these positions with direct contact with the children must have no criminal record.

You, as the director, are responsible for the day-to-day operations of the center. If, for some reason, you are not in the building during business hours, you must officially designate an individual to assume responsibility for center operations in your absence. This person must have full knowledge of center operations and be able to perform as the director. If the first designee is away when you have to be out of the building, a second person must be officially designated to handle the directorial responsibilities.

An Effective Administrator Develops and Manages Personnel Policies and Job Descriptions and Maintains and Safeguards Personnel Records

Child care is a service industry that depends on competent employees to make it successful. Thus, when hiring new personnel, you must make written personnel policies that clearly outline the operation procedures available for your staff. Detail specifically what the employee can expect and what is available to an employee of the center. Write your personnel policies to address the rights and responsibilities of the employee, keeping in mind the perspective of what is best for the program in terms of employee performance.

General Personnel Policies

Job Description

As previously stated this description should include all responsibilities the individual will have in the specific job category, including a statement of state requirements for the particular category. In Competency VI of this text we'll discuss how well-written job descriptions can protect you from certain legal liabilities and what should and should not go into a job description.

Employment Agreement

The employee agrees to work for a specified rate of pay in a specific position with the center. This agreement states that the employee has read, understands and agrees with all company personnel policies. The agreement may delineate a probationary work period before the employee achieves full employment status. If you choose to add any other stipulations in this document, you may do so, but all agreements should be reviewed by legal counsel for validity before being used by the early care and education program.

Most states endorse the doctrine of Employment at Will. Employment at will defines a relationship between the employer and employee in which either party can break the relationship with no liability provided that there was not an express employment contract that governed the terms of employment. Under this legal doctrine "any hiring is presumed to be "at will"; that is, the employer is free to discharge individuals "for good cause, or bad cause, or no cause at all," and the employee is equally free to quit, strike, or otherwise cease to work" (From Horace Gray Wood 1877 treatise).

Exceptions to the doctrine exist such as an employer may not discriminate when terminating an employee. If an employer is doing a workforce reduction, you do not have to go by seniority – you may take job performance into consideration.

Specific Personnel Policy Issues

Equal Employment Opportunity Statement

This statement advises the employee that the center employs without discrimination and without regard to race, creed, color, sex, age, national origin, or disability. The statement includes the concepts: employees are recruited and selected on the basis of overall qualifications; all employees will be treated fairly and all will be compensated on the basis of effort, comparable work performance, experience and contribution to the success of the program; all employees will have an opportunity for training, development and advancement on the basis of individual merit, aptitude, ability and potential consistent with the requirements of the center.

Provisional Period

Specify the purpose, length, benchmarks of the introductory period.

Work Schedules

Establish work hours before the employee begins work, including lunch times, break times, and number of days to be worked weekly. Designate where and how the employee is to record arrival and departure times. Clarify that an employee should not sign in before assigned work time, nor sign out late without express permission of the center director. Instruct employees to be at the assigned job site when the work shift begins and under no circumstances to leave the work site until relieved by another staff member. The children are never to be left unsupervised.

Salary Ranges/Pay Periods

Establish salary ranges for a particular position according to budget requirements, comparable pay scales for other programs in the area, job description, experience, and performance. Most increase reviews are done annually since most budgets are revised annually. Inform employees of pay period procedures - when pay day occurs, what time of day checks will be issued, and how much work time will be covered in each period. Overtime pay is paid at the rate of one and one-half times the employee's regular rate of pay. Non-exempt employees are entitled to overtime if they work more than 40 hours in a given week. It is not necessary to include in the calculation of overtime any hours paid and not actually worked, such as holidays and jury duty. Overtime must be authorized in order to be paid, but an employee cannot be forced to work overtime hours.

Absences and Sick Leave

The employee should be told what procedure to follow when notifying the center about an unscheduled absence. Employees should request scheduled absences well in advance to allow the director time to secure a substitute teacher. Paid sick leave is an optional benefit you may or may not wish to include in your benefit package. First examine budgetary constraints to determine feasibility of paying for sick days. If you choose to provide this benefit, establish criteria for eligibility including at what rate sick days will be earned, whether unused days will be paid, what calendar period will be covered, whether part time employees qualify for paid sick leave, when an employee becomes eligible for paid sick leave, etc. Some centers specify a number of sick days available in any one year and then pay employees for any unused sick days at the end of the year. Other centers just offer a set number of personal days which can be taken for any reason including illness.

Address excessive absences by advising the employee what action will be taken by the employer if the employee misses X number of consecutive work days. Also notify employees what action will be taken if they fail to report an absence from work.

Employee Records

All employees must have a completed job application on file. The employee must meet state requirements for age, education, etc. Falsification, misrepresentation, or the exclusion of pertinent information will be grounds for dismissal. It is a good idea to have employees complete a ten-year work history form to be kept in the individual personnel files. And each employee should submit to a criminal records check.

An I-9 form is required on file for each employee. This form documents the employee's eligibility for employment according to the U.S. Immigration and Naturalization Service. (See the sample I-9 form in this section.)

Some states require new employees participate in an orientation covering topics critical to the safe care of children. The state may specify what must be covered in the orientation. Whether your state requires an orientation or not, it is an excellent way to help a new employee feel more at ease and to assure yourself that all immediate aspects of early care and education and your particular program are covered. Have the employee sign a form attesting to such an orientation. You will also want to include current first aid and CPR certificates and other ongoing training in the employee's records. Require each employee to notify the director immediately if there is a change in pertinent personnel information (phone number, address, etc.). All employee personnel records are confidential.

Employee records contain sensitive information and it is important to safeguard social security numbers, birthdates, health information and any other facts that could lead to identity theft. Although emergency information may need to be available to staff, other sensitive information whether on the computer or in paper files should be protected.

Employee Benefits

Advise employees where the staff lounge, workroom and bathroom are located for use during specified break times. Advise them of designated assigned parking spaces. Disclaim the responsibility for the loss or theft of personal items and advise the employee if there is a secured area, such as a locker, where valuables may be stored.

If break time is to be paid, tell the employees how many breaks will be provided and when the breaks will be scheduled. Further discussion of compensation and benefits occurs in Competency VIII

Give employees pertinent information regarding payroll such as:

- How much time is covered in a pay period
- When and where paychecks will be issued
- Whom the employee should contact if there is a question regarding a paycheck amount or number of hours which were paid
- How overtime is recorded on time sheets
- How the employee accounts for sick leave, scheduled absences, or professional days
- The center policy for a lost check or for the issuance of paychecks prior to the scheduled pay day

If insurance is available through the center, advise the employee when he will become eligible for the insurance coverage, what procedures must be followed at that time, and what the coverage includes.

Cell Phones, Text Messaging, and Facebook

Use of cell phones and text messaging during working hours has created many problems for early childhood education and care administrators. If you chose to ban cell phones or any other electronic devices brought to the center by staff you might consider making a telephone available to employees in the employee lounge area. Specify when the phone may be used, how long calls should last, and what procedure will be used to relay phone messages to the staff. Instruct your staff in telephone courtesy and tell them what informational responses about the center should be given in the event an employee has the occasion to answer the phone.

Facebook has created new problems of confidentiality. There have been instances when staff do not understand that cute pictures of children may not be published on Facebook without parental permission and even with this permission, it is not advisable.

General Center Policies
Training and Meetings

Your state licensing agency may require your staff attend periodic training and development classes to meet state training requirements and promote professional growth. Your policies should clearly state staff expectations regarding attendance at staff meetings, parent conferences, and scheduled open house meetings.

Procedures for Releasing Children

Information about the proper procedure for releasing children to parents or other approved adults and how the teacher can identify approved individuals should be one of the first topics covered with a new employee. As part of developing management systems have written procedures to be followed by the staff when unauthorized people enter the center.

Train New Staff on Center Policies

- Employees' visitors during work hours
- Handling accidents involving children, specifying the treatment and reporting procedures
- Procedure an employee should follow when injured on the job (Explain about Workers' Compensation Insurance and what reporting procedure the employee should follow. Be sure to give your employees a list of doctors they may use in seeking medical treatment should they be injured.)
- The observation and reporting of suspected child abuse
- How to check children for signs of illness or possible abuse
- Supervision of children, including bathroom and playground times
- Smoking
- Use and care of classroom equipment and supplies (Advise whether or not certain materials can be removed from the center at any time.)
- State clearly the policy of the center on discipline. Many states prohibit corporal punishment and violators are subject to prosecution. Your policies might state that any child who is considered unmanageable should be brought to the director; that any violation of this rule, observed by any employee, should be reported immediately to the director; and the failure to do so could result in loss of employment and prosecution for not reporting known abuse.
- Handling biting incidents
- Confidentiality of records and information about children and staff
- Use of personal electronic devices

Performance Evaluations

Evaluation and review of an employee's work and work habits benefits both the employee and the organization. Such reviews should be conducted at regular intervals such as after completion of the provisional period and annually thereafter.

Federal Regulations

Here is what is required.

- Advise your employees of worker's compensation insurance.
- Review your expectations for employees to follow the blood-borne pathogens exposure control plan for the center as required by OSHA. If exposure does occur, the employee may choose to follow the treatment plan or sign a statement declining treatment.
- Include a policy statement indicating the center's compliance with the Americans with Disabilities Act.
- If you have at least 50 employees (within a 75-mile radius), you must include in your policies information that complies with the Family Medical Leave Act regarding an employee's time away from the job for family-related circumstances.
- Be sure to include your policies on sexual harassment, conflict of interest, use of company vehicles, and grievances.

State what disciplinary procedure will be followed if any of the individual company policies are violated. Document all infractions, disciplinary measures, and resulting employer/employee conferences. Sign and date the documentation and have the employee sign it. Then place a copy in the employee's personnel file.

Your company personnel policies should address all aspects of employment and be equally presented and applied to all employees. Have policies reviewed by legal counsel to be sure expectations are reasonable, legal, and equitable. The fairness doctrine must be applied as policies are administered, or the center is vulnerable to legal action. Review your personnel policies annually for needed revisions and updates.

Personnel Records

Employment Files

An employment file should be kept on each staff member and regular substitutes. The employment file should contain:

- Employment application
- Employment contract – if applicable
- A signed statement that the employee has been given a copy of the policies and has read, understood and is willing to comply with all
- Employment history (the length of the history varies by state)
- Orientation verification form
- Training certificates

- Current first aid and CPR credentials
- Verification of criminal records check if required by your state
- Signed statement from staff member attesting to employment qualifications

OSHA requires that medical records be kept separate. If your state licensing requires you to have staff medical records with the rest of the personnel file, it is suggested that you have a separate color coded file folder for this purpose. I-9 forms should be kept in a separate file.

Daily Attendance Records

Staff attendance may be kept in a number of ways. You may wish to keep an attendance roster designed like the attendance roster kept on the children or you may choose to keep an individual attendance record on each person reflecting annual attendance, absences, illness, vacation days, holidays, or professional leave days. Payroll records (time cards) will suffice as attendance records if needed. Attendance records should be kept on file for a minimum of six months.

Daily Time Cards

A time card recorded manually or punched by a time clock should be maintained for each employee. New cards should be provided weekly or by pay period. The time on the card should reflect the employee's time at work for which he is being paid. Some centers use computer software for this purpose.

Staff Roster

Create a staff roster that contains the name and home phone number of each staff person. This roster should be available at all times in case of an emergency or a need to get in touch with a staff person.

Substitute Roster

Also create a substitute roster that contains the names and phone numbers of substitutes who may be called in to work in the absence of a regular staff member.

Vacation Calendar

An annual calendar should be posted for teachers to indicate when scheduled vacations will occur. If the center prohibits certain times of the year from being used as vacation time, the calendar should indicate which days are not permissible.

Staff Work Schedule

Create a master work schedule indicating hours all staff members will work, where they will work, and how many days each week they will work those hours. Schedule adequate staff to maintain required pupil/teacher ratios at all times, but the work schedules should be concise enough to stay within the budgetary restraints of payroll.

An Effective Administrator Recruits, Selects, and Retains Staff

As a director, you face the challenge of recruiting, selecting and retaining staff by refining your personnel skills through research and solid employment practices. Research has shown that interviews are the least likely predictors of success on a job. Further, job skills alone are not predictors of successful staff in child care. In fact, only 30% of the job is typically skill related, while 70% of the job involves all other work behaviors. Education and experience in the early childhood industry do not necessarily equal outstanding job performance in the classroom. While an applicant's education and related experience are important factors to consider, they should not be the only considerations.

Recruitment Procedures

Criteria

Establish criteria for selecting a staff person for each job classification. Work with children involves planning a curriculum which provides activities that will enhance their social, intellectual, emotional, and physical development. Major considerations are the personal qualities and the applicant's attitude toward child care, children, and parents. Criteria should also be based on qualities and skills necessary to fulfill the job description.

Time Line

Establish a time frame for the hiring process. Allow enough time to advertise, interview, and make a selection before the vacancy is to be filled. Also allow for candidates who have to give notice to present employers before beginning work with your program.

Advertise the Vacancy

The advertisement should include a job title, brief job description, qualification, deadlines for applications and/or request for resumes, telephone number of address of the center and contact person. Advertisements may be placed in local newspapers, college placement offices, vocational/technical school offices, local employment agencies, and with information and referral agencies. Unless a secretary is available to field questions from prospective applicants, it would be wise to indicate that no phone calls will be accepted. Parents and existing staff members are good referral sources for prospective candidates. Post the advertisement on the staff bulletin board and on the parent bulletin board.

Review Resumes and Applications

If resumés were requested, review them based on your criteria. After you have screened the resumes, call those applicants you wish to interview to complete an application form. Job applicants also appreciate a brief letter notifying them that they have not been selected if that is the case. In such a letter you might state that, while you appreciate their interest, you have no position at present that exactly matches their qualifications.

If resumés were not requested, allow all applicants to complete an application form. The application form must contain the following information: name, current address, current telephone number, educational background, a statement that the person meets the age requirements of the state standards, and qualifying work experience, if applicable.

Gather Information

Optional information that may be requested is: work availability dates; a statement of the essential functions of the job that the applicant must read and initial; the applicant's history on his most recent job; the names, addresses, and telephone numbers of two references not related to the applicant who can attest to his ability to perform the job; and a statement to be signed by the applicant that he does not have a criminal record. As a rule of thumb, ask no questions that are not directly related to the applicant's ability to perform the job for which he is applying.

Employment applications cannot discriminate on the basis of sex, age, race, or religious preference. Applicants cannot be asked to disclose information about previous worker's compensation insurance claims nor be discriminated against due to qualifying disabilities.

JOB POSTING

Wanted: Individual with early childhood education background; loving, caring, outgoing, silly, enjoys playing in the mud, wet sand, shaving cream and the like; enjoys crawling around on hands and knees, meowing like a cat or slithering like a snake; must have calm speaking voice and able to read endless stories with zest, have eyes in back of head, and willing to change wet pants or diapers with a smile.

Needs to be creative, imaginative, fun, artist, scientist, psychologist, mathematician, who can put in long hours, enjoys parent contact – even when they are upset, and can do ten things at one time and never tires of giving a hand when asked.

Needs to understand basic plumbing – clogged toilets, able to do manual labor – shovel snow, hammer bookcases, fix broken tables, bikes etc.

Biggest pay incentive – a child's smile and a parent's appreciation of a job done well.

Selection Procedures

Once all applications have been received, it is time to begin the screening process. First screen for all applications meeting the minimum age qualifications for the position available. Then eliminate those who do not meet the minimum work experience and educational requirements. The remaining applications should then be ranked from most qualified to least qualified and interviews scheduled with the candidates you believe are most suited to fill the position.

In conducting the interview you may ask questions regarding willingness to stay in the position, satisfaction with the position, ability to work with others and the candidate's reliability. However, you must be sensitive to questions that appear discriminatory in nature that could be considered in violation of equal employment opportunity laws. These laws consist of the following.

- Equal Pay Act of 1963 - prohibits lower pay based simply on the gender of an employee

- Title VII - Civil Rights Act of 1964 - eliminates any form of discrimination in employment based on color, race, religion, sex, or national origin

- The Equal Opportunity Act of 1972 - gives the Equal Employment Opportunity
 Commission the authority to file suits in federal court against violators of the Civil Rights Act

- The Age Discrimination in Employment Act of 1967 - prohibits discrimination on the basis of age, against individuals who are between the ages of 40 and 64 inclusive, with the exception of cases in which age is a bona fide occupational qualification

- The Americans with Disabilities Act (ADA) of July, 1990 - prohibits employers of 15 or more individuals from discriminating against a qualified individual with a disability in application procedures, hiring, advancement, discharge, employee compensation, job training, and other terms, conditions and privileges of employment

Interviewing

If you want a high quality early childhood education center, hire high quality employees. Quality teams run quality centers. Good staff will help push you to the top.

There are no set rules as to what should be asked during the interview process, but the following guidelines might be helpful as you decide what questions to ask the candidate.

First, make a list of the characteristics that you see in your most valued employees. Then design questions you could ask a job applicant that would help determine whether she possesses these characteristics. Weight your questions, giving the most points to the characteristic you value most. Try this interview tool on several staff members to refine your questions. Then ask one of your best employees to join you in the interviewing process. You might also use an employment assessment tool designed by a professional to help screen for persons with the right qualities.

The questions you ask and any test you administer must be relevant to the work for which the applicant is applying.

The interview and the application form must concern matters that distinguish between those people who will better perform the job and those who will not.

Although you may not intend to discriminate, if you ask the wrong questions, you may cause the applicant to believe you are discriminating, and the applicant may file suit against you.

The Equal Employment Opportunity Commission issued the *Pre-Employment Inquiry Guidelines* in 1981 and the *Enforcement Guidance: Pre-Employment Disability-Related Questions and Medical Examinations* in 1995. These guidelines state that employers may not discriminate on the basis of race, religion, gender, pregnancy or planning to have a child in the future, marital status, number of children, child care arrangements, sexual preference, age, national origin, financial status, military record, or disability.

The guidelines indicated that some questions may or may not be considered discriminating based on the context in which they are asked. For example: Questions as to height or weight may be considered discriminating if they relate to gender or national origin unless their relationship to specific job requirement can be demonstrated.

Arrest and conviction records – questions relating to a job applicant's arrest record are improper, but you may ask about an applicant's conviction record.

In preparation for the interview, schedule a time when you can talk with the applicant without interruption. Review the candidate's application and formulate questions you feel will draw out responses. Be prepared to answer questions about the position regarding salary, benefits, and anticipated work schedules. Also be prepared to inform the candidate of the pleasant as well as the unpleasant aspects of the job.

In conducting an effective interview, make the applicant feel comfortable. Provide a thorough description of the position available and discuss benefits and opportunities associated with the job. Let the applicant do most of the talking as you guide the interview with open questions. Ask the applicant to tell something about himself and review the application, probing the accuracy of the information given. Pay careful attention to the applicant's reasons for leaving previous jobs and ask the applicant how he feels about the position at your center.

Test the applicant's knowledge and skills required for the position. If possible allow him to visit in a classroom and observe his skills with children. Obtain information on specialized knowledge the applicant has and determine if the applicant is over-qualified for the job or better suited for some other career. Determine if the applicant has personal characteristics required for the job, such as the aptitude for working with children, willingness to accept responsibility, emotional stability, reliability, and an ability to learn.

You may discuss the financial needs of the applicant in conjunction with the financial rewards of the job. If the candidate has specific monetary requirements as a prerequisite to accepting the job, these stipulations must be within the budgetary constraints of the center.

Sample interview questions might include:

- Why do you think you are good working with children?
- What experiences have you had working with children? Precisely what were you expected to do? Have you had any experiences planning lessons?
- If you had a choice, what age group would you most prefer to teach? Why?
- What is your philosophy regarding discipline?
- What do you think parents consider most important in good child care?

- How would you handle a typical classroom situation such as: one child biting another, a parent who is angry because a hat has been misplaced, bruises on a child's back or bottom, a child using bad language, toddlers who climb on tables, etc.?
- What hobbies or outside interests do you have that would help you in your job? Any special skills?
- Can you be flexible if the work schedules have to be altered on short notice?
- What do you see yourself doing over the next five-year period?
- Have you had any relevant training classes? Are you willing to grow professionally?

Do not ask:

- If the applicant is married
- If the applicant has children
- The applicant's age (You many ask if the applicant meets you states age requirements for working in early childhood education.)
- If the applicant has ever been arrested (You may ask, usually on the application form, if the applicant has ever been convicted of a felony.)

In going through the hiring process, consider recruiting both male and female applicants. We often hear the lament that there is a need for more male role models for young children, but low wages and the societal attitude that men are not so nurturing tend to dissuade men from applying and directors from actively recruiting male teachers. Many parents are uncomfortable with the idea of a male teacher, because they feel that their children will be at risk for sexual abuse. This reasoning is unfortunate and completely unfounded. It stereotypes males in an unsavory fashion and turns men away from careers with children. The children of today spend a significant portion of their childhood with women. They would certainly benefit from having a male figure who is both a leader and nurturer to balance and enrich their life experience.

Once you have settled on a particular candidate, contact the references provided to verify work experience before making a job offer. Legally employers cannot share assessments about former employees that could be considered libelous. In essence, as a director you cannot give a bad reference on a former employee as it puts your company at risk. A director can confirm that a person was employed and state the dates of his employment.

When you have selected a new employee and he has accepted the position, you should write a letter of thanks to those applicants who interviewed for the position but were not chosen. Keep their applications on file for future needs.

Retaining Staff

Employees who feel confident about their ability to perform the job and have a clear understanding of expectations are far less likely to leave their jobs than the employee who is never sure of responsibilities and expectations. Staff turnover can be minimized by carefully communicating job requirements and performance expectations. Begin with new employees by conducting an orientation covering the basic must-know information for the employee is to be successful. The orientation should cover personnel policies, salary information, complete job description, and any other relevant information regarding performance expectations. Follow-up evaluations and strong feedback, with generous specific praise and recognition of a job well done, are necessary to ensure an employee's continued success. Other center elements that contribute to staff retention are:

A High Quality Program

Each of us likes to work for a well-respected organization with a great reputation. You'll have more loyal staff if your center has the reputation for being the best in town.

Inclusion in Decision Making

The more an employee participates in setting the direction of the program, the more he buys into the mission and the more loyal he is to the team. Involve your staff in important appropriate decisions. Make them feel you respect them as professionals and respect their input.

Appreciation for Teachers

Encourage parents to express their appreciation for teachers. Teacher appreciation weeks are remembered for a long time.

Employees who fail to perform in accordance with program expectations and directives may have to be terminated. First, remember to follow the laws of your state regarding firing an employee. It is essential you seek and follow legal advice on this issue. Be consistent in your application of personnel policies and show evidence of good intentions in training an employee. Examine your personnel policies carefully. Do the policies reflect the company's goals? Are they flexible enough to allow discretionary decisions when needed? For example, do not state the violation of a particular policy is a firing offense unless you really mean to enforce it 100% of the time. Do not terminate someone in anger. All policies must be enforced consistently; otherwise the employer will lose in unemployment hearings. Make a practice of documenting conferences with employees who are not performing up to standard. You may wish to direct specific questions to your local labor office before deciding to terminate an employee.

An Effective Administrator Provides Staff Development Which Includes Orientation, In-service and Career Development Training, Understands Concepts of Adult Learning, and Motivates Staff to Participate in Training

An early care and education center is only as good as the people who work there day to day. New facilities and creative equipment are only the bells and whistles. The core of the program depends on the human element, the classroom teachers who work with the children and their families making the program an inviting place. Research shows the level of teacher training relates directly to the quality of care. Trained teachers are more in demand by parents who are increasingly more sophisticated in selecting care for their children. It is the director's responsibility to see teachers are informed, trained and motivated to be the best.

Beginning with new employees, provide an orientation program, either before or on the first day of employment, outlining must know information, particularly on health and safety issues. A complete orientation should contain the following points.

- Policies and procedures governing enrollees
- Emergency weather plans
- Employee's assigned duties and responsibilities
- Reporting requirements for suspected cases of child abuse, neglect or deprivation, communicable diseases, and serious injury
- General familiarity with health and safety requirements for caring for the children (You will require employees to achieve in-depth knowledge of health and safety issues later.)
- Childhood injury control
- Employee training requirements
- Disciplining children

Center disciplinary policies should be discussed in detail. Instruct inexperienced teachers not to raise their voices, speak sharply, threaten children or issue unwarranted ultimatums. There is no place for sarcasm or humiliation in the early care and education program. Children need to have their self-esteem promoted, not destroyed by an unwitting adult. New teachers should be cautioned that food cannot be withheld from children as a means of discipline. Provide new staff members with positive techniques to employ with the children in lieu of harsh punitive methods.

New teachers who have limited training in child development should be given developmental expectations for children in their class' age group, curriculum goals and objectives, and suggested transition techniques. The most important task a director can do in the mentoring process is guide the teacher with good feedback and positive reinforcement, be a role model for good teacher/child interaction. Some centers have a well-developed mentoring program in which they pair a new teacher with an experienced teacher. The new teacher spends time observing the experienced teacher and meets with him regularly to ask questions and to discuss his own progress. The mentoring period may last six months to a year. Some programs give mentors a bonus at the end of the mentoring period.

Safety issues are critical for all staff, but especially for new teachers not familiar with the inner workings of the program. Plan to assist new teachers during the first few days of work as they get acquainted with children and parents. It takes time to know who is authorized to pick up children, and a new teacher should be given explicit instructions about identifying any adult with whom he is unfamiliar. Point out emergency evacuation procedures, where medical treatment supplies are kept, and where parent information records are stored in case of an emergency situation. Discuss playground safety measures as well as classroom safety rules.

Professional development workshops covering relevant topics are a means of qualifying new teachers and rejuvenating experienced staff. Conduct a needs assessment based on staff experience, prior training, and observed classroom performance to determine what training workshops would be most beneficial to your program. Specific workshops should be tailored around specific needs, or make individual recommendations to the staff regarding outside seminars. Unless the workshop is generic to all age groups, teachers should focus on those training sessions that deal with the age child with whom they work.

When researching what professional training is available, you will find a wide array of classes and presenters. Some classes will have a lecture format, some audio-visual materials, and others hands-on participation. All of these different presentation styles should be taken into consideration before choosing a particular training class to have the class be meaningful and have applicative value for the participant. You want staff to gain good information from a training class, so encourage them to choose classes that appeal to their individual styles of learning.

If possible, review various presenters looking for those with the most audience appeal. A good presenter incorporates good techniques to address various learning styles and will offer programs rich in different kinds of sensory stimulation. Adults learn in a variety of ways, and research shows that some people learn more by what they see, while others learn more by what they hear. For adults, the information being presented must have relevance in some way to their prior life experience if it is to be incorporated into their mainstream knowledge. An effective training class will focus on the high points of the topic to be covered, involve the participants as much as possible, and allow a question and answer period. The best time to attend a training class is between 10:00 A.M. and Noon, because during this time period people have a high retention rate, are very alert, and quite possibly will remember what they learn more than at any other time of the day.

With quality linked directly to the level of training, it is imperative the director encourage his staff to see training as a means of professional growth and personal fulfillment, not just a means of satisfying a ten-hour job requirement. Professional workshops help the classroom teacher keep abreast of new information, affirm what he has already learned and practices, and renew his enthusiasm for work. Workshops can become a gathering place to interact with peers, share ideas, and experience camaraderie with others in the same profession.

If you sense any of your teachers wish to do more in the way of professional development than the minimum requirement, be sure to tell them of options for obtaining a credentialed status such as those listed below. There are two types of credentials for individuals.

Certified Childcare Professional (CCP)

This is an individual credential offered through The NECPA Commission, Inc.

Competency V: Management and Human Resources

Child Development Associate (CDA)

This is an individual credential offered through the Council for Early Childhood Professional Recognition. The evaluation measures are CDA competencies and functional areas, professional resource file, formal observation and written assessment.

Directors face a challenge in motivating teachers who are not interested in professional growth. Unfortunately, all directors will encounter some individuals who are content to work day to day with no thought of increasing their level of knowledge or expertise. These individuals balk at training requirements, using the excuse that they already have enough training and the classes infringe on their personal time. There are ways to motivate these people and encourage the rest of the staff as well:

Schedule regular staff meetings that provide time for the staff to share problems and brainstorm solutions. Guide the teachers to decide for themselves which of their skills are weak and could stand improvement. Then you can develop an instructional class or recruit a presenter to cover the specified topic.

Provide an incentive program that encourages staff training participation. The incentives may be monetary rewards, salary increases, verbal recognition at staff meetings, or formal written recognition in the parent newsletter or on the parent bulletin board. A director might offer an extra floating holiday to teachers who train beyond minimum requirements. You might hold a recognition banquet annually for teachers and spouses or recognize an employee of the month. Any reward is feasible as long as it accomplishes the job of saying well done to a deserving staff member.

If possible develop a career ladder within the child care program that allows the teachers to move from assistant teacher to lead teacher to assistant director to director. This scale must be carefully conceived to reflect realistic salary adjustments and experience/performance criteria. The lack of management-level positions can be a drawback to the career ladder unless the center is part of a large corporation.

An Effective Administrator Provides Guidance and Supervision for Each Employee

Every team must have a leader to provide supervision and guidance if quality performance is to be achieved by the team as a whole. The staff looks to you for leadership, and parents view you as a pivotal factor for quality child care delivery system. You set the program standard as you model appropriate professional behavior in every aspect of your job performance. When dealing with children you should demonstrate knowledge of child development and appropriate behavioral expectations. Your attitude should reflect concern for children's welfare as you treat them with courtesy and respect, not disdain, impatience, or sarcasm. This includes:

- Communicating clear expectations for performance
- Supporting staff in their development and accomplishment of professional goals and objectives

Competency V: Management and Human Resources

- Motivating and challenging staff to set a high standard
- Observing objectively and giving constructive feedback in a way that helps staff to grow professionally
- Supervising and monitoring staff so that quality job performance is recognized and inadequate job performance leads to remediation and/or termination when necessary
- Using knowledge of different supervisory styles and methods to meet individual needs of staff
- Modeling appropriate behavior and professional dress

Parents should be treated courteously and respectfully. As the director, you model the concept of the customer is always right even when the customer is not right. You must always be willing to listen to parent concerns and complaints without becoming defensive and then resolve the problem immediately, if possible, or mediate an agreeable compromise.

With the staff you lead by being clear and concise in expressing program performance expectations and fair in addressing any conflicts that may arise. It is inappropriate to discuss one staff member with another or to treat one staff person differently from another. If you are to have the respect of the staff and unquestioned loyalty to your leadership, the measures you take for treating non-performance must be consistent for all situations. The major emphasis should be providing both leadership and support to create a harmonious working environment that encourages teachers to work together, support one another, and do what is best for the children.

To keep everyone on a positive, progressive track, staff should have a clear understanding of performance expectations and quality delivery standards. The first step of this communication process is written standards reflecting the early care and education program's overall philosophy. You define goals you have for the children, curriculum you use, how discipline is handled, values your program supports, roles your program plays in the community, etc.? Provide teachers with a written job description delineating work responsibilities including classroom supervision, preparing lesson plans, implementing age-appropriate activities, general housekeeping duties, and working with other staff members to provide a comprehensive program for young children.

State clearly what standard of performance is expected of each employee. Tell them:

- What dress code you require for your employees
- What behavior is expected as center representatives at all times in the community
- What the employee's responsibility is to keep information on other employees and on children and families strictly confidential
- The requirement that all employees have knowledge of state licensing regulations and they will be held accountable for compliance with all rules and regulations

Quality assurance is not always something achieved by providing people with written expectations. You will need to follow up with both formal and informal observation techniques to see each teacher's skills are strong enough to provide quality delivery of the program. Assess each teacher for quality points and build on those skills to strengthen any areas of weaker performance.

Quality begins with a teacher's attitude – is it positive or negative towards work situations? Is he receptive to constructive critiques of his job performance? A good teacher likes and respects the children with whom he works. He wins their affection through kindness and understanding. His tone of voice is controlled and does not get louder to reach above the voices of the children. He speaks clearly and concisely, giving simple directions reinforced by smiles of support and encouragement. He lends assistance when it is needed, but allows the children to practice becoming independent and to choose their work from many varied activities and learning opportunities. A good teacher sets positive limits and boundaries so the children know what expectations are, and he does not demean a child who falls short of these expectations. He spends time observing each child in his care, recognizing traits that make each child unique.

A good teacher respects parents and understands a parent's need to know what has happened to their child throughout the day. A good teacher likes himself. He takes care of himself physically to maintain the stamina needed to keep up with young children, and a good teacher realizes each day is not only a learning experience for the children, but for himself as well.

Being a good teacher is not something accomplished all at once. It takes a person with potentially good skills, time, training, and experiences with children to develop the "quality points" mentioned above. You can guide this learning process and help the teacher grow professionally by providing regular feedback on observed classroom performance. The observations should not only point out weak areas, but strong ones as well.

Feedback should be provided to all teachers on a regular basis. Otherwise, sporadic feedback given randomly is perceived as being pure criticism, and it is not well received by the staff nor will it achieve the desired changes. Comments regarding observations of performance should be made in a non-threatening manner and accompanied by alternatives for strengthening weak skills.

For example, if a teacher is observed scolding the children for loud voices, running in the hall, or being disruptive at nap time, you could help the teacher learn about positive ways of giving directions that reverse the need for negative comments. The teacher could learn to signal to the children or speak to them individually when voices are getting too loud; instead of saying don't run, the teacher could tell the children how he expects them to move through rooms or halls; when a child is disturbing others, the teacher could remove him from the rest of the group or offer the child an alternative activity. In essence, you can help the teacher learn to reinforce positive behaviors rather than focusing on negatives.

Generally speaking, you will find that most of the staff will welcome constructive critiques and feedback, which will enable them to grow professionally. In those situations where a teacher resents the feedback or simply lacks the aptitude to make necessary changes, you must make a decision about the employee's future with the center by considering the following questions.

- Has the employee demonstrated enough ability to warrant further training effort?
- Is the employee suited to the age group with which he is presently working, or would his skills be better utilized in a different class?
- Does the employee need to be formally reprimanded and the process for termination set in place?

If the director reaches the decision to formally reprimand the employee, he should document his conferences with the employee. In this documentation, the director indicates what issues were discussed in the conferences, and that he notified the employee that further infractions will result in termination.

To be an effective administrator, a director needs to understand his personal strengths and weaknesses in dealing with people. Commercial evaluation tools are able to provide insight on personality traits that directly influence behavior styles. Dominant personality traits would be highlighted along with information on recognizing dominant traits in others. This information could prove beneficial in determining which personality types work well together, how one personality type responds to other personality types, and how you can effectively respond to the various personalities of the staff. Evaluation tools are available through communication consulting companies, adult education programs at local colleges and universities, or advertised through child care industry publications.

Your ability to supervise the staff effectively through observation, constructive critique, and positive feedback can make the difference between mediocrity and excellence. Exhibit a sense of pride that child care is your career choice. By holding the position in high esteem you reinforce the self-worth of everyone who works for you, and ultimately the children reap the biggest reward of all - teachers who care about themselves and the quality of work they perform.

An Effective Administrator Develops and Manages a Formal Staff Evaluation Process Which Is Based on Observation and Opportunities for Regular and Continuous Self-evaluation

Classroom teachers who are truly interested in doing a good job welcome both positive and negative comments from the director. Many times people are not aware they are doing something wrong until it is brought to their attention, and more often, people appreciate knowing their supervisor sees them doing a good job. Staff morale is boosted immeasurably by knowing the director values the teachers enough to make their classroom performance a priority.

You can employ several techniques in completing classroom observations. The informal method is to stop in a classroom at random times throughout the day to assist the teacher if needed, chat with the children, or deliver any miscellaneous materials. During these times a director with a keen eye can assess what is taking place in the classroom. Pay particular attention to safety and hygiene issues with the children. Are teachers sanitizing changing tables after each diaper change? Are teachers washing their hands after wiping noses or changing diapers? Are teachers responsive to individual children - do they talk to children with nurturing voices? What is the tone of the classroom? Does it feel relaxed, warm, tense or frenzied? Are the children content, calm, anxious, or frustrated? Are children free to select their own activities or is every moment of the daily schedule teacher directed? Quick, sensitive observations can be accomplished in less than five minutes. When you do note a problem, point it out immediately in a non-threatening manner. An immediate response to observed problems lets the staff know that you are tuned into quality performance and expect to see it happen center wide.

A formal evaluation method should include a written instrument designed to rate performance based on established criteria that have been made available to the classroom teacher. You can develop this formal rating system based on expressly delineated responsibilities, job description requirements, center policies, center philosophy, and state rules and regulations. This formal evaluation tool should be thoroughly explained to the teachers in terms of content, when it will be used, what purpose it serves, and what impact, if any, it has on future employment. Teachers should have a copy of the evaluation to avoid misunderstandings about company expectations. Formal evaluations are generally done on an annual basis and may be tied to performance reviews for salary increases.

Formal evaluations may also be multi-faceted in that they allow for feedback from many sources in generating a comprehensive review. The basic instrument, as described above, allows the director to make written observations based on the stated criteria. A second component would allow the employee to do a self-critique based on the same criteria. A third component would allow parents to make a written response based on the criteria of which they would have knowledge. The parental component could even be included in an assessment of the entire program. Such an assessment would give parents an opportunity to rate not only individual staff members, but the general services of the entire program as well. Parents should be given an opportunity to comment on fees as compared to services rendered. Data gathered from all three components can be compiled and used to upgrade staff performance and center services.

Providing teacher feedback must be a priority with any director who wishes to improve the quality of the child care program. Offer this feedback regularly and consistently so it will have an impact on center operations. Professional growth is an ongoing process that will suffer if evaluations only occur once a year. Set aside one day each week to meet with individual staff members to share their observations and hear their concerns. Even if it is impossible to see all staff members in one day, cycle through so that you see everyone over a two week period. Any problems observed in the classroom should be addressed quickly to avoid having the teacher get in the habit of doing something wrong. Frequent conferences set the stage for staff to succeed.

A good director will empower the staff to be an integral part of the professional growth process. Allow teachers to have input in what evaluated criteria is truly important and allow them to set personal goals in achieving higher performance standards. Incentives to promote and recognize quality performance might include: recognizing an employee of the month with a plaque that is prominently displayed in the parent traffic area; submitting a recognition article to the local newspaper; designating a choice parking place for an honored employee; providing an extra paid holiday; or taking a different teacher to lunch each week. People need more from a job than just a paycheck. A pat on the back, a supportive smile, and an occasional thank you will go a long way in rewarding teachers for a lot of hard work and dedication.

Summary

Demonstrating competency in staff management and human resources, an effective administrator:

- Provides a mechanism that defines tasks, job roles, the distribution of authority, quality standards, and concepts of teamwork and decision making within the program

- Develops and manages personnel policies and job descriptions and maintains and safeguards personnel records

- Recruits, selects, and retains staff

- Provides staff development which includes orientation, in-service and career development training; understands concepts of adult learning and motivates staff to participate in training

- Provides guidance and supervision for each employee

- Develops and manages a formal staff evaluation process which Is based on observation and opportunities for regular and continuous self-evaluation

If you feel you lack confidence in any of the skills listed above, please go back and review the appropriate section in this chapter.

Competency VI

Educational Programming

Competency VI

Educational Programming

Learning Objectives:

- To understand that contemporary learning concepts are based on theories developed over time

- To gain confidence in the understanding of basic information regarding the development of the brain

- To understand developmentally and culturally appropriate practices

- To be able to select and use curriculum, materials, and equipment for the best early childhood education practices

- To be able to select and use assessment tools and strategies

- To gain an understanding of the value of national accreditation, standards, and evaluation tools

An Effective Administrator Understands that Contemporary Education Theories Come from Concepts Developed Over a Period of Time

Early childhood education has been influenced by theorists interested in understanding the complex social interaction of humans, how we learn, and the influence that environment has on our ability to learn and function. European and later US research has given rise to learning practices and methodologies. The following is a brief introduction to the theories and theorists who have influenced the development of early childhood education.

Scaffolding and the Zone of Proximal Development

Lev Vygotsky (1896 –1934)

Lev Vygotsky is important because of his view of human cognitive development and because he expounded the importance of understanding how social, cultural, and societal influences affect one's development. This translates in early childhood education to indicate social interaction as a stimulus for cognitive development. It further translates to teachers needing to adjust experiences in the learning environment to the background experiences brought to the class by the children.

Two important terms come from Vygotsky – "ZDP" Zone or Zone of Proximal Development and the theory of Scaffolding. Vygotsky saw language as a crucial tool for cognitive development. A child will learn how to think because words assist the transmission of thought.

He defined the ZPD as the distance between what a child can accomplish during independent problem solving and what can be accomplished with the help by a more competent member of the culture such as a teacher. This help consists of supported learning with the teacher's role being very specific and sensitive. The role of the teacher is to keep the tasks in the ZPD slightly above the child's level of functioning; the teacher is not to simplify content but to provide unfamiliar content.

Theory of Cognitive Development

Jean Piaget- 1896-1980

Jean Piaget presented the Theory of Cognitive Development which promotes the idea that children learn in distinct stages. He proposed the environment and heredity have a profound impact on how children learn. Piaget also believed children should be allowed to choose from an array of activities, have concrete experiences appealing to the five senses, and move at an individual pace with minimal teacher direction.

Piaget posits that knowledge is active construction, not passive copying. Construction is the only way we can deal with the countless missing events in our day to day experiences.

The root metaphor underling Piaget's theory of knowledge is change. The teacher should think of the world as a process, not as a series of categories. Knowledge is the understanding of the process by which objects and events change. Only when children understand this process are they able to cope with the apparent discontinuities of their everyday world. Knowing is more than doing, knowing is also reflecting on how the doing was done.

Good education provides the student with the means to construct and use knowledge. It provides an environment where children have ample opportunity to experience changes (discontinuity) in all four areas of knowledge, and freedom to construct an understanding bridging the differences (continuity). There are two processes at work here.

- The process of assimilation - applying general schemes to different objects and events in the environment.
- The process of accommodation - when the environmental input and the organism are so discrepant the organism is forced to change (Schemes are modified to adapt to the input.)

The Four Stages of Cognitive Development

Please note that the order of the stages is fixed. No stage can be skipped as the development of the stages is cumulative.

1.) Sensorimotor Stage (birth to 2 years)

Children come to understand their environment through their own actions (practical intelligence).

2.) Preoperational Thought (2 to 7 years)

Child grasps symbolic language/representation, understands the operation of function. But function is seen as a one way relation.

3.) Concrete Operational Thought (7 to 11 years)

The child has the ability to mentally reverse actions, moves beyond the stage of mere perception.

4.) Formal Operations (11 + years)

Child is thinking about thinking.

Children move along three dimensions in their understanding of and interactions with the physical and social world.

- Reactive to Active
- Absolute to Relative
- Empirical to Logical

Attachment Theory

John Bowlby (1907-1990)

John Bowlby described attachment formation as bi-directional emotional bonding. Translation: Bowlby's attachment theory emphasizes the importance of the relationship between the child and the caregiver. It is important for a child to be securely attached to another. The secure attachment allows the child to explore and develop. It is interesting to note that cross-cultural research has shown that babies form attachments to multiple caregivers.

Stages of Bonding

- Early months - show great interest in all people
- Four to six months - begins to prefer certain familiar people
- Six months - intense desire to be with certain familiar caregivers
- Six to eight months - stranger anxiety

Types of Attachment

Secure

Child plays happily within a strange play setting, if parent is present. Child may cry when parent leaves the group but will greet parent joyously when they return.

Insecure Avoidant

Child may or may not cry at parent's departure from a strange play area. Child ignores and moves away from parent when they return.

Insecure Ambivalent

Child very upset when parent leaves a strange play area. Child continues to be inconsolable when parent returns, clings to them, angry rejection.

Variations in Infant Attachment

Babies of many cultural groups around the world fall into secure or insecure categories of attachment at approximately the same rates as American infants.

Although Japanese and Northern German infants seemed to become excessively distressed at separation, this could be the result of cultural values and socialization practices.

Cultural differences in attachment may also be genetically derived. Babies of some cultural groups may have timid or cautious personalities.

Parenting behaviors matter. Responsiveness and warm physical contact lead to secure attachments. Responsiveness involves carefully interpreting babies' signals and responding appropriately.

Great care must be taken not to misinterpret cultural expression of warmth and responsiveness. A child with special needs bonds as securely as typically developing children.

The Humanistic Theory
Abraham Maslow (1908-1970)

Abraham Maslow developed the Humanistic theory that all people are driven by basic needs. If basic needs and capacities (which are neutral, pre-moral, positive and good guide one's life) one grows healthier and happier. Sickness is certain if one suppresses or denies these basic needs. There are higher and lower needs hierarchically arranged in levels of potency, the fulfillment of higher needs relies upon gratification of the lower more potent ones. The higher aspects of human nature rest upon fulfillment of the lower needs.

Maslow's Hierarchy of Needs

The identified needs are listed below in descending order.

- Self actualization/Spiritual/Transcendental: The ability to realize one's potential, desire for personnel and spiritual growth and development and to continually improve one's life
- Self Esteem: Ego, the need to feel significant
- Social Needs: Belonging, affection, love, respect
- Safety/Security: Assurance of survival
- Basic Survival: Physiological needs such as food, shelter

Psychoanalytic Theory
Erik Erikson (1902-1994)

Erickson believed humans develop throughout their entire life span. This contradicted Freud who believed the human personality was shaped by the age of five.

Erickson stated there are eight psychological stages encountered throughout life. Each age or stage of development is characterized by a struggle between two emotional states, one positive and one negative. The emotional struggle in infancy is between trust and mistrust. Emotionally healthy babies come to understand they have nurturing, responsive caregivers who meet their basic needs. They come to view the world as safe and predictable. Therefore, attachment formation is a critical part of achieving trust and allowing babies to come to know and bond with caregivers. Erickson stated that each of us must pass through and successfully resolve developmental crises throughout life. The psychological stages are:

- Trust vs. Mistrust (Birth to 18 months)
- Autonomy vs. Shame and Doubt (18 months to 3 years)
- Initiative vs. Guilt (3 to 5 years)
- Industry vs. Inferiority (6 to 12 years)
- Identity vs. Role Confusion (12 to 18 years)

- Intimacy vs. Isolation (18 to 35 years)
- Generactivity vs. Stagnation (35 to 55 or 65)
- Integrity vs. Despair (55 or 65 to Death)

Behaviorist
B.F. Skinner (1904-1990)

The Behaviorist theory promotes the idea that behaviors are learned from the environment and can be increased or decreased by using the reward system. B.F. Skinner developed the technique known as behavior modification. It is commonly used in preschool classrooms to decrease or eliminate undesired behavior by way of time-out or redirection to an alternative activity. Some important aspects of this theory are:

- Operant conditioning: Behavior is altered by manipulating consequences
- Positive reinforcement: Presents a consequence that increases the frequency of the behavior it follows
- Negative or removal reinforcement: Increases the frequency of a behavior it follows by removing an undesired consequence
- Extinction: Reinforcement is removed all together, so behavior decreases and ceases
- Punishment: Any consequence decreasing the frequency of the behavior
- Shaping: Method of successive approximations in which only ever more accurate behaviors are reinforced. Dropping a bird seed path…

Theory of Multiple Intelligences
Howard Gardner (1943 to Present)

Gardner's theory of multiple intelligences contradicted earlier thinking of intelligence was a single inherited entity. His theory of multiple intelligences – people are prone to learn in various ways is widely accepted today. His theory questions the validity of IQ tests as the only measure of intelligence. His theory also challenges Piaget's work proposing children learn in distinct stages. Instead, Gardner proposes that at any one time a child may be at different stages of development. Gardner's intelligences are:

- Linguistic: Facility for written and spoken language
- Musical: Love music-sensitive to sounds
- Logical: Abstract conceptualization/math
- Spatial: Adept at visualizing and creating pictures and objects
- Kinesthetic: Body awareness

- Intrapersonal: Inner feelings
- Interpersonal: Learn through interaction
- Naturalist: Organizing, sorting
- Existentialist: Spiritual

Others

In addition to the above mentioned experts, there are several contemporary authors and speakers from the U.S., such as:

- Ed Ziegler who has noted the importance of play
- Eric Jensen who has written about knowing how the brain works in order to facilitate a proper learning environment for children and students of all ages including noting the importance of play
- Pam Schiller who has discussed windows of opportunity for learning
- Pamela Phelps who speaks to how to support children's success
- Elaine Johnson who speaks to the importance of knowing how the brain functions as a fundamental base to construct learning environments

An Effective Administrator understands that Brain Research has reaffirmed the Importance of High Quality Early Childhood Education

Creating a Brain-Friendly Environment- Learning Styles, Teamwork

The key to all instruction begins with engaging emotions and experience, raising curiosity with relevant and meaningful information and presenting a brain friendly formula to create optimal learning environments for lifelong success. As stated by Marcus Conyers and Donna Wilson, "The brain learns best by using relevance, emotion, patterns, and context to create meaning" (Conyers & Wilson, 2005).

The resource information and strategies of a brain friendly model adds an exciting and effective dimension to all aspects of our jobs as managers and as leaders in our centers.

This is important information that can positively influence communication for supervising and developing a motivated staff team.

This is important information that can assist us in our ability to select and train staff.

This is important information that can have a positive influence on communication with parents for better enrollment and student retention.

Understanding the way the brain functions with all its emotional, instinctive, and cognitive differences aids in understanding the importance of the body/brain connection, nutrition, exercise, and physical safety in our centers.

Parent forums and staff professional development meetings are all important components that affect the success of our program both in and out of our classrooms. The initial workshop for us as directors, for staff to effectively implement strategies in the classrooms and for parental support of our program needs to focus on the importance of a quality early age education in a brain friendly environment. It is essential that we experience the power each of us and our staff and children hold in the ability to understand and develop an awareness and 'metacognition' (Wilson & Conyers, 2006) of how to use our brains.

The Four Fundamental Forces of Learning Model for Boosting Student Achievement (Wilson & Conyers, 2005) are:

- Force 1 – Professional Development and Teacher Preparation
- Force 2 – Physical/ Mental Health and Safety
- Force 3 – Parent Support, Mentors, and Peers
- Force 4 – Pre-K, Pre-Natal, and Prior Knowledge

Facts about the physiological structure of the brain, how the brain functions according to neuroscientific information, and theories on how the brain processes information, experiences and emotions in its ability to learn are the reasons behind the development of this environment for effective pedagogy for staff and students of all ages.

In our journey to develop the most effective brain friendly environment that meets your centers unique mission, we are also striving to develop strategies that ensure a positive state of mind with the ability for everyone involved in our organization to gain meaning in their own personal and professional lives. Relevance and meaning attracts our attention for ultimate retention of these necessary strategies. The relevant strategies in return will give us the ability to transfer information and implement our most important instruction for success in the classrooms and in our centers.

The concept of "Driving Our Brains" (Wilson & Conyers, 2006) through metacognition to understand the world and learn from life experiences is an interesting phenomenon. Metacognition translates to thinking about thinking. A skill many times we ignore in the hustle and bustle of our daily lives. However, learning to become aware of the purpose in the background of all that we do strengthens our intrinsic motivation to be the best possible professionals.

A second crucial skill to possess is the ability to stay in a state of mind of practical optimism. Practical optimism is the foundation upon which to build positive attitude and strong motivation. This brain friendly initiative teaches us to focus on a process and methodology rather than on specific curricular content or material. The priority is to empower our staff and students with the necessary skills and strategies for lifelong personal and educational success (2006). Everyone who has the ability to develop these skills will have the ability to succeed in all academic and experiential learning opportunities regardless of subject content and more importantly life challenges.

Therefore a major focus in this course is to understand how to develop a cooperative learning environment that encourages teamwork and practical optimism as a basis for the success of our centers in all areas of management and leadership.

"Every student is as unique as a fingerprint" (Wilson & Conyers, 2002). "In the end, it is not standardization that makes a classroom work. It is a deep respect for the identity of the individual" (Tomlinson, 1999, p.12).

This concept is also true for everyone involved in your center. Everyone is as unique as a fingerprint. The ability to recognize each person's unique strengths and weaknesses and the ability to respect each person's contributions builds a solid foundation for an effective team.

It is the responsibility of every leader to understand and apply strategies on the most effective methods to appreciate each member of this team.

You, as the leaders, will experience your power. Your staff will experience the power and the students will experience the power they hold. This power is translated into the ability to understand and develop an awareness and metacognition of how to use our brains to gain confidence in our ability to be the best we can be in our professional and personal lives.

Facts about the physiological structure of the brain, how the brain functions according to neuroscientific information, and theories on how the brain processes information, experiences and emotions are the reasons behind the development of this environment for the most effective management and leadership potential.

Developing a sense of pride, self-esteem and confidence is a vital ongoing part of this program. Effective proven techniques to motivate staff and students to discuss, present, brainstorm, and encourage creativity and teamwork is all integrated into this philosophy. One of the most stimulating challenges of this kind of program and environment is the constant encouragement of the ability to look for the solutions rather than the more passive desire to dwell on the problem.

Brain Basics

The brain only weighs about 3 pounds but makes up critical portions of the nervous system with nerve cells connected by nearly one million miles of nerve fibers. The nerve fibers run throughout the body connecting the body and brain and giving humans extraordinary flexibility for learning. The human brain has the largest area of uncommitted cortex of any species on earth with the cortex being the process center for higher level cognitive thinking (Jenson 1998).

The limbic system is our mid brain and is the center for our emotions which can be considered the gateway to learning from the lower part of our brainstem. It is important to activate positive emotions at all times for optimal learning (Conyers & Wilson, 2005).

The theory of interconnected neurons and the importance of students being able to assess the relevance of information to their own lives for their own physical well being and cognitive development gives a better physiological understanding of the importance of positive social interaction and cooperative learning in this process (Sylwester 2001). In addition, neurons and molecules that have attached emotions to them affect memory in conscious and unconscious brain and body reactions (Pert 1999).

Specific exercises such as BrainObics and Brain Gym connect the left and right hemispheres, activate the cerebellum for movement coordination, and the occipital lobe for visual processing, and being so close to the cerebellum, develop visual kinesthetic connections (Conyers & Wilson, 2005).

Everyone is more attentive and better prepared in a center and classroom that plans for exercise and movement.

The brain is the only part of the body that does not reproduce new cells therefore we must make as many connections as possible between existing cells.

In order to increase intellectual potential the more new information and experiences we can create for our children the more we are developing their intellectual potential.

There are two kinds of cells in our brain. 90% of the cells are glia cells and 10% of the cells are the neurons. These neurons are considered the cells for learning. Each of these cells can make 100's or 1000's of connections.

- Neurons pass on information.
- Neurons can receive signals from thousands of other cells.
- Neurons contain a cell body, dendrites, and axons.
- Dendrites branch out along axon branches, repeatedly sending signals to thousands more neurons.
- Synaptic reactions arrive from dendrites to the cell body.

Neurons process information and convert electrical and chemical signals back and forth. Electrical pulses travel across synaptic gaps from one neuron to another by neurotransmitters (chemicals) making new connections to cells.

Therefore, where we once believed that it was each section of our brain that functioned in and of itself in coordinating our body functions, we now know it is really the connections made between these cells in the different sections that affect us the most. This information tells us that it is really the outside world with its smells, sounds, tastes and touch that is the brain's real food for making countless neural connections.

From a physiological perspective:

- The brain is energy inefficient. It is about 2% of the adult body weight but it consumes about 20% of the body's energy.
- The main source of energy for the brain is blood. The blood supplies nutrients like glucose, protein, trace elements and oxygen.
- The brain gets about eight gallons of blood each hour, about 198 gallons per day.
- "The Body-Brain System is 45% to 60% water. Stay hydrated" (Wilson & Conyers, 2006, p. 28)

It is important for staff and children to be interacting and learning in a mobile environment with plenty of water and drinks available.

However, what the brain does best is learn. The brain rewires itself with every new stimulation, experience and behavior.

Emotions and the Brain

Stress and the Brain

A stressful moment for a child or adult can be a simple put down or embarrassing moment. It can mean an argument with mom or an uncomfortable moment with a friend. It could be the sound of a screaming voice or a mean look from the director or teacher. It can be a sudden pop quiz or a timed standardized test for older children. It can be isolating a child in 'time-out' that will only add to this child's stress and frustration rather than calming him down.

Chemicals (adrenaline/epinephrine) are released that block pathways & the brain & body go into emergency mode. The result is that the body is now soaked with emergency mode chemical responses that send all our oxygen to the muscles in our body. It is good if we need to fight, freeze, or get away. It is bad if we need to learn. This mind/body effect can last up to 48 hours.

Knowing that this chemical response in the brain can last up to 48 hours, let's understand ways we can help relax the brain and help the student or child return to the state of mind in which he will be able to continue learning.

A happy brain is a brain surrounded in an environment of:

- Cooperative learning
- O.K. to make mistakes
- Risk taking
- Team work
- Support
- Respect for diversity

A sad brain lives in a stressful environment with very little interaction and input.

Knowing what we know about stress and the brain, we can truly appreciate the odds we place against our children on standardized tests such as the SAT college exams. Yes, many adults and students have learned to deal with their stress and are able to manage their emotions to the point where they can productively take the test or function under stress. However, many will not be mature enough or capable of doing this. Even those who have the ability to think under these conditions are still naturally working with a terrible disadvantage. And so, how accurate are these scores or is the work we anticipate from an employee or child?

How the Brain Learns Best

Pattern Making

The brain wants to know what is about to happen. There is security in being able to get ready and anticipate an order of events. Let staff in meetings and children in the classroom know what the plan will be. Develop a plan, list the events, or display a schedule.

Emotions create a safe and secure environment. Avoid stressful activities, embarrassing situations and isolated pressure for performance.

Relevance

As we have already mentioned the information must be meaningful. If children like to take trips or play games, now is your opportunity to invent that new Fisher Price game for teaching the way the brain is most receptive. We activate and engage positive emotions with the students themselves when children are taught that education is really learning to learn from everything around us. Within the confines of a center or school building, home or the scheduling of field trips we must intentionally plan on ways to integrate textbook facts into meaningful experiential context.

Strong Intrinsic Motivation Raises Everyone's Attention Level

Wouldn't you love to know the formula that would rid our staff and children of the frustrating apathy that exists so often? What does it take to abolish the word apathy from our vocabulary, or "I can't", or "I just want to watch another T.V. show!", or "I'm bored" or "I cannot change the way I have been doing it for too many years." Our list of excuses can easily go on and on. Instead we need to create situations of energizing motivation. New studies on the brain may just be the information we need.

It is very difficult to learn when we do not care or think we care to learn. This happens when we are required to perform, when we must work alone with no interaction and input, and when the information we must learn is not relevant to our lives. Picture the classroom with rows of chairs and desks isolated from each other. The dittos are passed around and it is not permissible to share information because sharing is now considered cheating. In this classroom structure, the teacher has the burden of interacting with each student in the class; the alternative being the student has no interaction. In a class of 25-35 students this is extremely difficult. The teacher resorts to lecturing, redundant dittos and testing. If there are no visual aids and the students must be called on one at a time in order to respond or ask a question, the brain is now in passive, apathetic mode. It has been proven that the brain can only pay attention in this situation for about 20 minutes. What to do when the brain shuts down? Interaction and physical movement will energize the brain. Be careful not to leave your child in a passive mode for more than an hour or two or your child's brain cells will begin to self-destruct. Same with staff and professional development trainings.

We increase intrinsic motivation in our staff and children with:

Choices of what to learn (content), how to learn (projects), and with whom to learn it (Partners)

Relevance through personal connection

Engaging the learner in the process physically and emotionally

Strategies to Increase Intrinsic Motivation among Staff, Children and Parents

Take a blank sheet of paper, a writing utensil in hand, and help me draw a picture that illustrates a place where an adult or child will feel motivated to participate. Can you draw in the following ingredients?

- A threat free environment where we work together as a team

- The team is setting goals that are meaningful to them according to the mission of your center.

- Create a positive climate through positive interaction, music and room design. We all have our ups and downs; however, there must be a professional commitment to a consciously positive attitude when working with staff, parents and children. Smiles, soft, sensitive and exciting voice tones, along with colorful visual aids for materials and research make me feel good already. If a positive attitude structure is planned, the teacher looks forward to the day as much as the children. The staff and parents look forward to professional development and training as much as the director.

- A positive climate activates and engages positive emotions, ways to engage staff and children in the positive learning experience is through role-playing and drama, music and art activities, celebrations and non-competitive games

- Feedback in the center with staff and parents and in the classroom between the teacher and the children as well as between the children themselves

Teamwork and cooperative learning groups are better opportunities for positive interaction, taking the burden off the instructor, director or teacher to be the sole source of information and interaction. Remember, to achieve these results, a director must:

- Eliminate threat
- Set goals
- Create a positive climate
- Activate and engage positive emotions (e.g., drama, music, art, celebrations, non-competitive games)
- Increase feedback

Where we once believed it was the genetic structure of our brains that had the most influence on our intellectual potential and motivation, we now know it is the environment around us that influences these assets for lifelong success.

Learning Style Differences and the Way We Think and Communicate

Every member of our center team brings talents, learning style preferences and different perceptions. Perception is influenced by the way each person's brain developments in the cultural, genetic, experiential and academic environments in which he/she lived and grew. An object is the same but an image of this object to the consciousness is different depending upon this perception. Carter also describes that without experience an individual cannot conceptualize objects. Furthermore, even though the ability to recognize may develop in specific areas of the brain, recognition is complete only when memory brings up associations for what is being recognized (Carter, 1998). This information is important to understand how these varied life experiences may impact our centers.

In addition, when developing a curriculum for our children this information emphasizes the importance of experiential learning for all children's conceptual understanding, overall retention and ability to transfer and apply concepts learned. Experiential learning involves activating areas developed in the brain of all the learning styles while making multiple associations between these areas for more accurate recognition and recall. Memory strategies are described through the involvement of the episodic memory, the motor memory and the taxon memory. In contrast to the traditional educational philosophy of auditory instruction through lecture in which only five percent of the lecture is retained from the taxon memory of left hemispheric learning through hearing and verbal details and facts, it is most important to use right hemispheric memory strategies.

Most effective retention and recall happens with happy life experiences in the episodic memory area or with learning by doing and seeing through the motor memory area. Once a person learns how to ride a bike it is rare that this skill will be forgotten as it is wired into the motor memory (Conyers & Wilson, 2005).

Creating positive learning experiences with staff and students seeing and using the information is the foundation of an effective program and educational curriculum.

An Effective Administrator Implements Curriculum Reflecting the Most Accepted Practices in Child Development and Implements Programs Addressing All Aspects of Early Childhood Education

Developmentally Appropriate Practice (DAP) and Early Care and Education Curriculums

The domains of development (physical, social, emotional, cognitive) are closely related. Development in one domain influences, and is influenced by, development in other domains. Development occurs in a relatively orderly sequence, with later abilities, skills and knowledge building on those already acquired.

Development proceeds at varying rates from child to child as well as unevenly within different areas of each child's functioning. Early experiences have both cumulative and delayed effects on individual children's development. Optimal periods exist for certain types of development and learning. Development proceeds in predictable directions toward greater complexity, organization and internalization.

Development and learning occur in, and are influenced by, multiple social and cultural contexts. Children are active learners, drawing on direct physical and social experience as well as culturally transmitted knowledge to construct their own understanding of the world around them.

Development and learning result from interaction of biological maturation and the environment that includes both the physical and social worlds that children live in. Play is an important vehicle for children's development across the domains as well as a reflection of their development.

Development advances when children have opportunities to practice newly acquired skills, as well as when they experience a challenge just beyond the level of present mastery (the zone of proximal development). Children demonstrate different modes of knowing and learning and different ways of representing what they know.

Children develop and learn in the context of a community where they are safe and valued, their physical needs are met, and they feel psychologically secure.

Developmentally and Appropriate Practice (DAP)

Here are some things to remember regarding DAP.

- Practice is a purposeful action and experience
- Appropriate practice is a purposeful action and experience within a social context
- Appropriate practice contains an inherent dynamic of change
- Age appropriateness
- Individual appropriateness
- Social
- Cultural appropriateness
- Play- oriented/child–initiated/child-directed plan and learning

An Effective Administrator Understands How Children Grow and Develop, Why Children and Parents Experience Separation Anxiety, and is Able to Direct Staff to Productively Work with Children

In order to accomplish these things, an effective administrator:

- Applies DAP for infant, toddler, preschool, school-age, and multi-age groups
- Gives direction and support for the proper handling of common early care and education activities such as diapering, feeding, toilet training, peer interactions, and multiage groups
- Ensures that school-aged children are involved in program decisions
- Manages children's enrollment and transitions and gives attention to separation and adjustment anxieties of children and parents
- Uses assessment to support curriculum
- Supports age-appropriate behavior management techniques and assists staff to handle conflict resolution and crisis management situations in order to minimize violent behavior

Implementation of Early Childhood Principles for All Age Groups

As center director you are responsible for planning and implementing a total early care and education program reflecting its underlying mission, goals and objectives. To be successful you must understand children of all ages and have a thorough knowledge of the various stages of child development plus have familiarity with a variety of educational strategies to promote and enhance these developmental stages. You are charged with placing children in developmentally appropriate classroom situations, led by competent teachers trained to promote social, cognitive, emotional, and physical development in their classrooms.

If you do not have a formal educational background in early childhood education and child development, enroll in college level courses in ECE. If that is not possible, we encourage you to seek out continuing education in early childhood education, read books and periodicals faithfully so you will be capable in hiring and supervising teachers, developing a curriculum supportive of excellent educational practices, accurately assess individual children's development, and speaking knowledgeably with parents and fellow educators.

In an early care and education center each age group exhibits certain developmental characteristics that have to be addressed in terms of (1) care and supervision, (2) learning activities, and (3) age appropriate equipment. The following information on each age group focuses on these three areas:

Infants

Children from six weeks to eighteen months need a great deal of individual care. This age span encompasses a wide array of developmental characteristics and physical needs that must be addressed child by child. Each infant will be on an individual schedule that may or may not coincide with the schedules of other children in the group. Proper pupil/teacher ratios must be maintained at all times, and additional staff should be available to help during feeding times or emergency situations such as a child becoming ill and requiring one-on-one assistance. Babies who are too young to hold bottles must be held for bottle feedings. Bottles cannot be propped in beds or infant seats because of the risk of choking and the need an infant has to be nurtured during feeding times. Pediatricians warn that propping bottles can cause milk to pool in immature Eustachian tubes resulting in bacterial buildup that leads to ear infections.

Request parents to complete a feeding chart upon enrolling an infant in the program. This chart should indicate what the child is currently eating, the amount, and the intervals the child is being fed. As the infant matures and her feeding habits change, parents should update the feeding chart. Never give children food or milk the parents have not prescribed. Insist baby formula be prepared at home and brought to the center daily, clearly labeled with the child's name and the current date. Do not store formula overnight.

Parents should label all items belonging to each child. Clothing, bedding, bottles, and pacifiers must all be marked and should only be used by that child. Each item of sleep equipment, including cribs, cots, mattresses, blankets, sheets, etc., should be cleaned and sanitized before being assigned to another child. Children should not share bedding. Infants' linens (sheets, pillowcases, blankets) should be cleaned and sanitized daily, and crib mattresses should be cleaned and sanitized weekly and when soiled or wet.

The U.S. Centers for Disease Control warn us not to wash or rinse clothing soiled with fecal material in the early care and education setting. You may empty solid stool into the toilet, but be careful not to splash or touch toilet water with your hands. Put the soiled clothes in a plastic bag and seal the bag to await pick up by the child's parent at the end of the day. Always wash your hands after handling soiled clothing. Explain to parents that washing or rinsing soiled diapers and clothing increases the chances that you and the children may be exposed to germs that cause diseases. Although receiving soiled clothes isn't pleasant, remind parents that this policy protects the health of all children and providers.

Infants will progress through a variety of developmental stages as they mature. Physically, a baby will master rolling over, sitting up, crawling, pulling up and practicing constantly until he is mobile and walking. Emotionally and socially, he will learn to respond to adults, distinguish between voices, recognize familiar faces and become alarmed when he sees a stranger. Cognitively, he will begin to demonstrate memory, smile in recognition, begin to follow simple instructions, intentionally act, and explore with hands and fingers.

All of these developmental steps necessitate a stimulating environment that allows the young child to progress at will. The only time an infant should spend in a crib is when he is sleeping. Otherwise he should be allowed freedom to move about the classroom to achieve maximum physical, sensory and social experiences. Teachers should interact with infants throughout the day, talking to them, singing, and making sounds that the children can mimic. Diapering and feeding are opportune times for individual attention and nurturing conversation.

The infant area should be equipped with a crib for each child, feeding table or individual high chairs, rocking chairs or hammocks for teachers holding children, and an array of developmentally-stimulating toys. Mirrors should be placed on floor level to allow an infant a wonderful opportunity to vocalize and interact with his image. Soothing music is appropriate.

Toddlers

Toddlers experience the same hygiene needs as the infants. These children are still in diapers, so the same diaper changing techniques should be used. Proper sanitation, hand washing, and diaper disposal steps should be followed.

Children in the toddler age group, thirteen to twenty-four months, are becoming more physically independent and are learning to feed themselves. This learning process can become extremely messy at times, and it may seem that toddlers wear more food than they actually get into their mouths. Teachers must have a great deal of patience and an abundance of washcloths on hand after mealtimes. Pacifiers and bottles should be weaned at this stage to avoid the spread of germs when these items are inadvertently shared and to avoid possible speech problems that can result from teeth becoming misaligned from prolonged sucking on bottles and pacifiers.

Toddler care still requires a great deal of physical maintenance, but social supervision is now becoming important as these little people become mobile and interact with their peers. The toddler is still very egocentric and has no concept of where he fits in to the rest of the world. Therefore, sharing is not something he understands and he will go to great lengths to see that he gets his way.

Toddlers are constantly on the move, and knowledgeable teachers have realistic expectations that this group cannot possibly be still. The accepted rule of thumb is that a child's attention span is about a minute longer than his age, so it stands to reason that activities for this age group must be intense and brief.

Physically, the toddler spends most of his time and energy refining large motor skills. He tends to walk with his feet wide apart, head forward and his arms out. He enjoys objects that he can push or pull and he likes holding objects in both hands. Stacking/un-stacking and carrying/dumping are favorite activities. Attempts at art will produce scribbles.

Socially and emotionally he is very egocentric. He likes being assertive and independent, but he will cry when left alone. He is very enthusiastic and generally friendly and he will often refer to himself by name.

Cognitively, he is beginning to make visual discriminations. He can name objects in a book, work simple shape puzzles, mimic adults, and follow one-step directions.

The most common inappropriate behavior with this age group is biting. You will need to help both the parents and teachers understand that this behavior is not the result of devious planning or overt attempts to be mean to others. Oral gratification is primary for a young child. Everything goes to the mouth, including other people. Toddlers do not discriminate where they bite other people, so unfortunately, cheeks and backs are bitten as often as arms and legs. Sometimes even noses are bitten.

Researchers have suggested a number of reasons for biting including anger, teething, or self defense. However, the most common reason is frustration. Biting is a form of communication between two non-verbal participants even though it has negative consequences. The director must help all concerned parties realize that very likely the biter has no awareness that he has caused pain to another. The biter should not be disciplined by his parents at the end of the day, because he will not remember ten minutes after the incident occurred. When biting does occur, however, all attention should be focused on the child who was bitten and an effort should be made to redirect the biter to other activities. Offer the biter an alternative such as a cold teething ring to bite if he continues to display a need to bite others. All biting incidents should be recorded.

Although biting is a fairly common occurrence in toddler classrooms, there should be an investigation to determine if the problem comes from classroom management or may have contributing factors from the home environment. If biting is a persistent problem in a classroom, it is important to look for patterns in classroom activities that contributed to the problem. Did the biting take place at the same time each day or when similar types of activities occurred. If you find out such to be the case, you may need to change the management of the classroom to reduce incidents. Needless to say, one of the greatest frustrations of parents is to have their child bitten.

Toddler room equipment should be low and manageable. Establish limits and boundaries to help toddlers learn that tables are for eating while big play pieces are for climbing. Toys for this age group should include push toys, balls, large manipulative, stacking blocks or bowls, large books, shape sorters and simple puzzles. Large climbing pieces should be available to focus on large muscle development.

Two-Year-Olds

The two-year-old is rapidly moving up the developmental ladder. He embraces life with an abundance of energy and enthusiasm and will generally run unchecked until the adults in his life start setting limits and boundaries. Teachers of two's need to have consistency in daily routine and provide activities that are still short and intense to accommodate a short attention span. Teacher expectations should be voiced and repeated regularly to provide guidance for this age group.

The two-year-old has mastered a great deal of large muscle control. He enjoys climbing into things and using his whole body to express emotion. He can feed himself and help undress. He is beginning to develop a preference in using his hands, but he is still awkward with small objects. He is very sensory oriented and has difficultly relaxing.

Socially and emotionally, the two-year-old is still very self-centered. He enjoys parallel play, but he is unable to share. He thrives on routine and is resistant to change. He is easily distracted and is somewhat impulsive.

Cognitively, he is making great strides. He understands familiar concepts but still has a limited attention span. He enjoys water play and he explores by touching and tasting. He can name many objects in books and he can recall where toys are left.

Two's enjoy a variety of activities allowing sensory exploration. They enjoy music, books, riding toys, water tables, wooden puzzles, peg boards, dress-up clothes, and unit blocks. Art activities might include drawing with magic markers and finger painting. Two's still do not have fine motor control so crayons and paint brushes need to be thicker for easier grasping.

Two-year-olds need classroom equipment that is low and manageable. They are still refining large muscle skills and will continue to climb, so a large climbing piece is recommended.

Three-Year-Olds

Three's are generally categorized as the most harmonious group of children in the program. Their dispositions are usually very bright, and teachers find three's are truly adult pleasers. They bond with their teachers and are intent on following the daily routine. They enjoy their classmates and work toward becoming very social little people.

Physically a three-year-old feels quite satisfied with his ability to make his body do what he wants. He is toilet trained, walks well and is beginning to lose his babyish appearance. He likes riding toys and can master a tricycle. He is beginning to use fine motor skills and can grasp with his thumb and forefinger. He is able to put on and take off some clothing, including buttons. He can hold a cup in one hand and can balance on one foot.

Socially he seeks recognition from adults by doing what they ask of him. He enjoys developing friendships and will begin playing with others in his class. He may create imaginary playmates and at this age nightmares and phobias may begin. The three year-old thoroughly enjoys dramatic play and enjoys imitating adults. He is very independent and may exhibit occasional frustration and jealousy.

Cognitively, he is very curious. He is always asking why and he enjoys guessing games. His attention span is still limited but now he can carry out two to four directions in a sequence. He is beginning to establish number concepts and understand cause and affect relationships. He recognizes various sizes and shapes and he can name and match colors.

The three-year-old classroom should contain water play materials, musical instruments, climbing pieces, unit blocks, fine motor manipulative, homemaking area, dramatic play area, books, record or tape player, and an art center. Thick crayons should still be used with this age group.

Four-Year-Olds

The four-year-old has reached the pinnacle of the preschool ladder. His physical and mental confidence say he can do anything he wants. Teachers of fours spend a great deal of time simply monitoring behavior to keep it within reasonable boundaries and limits.

The four-year-old has become totally physically adept. He is very active and his body has acquired that longer, leaner look attributed to older children. He enjoys walking, running, hopping, standing on one foot and he tends to be quite acrobatic with his movement. He is able to dress himself, even lacing his shoes. He has mastered fine motor control and can hold a paint brush or crayon in an adult manner.

Socially, the four-year-old is quite explosive. He enjoys a feeling of power and testing limits. He is bossy, argumentative and easily over stimulated. He enjoys developing special friends, but will hit others and insist on having his own way. He has a terrific sense of humor and may like to tell tall tales. He still has difficulty accepting responsibility for his behavior and will want to blame it on someone else.

Cognitively, he is full of questions. He wants to know how things work and is full of ideas. He enjoys a variety of materials and his dramatic play closely parallels real life experiences. He is beginning to recognize several printed words and his attention span is increasing, making it easier to focus on a task.

The four-year-old classroom should include water and sand play areas, climbing pieces, balls, unit blocks, props for roads and towns, more complex puzzles, and manipulatives including attribute blocks, dramatic play clothes and props, a variety of books and a variety of art materials.

School-aged Children

School aged children have different needs than children in the preschool program. They have been in a structured environment at school and view the after-school program as a place to relax, have a snack, perhaps do homework and enjoy some recreational activities before going home. Children in this age group may range from five years to twelve years with each age having its own set of characteristics and behaviors. Mixing all of these ages may prove to be a challenge, and teachers working with this group should make an effort to separate older and younger children if possible.

Physically, we continue to see body changes, with girls changing faster than boys. Self concept is linked closely to body image, and sexual development begins to occur with the onset of hormonal changes and an exhibited interest in the opposite sex.

Emotionally, school agers begin to develop an idea of self. They are pondering who they are in this world and what values they hold important. Younger school agers still express emotion readily, but older children tend to repress emotion, are afraid of criticism, ridicule, and the opinions of others. Adults working with these age groups need to acknowledge and validate each child's feelings. At this age some children begin to conjure up fears of things beyond their control such as AIDS, wars, and horrific news events. It is also during these years that children begin to recognize the inconsistencies in adult behavior (e.g., the double standard and do as I say, not as I do).

Socially, school agers need friends and need to feel accepted. Adults should acknowledge sex role performances but avoid stereotyping by sex. Do not inhibit girls from being athletic or boys from being artistic, but regardless of choice, encourage a child's efforts. Children need time to be by themselves. They have been with peers at school all day and, if needed, me space is vital.

A program for school agers should include lots of physical activity. Activities should be balanced to include some structured time versus some unstructured time. This group also needs some quiet time for reading or homework with teacher support when requested. It is very important to allow older children to have a say in what happens to their time. Do not be afraid to include and empower the children in the decision making process.

Giving Direction and Support to Common Early Childhood Education Activities

Diapering

Proper diapering techniques are a major issue in the care of infants. A child or baby can never be left unattended on a changing table. Thus, all diapers, diaper creams, wipes, etc. must be ready for use before the child is placed on the table and a hand washing sink should be adjacent to the diaper changing station. The US Centers for Disease Control offers diaper-changing recommendations. Diaper changing areas should:

- Only be used for changing diapers
- Be smooth and nonporous
- Have a raised edge around the area to prevent a child from falling off
- Be next to a sink with running water
- Not be used to prepare food, mix formula, or rinse pacifiers
- Be easily accessible to providers
- Be out of reach of children

Diaper changing areas should be cleaned and sanitized after each diaper change as follows.

- Clean the surface with an approved sanitizing agent.
- Follow product and state guidelines.

Competency VI: Educational Programming

RECOMMENDED PROCEDURE FOR DIAPERING A CHILD

1. Organize needed supplies within reach: fresh diaper and clean clothes (if necessary); dampened paper towels or pre-moistened towelettes for cleaning child's bottom; child's personal, labeled ointment (if provided by parents); trash disposal bag
2. Using only your hands, pick up and hold the child away from your body. Don't cradle the child in your arms and risk soiling your clothing.
3. Place approved rolled paper between the child and the diapering surface.
4. Lay the child on the diapering surface.
5. As required, put on glove(s)
6. Remove soiled diaper (and soiled clothes).
7. Put disposable diapers in a plastic-lined trash receptacle.
8. Put soiled, reusable diaper and/or soiled clothes WITHOUT RINSING in a plastic bag to give to parents.
9. Clean child's bottom with a pre-moistened disposable towelette or a dampened, single-use, disposable towel.
10. Place the soiled towelette or towel in a plastic-lined trash receptacle.
11. Wipe child's hands with disposable wipe if child touches their genital area or any other area deemed not clean.
12. If the child needs a more thorough washing, use soap, running water, and paper towels.
13. Remove and dispose of your gloves in a plastic-lined receptacle.
14. Wipe your hands with a disposable wipe and preferably in running water with soap.
15. NEVER leave a child alone on the diapering table.
16. Diaper and dress the child.
17. Wash the child's hands under running water.
18. Sanitized the diapering surface immediately after you finish diapering the child.
19. Return the child to the activity area.
20. Clean and sanitized with an approved agent, the diapering area, all equipment or supplies that were touched, and soiled crib or cot, if needed.
21. Wash your hands under running water.

Medications

Early care and education centers are frequently called upon to dispense prescription medication to young children. Parents must complete medication forms and the medicine should be dispensed according to the form directions and the form documented accordingly. No child should receive any medication without written authorization from the parent.

Language Development

Language development for preschoolers begins at birth. Children learn language skills by imitating the language they hear, so it is important adults who work directly with children have good language patterns.

Babies turn their heads in response to voices and cry to verbalize their needs. Babies progress from cooing to gestures to babbling to imitating sounds to producing their first words. Toddlers expand on this development by uttering two-word phrases, repeating adults' words, responding to direction and verbal requests and having a working vocabulary of five to fifty words.

The two-year-old begins using two to three word sentences. He is still learning to produce certain sounds causing errors in pronunciation. He enjoys nursery rhymes and repetitive rhythms. He cannot express his emotions verbally and may get frustrated if the adult cannot understand him. He can now match words with objects and has a working vocabulary of 50 - 300 words.

The three-year-old enjoys talking. He likes new words and has increased his use of pronouns and prepositions. He is able to pluralize nouns and add "ed" to indicate past tense for verbs. He may still make some sound substitutions and his working vocabulary is now from 300 -1,000 words.

The four-year-old likes both words and talking. He can respond readily to verbal directions and enjoys singing along or reciting poetry. He can join sentences together and by the time he turns five will have a working vocabulary of 1,500 words.

Toilet Learning

As children mature physically they begin to gain bladder and bowel control. Once the child is able to manage his clothing with minimal assistance and shows an interest in toilet training, it is time to begin the process. Children who are training should be taken to the bathroom at regular intervals throughout the day and asked frequently if they need to go. However, because they often do not want to interrupt their play with a trip to the bathroom, they may say "no" when the right answer is yes. Successful toileting should be highly praised and minimal attention given to toileting accidents. A child should never be made to feel badly because he has an accident in his clothes. Toilet training takes time and patience and to be completely trained, bladder and bowel, may take several years. Parents with unrealistic expectations for this skill should be counseled and made aware of the serious psychological damage that can occur if children are forced to train before they are ready or are humiliated when accidents occur.

Anytime between the second year and fourth year, the toddler may show signs that she's ready to start toilet training herself. Staff should be trained to watch for key indicators of a child's readiness to begin toilet training.

- Regular, predictable bowel movements
- The ability to pull her pants up and down

- Interest in others' bathroom habits and in wearing underpants – basically, wanting to be like others around her
- Some demonstration – such as squatting, grunting, or even telling you that she's having a bowel movement

Remember even if the child shows all of these signs, but is still not interested in using the toilet, don't push the issue. Remember, it's got to be up to her.

Curriculum and Learning Styles

A curriculum is a plan of instruction that details what students are to know, how they are to learn it, what the teacher's role is, and the context in which learning and teaching will take place. For more than one hundred years, theorists have worked to understand how learning takes place. We have seen from the brief sketch of the theorists the foundation for the development of DAP. The development of curriculums and teaching methodologies currently in use in early childhood education came from the same sources.

Teachers are expected to teach content that is challenging but achievable, is important and worthwhile, builds on prior knowledge and extends learning, and respects the child's home culture and encourages participation in shared culture of the class.

Quality early childhood education programs have two basic components: (1) providing a safe, nurturing and caring environment for children and (2) providing a stimulating environment leading to learning, positive growth and development for children. You are responsible for managing a program that addresses these components. Look carefully at your center's philosophy and goals when making decisions on the curriculum model you will use.

Creative Curriculum
Dodge, D. Teaching Strategies, Inc.

This curriculum is designed for children birth through pre-kindergarten. It also includes assessment materials. The basis of the curriculum is "learning through purposeful play" facilitated by intentional teaching practices. The main features are:

- Creative Curriculum offers teachers guidance, support and freedom to be creative and responsive to children
- Children learn from their daily interactions with their environment
- A carefully organized and rich environment is the foundation for Creative Curriculum
- Central to the use of environment is an understanding of the potential of various materials to enhance learning and teaching
- Focus on developmental progress
- Focus on interest areas
- Fosters creativity

- Rooted in theory and practice - teachers should recognize interplay between socio-emotional, cognitive, and physical growth
- Erikson - Trust, Autonomy, and Initiative
- Piaget – Hands-on Learning (active exploration)
- Recognizes culture as an integral part of the child's life

The Project Approach

L.G. Katz and S.C. Chard define the project approach as an in-depth study of a particular topic that one or more children undertake. Work on a project should extend over a period of days or weeks depending on the children's ages, interest, and topic. Unlike spontaneous play, projects usually involve children in advanced planning and in various activities that require several days or weeks of sustained efforts.

Project work as an approach to ECE refers to a way of teaching and learning as well as to the content of what is taught and learned. The approach emphasizes the teacher's role in encouraging children to interact with people, objects and the environment in ways that have personal meaning to them. As a way of learning it emphasizes children's active participation in their own studies.

The Project Approach aims to:

- Cultivate the life of the young child's mind
- Improve the learners understanding of the world around them
- To strengthen children's dispositions to go on learning
- To provide a balance of activities which include spontaneous play and systematic instruction
- To help adults and children to see school as life – school experiences are real, the stream of life's experiences do not occur in categories such as science and history (The content of life experience is more like events and topics all mingled and blended, rather than discrete disciplines.)
- For children to experience the class as community - community ethos is created when all of the children are expected and encouraged to contribute to the life of the whole group - even though they may each do so in their own way.
- To help teachers see their work as challenging- a curriculum that limits the teacher primarily to daily instructional lessons or to setting out the same toys and materials day after day can quickly become dreary and devoid of intellectual challenge.

Bank Street

This approach emphasizes the importance of the educator's concern with emotions and their role in learning and development. Its objectives are:

- Enhancing competence - ego strength and skills
- Identifying self qualities/self worth - individuality or identity
- Participating, communicating - socialization
- Synthesizing inner and outer worlds - integration of function
- Specific objectives:
- To serve the child's need to make an impact on the environment through direct physical contact and maneuver
- To promote the potential for ordering experience through cognitive strategies
- To advance the child's functioning knowledge of his/her environment
- To support the play mode of incorporating experience
- To help the child internalize impulse control
- To meet the child's needs to cope with conflicts intrinsic to this stage of development to facilitate the development of image of self as unique and competent person
- To help the child establish mutually supporting patterns of interaction

The Reggio Approach

The Reggio Approach fosters children's intellectual development through a systematic focus on symbolic representation. Young children are encouraged to explore their environment and express themselves through all of their available "expressive, communicative and cognitive languages" whether they be words, movement, drawing, painting, building sculpture, shadow play, collage, dramatic play, or music…

Characteristics of Reggio Approach include documenting three key functions.

- Children should be provided with a concrete and visible memory of what they said and/or did to serve as a jumping off point for next steps in learning.
- Educators should be provided with a tool for research and a key to continual improvement and renewal.
- Parents should be provided with detailed information about what happens at school in order to foster input and support.

An impressive feature of the Reggio Approach is the way the young children are involved in extended in-depth investigations; what we commonly refer to as project work.

Some specific features of the schools are:

- Piazza- meeting area, town square
- Ateliar – expressive arts studio
- Atelierista – promote the use of visual languages as a construction of thoughts and feelings within holistic education, provides a place for children to become masters of all kinds of techniques- paint, clay, drawing (all symbolic languages), assists adults in understanding the processes of how children learn, provides a workshop for documentation, visual artists, collaborator, interpreter, protagonist, resource
- Mini ateliar – expressive art studio within classroom
- Pedagogista – Role of Pedagogista – to sustain and implement the philosophy of the system, offer professional development, support reflection and enrichment, construct meaningful alliances, support collegiality, promote value of exchange and discussion, promote cultural and social growth of systems for children, resource and reference point, a link

Additional features of the Reggio Approach are:

- Very visual
- Process is important

Montessori

Maria Montessori was born in Ancona, Italy 1870, and died in Holland 1952. She was the first female physician in Italy. In her medical practice, her clinical observation led her to analyze how children learn, how they build themselves from what they find in their immediate environment. So she founded the first Casa dei Bambini (Children's House) in Rome.

Today there are nearly five thousand private and two-hundred public Montessori Schools in the U.S.

The premise of the Montessori approach is that children teach themselves

Children under age six have extraordinary powers of the mind. They have a universal ability to absorb knowledge from their surroundings just by living – "the absorbent mind"

Children need to explore and discover in order to be calm.

The Montessori Preschool classroom allows children to move, touch, manipulate, and explore. It gives them the freedom to choose their own work without unnecessary interference from adults. In this environment they learn to work independently, based on their own initiative, which builds concentration and self-discipline.

Montessori education enhances young children's knowledge in the present, and establishes the foundations for true comprehension on a more abstract level later in life.

Four distinct classroom areas are included in all Montessori schools.

- Practical life
- Sensorial
- Mathematics
- Language

No subject is taught in isolation. Most work is done individually.

Adults work to perfect the environment while the child works to perfect themselves.

Practical life experiences allow child to function independently in the adult world. These experiences include:

- Care of person
- Care of environment
- Development of social relations
- Movement

High Scope

The High/Scope Research Foundation

High/Scope has curriculum for infants through preschool emphasizing adult-child interaction and a carefully designed learning environment. The program has four guiding principles.

- Children construct knowledge through active involvement.
- Children develop capacities in a predictable sequence and adult support contributes to a child's intellectual, social, emotional, and physical development.
- Consistent adult support and respect for children's choices, thoughts, and actions strengthen the child's self esteem, feelings of responsibility, self control, and knowledge.
- Careful observation of individual children's interests and intentions is a first step in understanding their level of development and in planning and carrying out appropriate interactions.

The High Scope Model assumes children learn when they are actively engaged and involved in interactions with people and materials in their environment.

Emergent Curriculum

This is a learning approach based on the children's interest as well as the teacher's interests. It is a process allowing children to learn thru experience, make choices and be creative. Children develop intense interests in a variety of ideas and objects. Teachers should take advantage of this natural curiosity and eagerness to learn by providing opportunities to explore subjects in a variety of ways.

Curriculum is what teachers want children to learn. Effective curriculum is rich in opportunities for acquiring academic, intellectual, social, and life skills.

The Role of the Teacher

First and foremost the teacher must consider the ages of children and what life experiences the children bring to the program. Planning should include basic skill development as well as enrichment opportunities to enhance what children have already experienced and learned.

Teachers should plan a curriculum that includes activities for skill development in the areas of art, social skills, music, language, literacy, math, and science. Large and fine motor skill development should be encouraged through the use of appropriate classroom materials and equipment. A variety of outdoor activities should be included in your developmental program.

The teacher can spend her time observing and visiting the children as they work, contributing to their play, asking questions, and using encouraging words. She can help the children transition from their work and play to meal time, outdoor activities, and naps. She will be able to use her soft voice and spend time each day observing each child and enjoying each child.

The teacher must be ever-vigilant for opportunities to create learning experiences for children. The observant teacher gathers information from the children to plan new interest centers and introduce new materials to spark their interest. Listening to children as they play gives you clues to their interests and what they want to learn. This guides changes in materials and room arrangements. For example, discussions among children about storms might suggest a weather interest center. You could put books about weather, simple thermometers and barometers, pictures of hurricane reconnaissance planes, satellite weather maps, etc. in the center. Be alert to the children's new fascinations and be prepared to capitalize on their eagerness to learn.

Children have varied learning styles and therefore find it easier to learn in an environment that offers auditory, visual and kinesthetic opportunities. The most effective learning environment is one in which the teacher observes each child and creates a learning environment of differentiation where the instruction meets the needs of the individual child.

Free play as part of the curriculum is a time for children to develop specific important skills as independent learners. It is not a time for teachers to do lesson planning, socialize with other staff or engage in any other work that does not involve the children. It is an opportunity for the teacher and staff to socially interact with the children, to encourage certain behaviors and activities, to observe and to document for ongoing consistent assessment of the individual child and to focus on informal teaching opportunities.

Once you have chosen curriculum and have scheduled appropriate activities, make sure each classroom is properly equipped with sufficient materials and equipment to carry out a successful learning experience. Art materials should include liquid or tempera paint in assorted colors, finger paints, large crayons, scissors, wide paint brushes, manila drawing paper, newsprint, assorted construction paper, finger paint paper, butcher paper, magic markers, glue, paste, etc. Specific art project items can be purchased on an as-needed basis. Toys, manipulatives, dramatic play materials, science center materials, blocks, and musical equipment should be selected on an age-appropriate basis. Remember many materials can be made, such as paste or play dough. Find creative uses for simple household materials such as shaving cream or Jell-o. Ask parents, suppliers, and community businesses to donate materials that can be used in art or science projects. Examples might be newsprint, fabric, egg crates, plastic jugs, etc. It is not necessary to purchase all of your materials.

An Effective Administrator Ensures Appropriate Room and Space Arrangement and Supports Effective Space Design Based on Knowledge of Environmental Psychology and Childhood Development

Putting thought into classroom arrangement will pay off in a number of ways. Children in well-designed classrooms are presented with opportunities for choice and self-directed activity resulting in increased learning, fewer aggressive behaviors and less adult intervention. It is conducive to a lower noise level demonstrating that children are busy and interacting in positive ways. Teachers have more time for observation and supportive dialogue and need less time for redirecting. The daily classroom experience is more pleasant for both child and teacher.

How can you design your classrooms to create an environment that will be most conducive to the total development of children and positive daily experiences? The following principles of effective classroom design help achieve the optimum environments.

Classrooms

Well designed classrooms result in happy, busily engaged children and relaxed teachers. Children come to school eager to participate in interesting learning activities where they can explore to their hearts' content. The classroom should give each child opportunities for both active and quiet play, group activities and individual time. The child in the well-designed classroom will be more likely to know what she wants to do, where the materials are for her work, will be able to get those materials for herself, use them, and know where to put them when finished.

The room must be large enough for children and staff to move about freely and to use learning centers without encroaching on other activities. There should be adequate space for larger group activities as well. Room design should include space for the storage of materials and children's personal belongings.

Ideally there should be at least 30-50 square feet useable space for each child. When children are too crowded, their stress level increases (not to mention the teacher's stress level) and they become irritable and frustrated.

Appearance

Recent studies have shown neutral wall colors rather than bright primary colors are better in early care and education centers and preschools. Neutral colors such as beige, ecru, and grays are more calming. They help children distinguish between background and objects displayed on the wall. (figure-ground perception) Children are able to focus on pictures and learning materials against a neutral background.

Lighting

Light affects the mood of a classroom, particularly the right kind of light. In absence of natural light there should be an abundance of artificial lighting (is needed). Fluorescent lighting gives a cold and sterile feeling. Incandescent lighting is more warm and comfortable. Task lighting in some areas can be effective. Plenty of low windows bringing in natural light and offering a connection with the outdoors are an added benefit. Being able to look outside during the day helps us maintain a happy attitude.

Air Circulation

Air quality has a lot to do with positive outcomes in the classroom. Children and adults need fresh air and comfortable temperatures. When air is stale, we become lethargic and less alert. Many centers being built today are incorporating air filtration systems that reduce the spread of contagious diseases and allergies.

Flooring Materials

Flooring is another consideration. Carpet enhances the warm, homey feeling of the room, absorbs sound, and is softer when children take inevitable falls. Carpet should be a low pile, non-allergenic, and anti-microbial and meet fire safety standards. A strict cleaning regimen to keep carpet safe and attractive is a must. Some areas of the room, such as a diaper changing area, food preparation area, painting or water play area, should not be carpeted. You may want to consider tile flooring and area rugs over the tiles. Tile flooring is easier to clean and area rugs that acquire permanent stains can be easily replaced.

Arrangement

The goal of good room arrangement is to have a variety of safe, accessible centers or areas that entice children to explore, learn, and create while interacting positively with one another. The teacher's role should consist of interaction and observation facilitating learning through the interests of the children. Be sure to allow sufficient traffic space so children and adults do not have to go through one center to get to another one.

Interest Centers

Centers should be large enough for several children to play or work together. There should be materials and equipment for several children. Sufficient materials allow children to focus on the activity and not on waiting their turn. Many materials can be real items rather than purchased toys.

One does not have to spend a fortune to create well-equipped, intriguing interest centers. Tap the resources of parents to assist you in filling themed prop boxes.

The placement of the interest centers is important. Children should be able to work undisturbed as long as they like and then move on to another area that interests them. Some centers have a lot of cross-over material that works well side by side. Observe how the children use the materials to determine this.

Interest centers should be clearly defined with low walls (2' shelves are perfect) or changes in the floor levels (using platforms or lofts) or even small fences or cardboard murals the children have created themselves. This definition helps children focus on the activities in the center and helps them keep materials in their proper places. The smaller spaces created by the divisions reduce the large-group stress often experienced by young children.

Certainly there will be times when a child will want to move equipment from one center as part of their play. Set rules about where items are to be placed at the end of the play time so others can find and use it later.

Make literacy a part of every center. A book about tractors in the block area, a cook book in the play house, or chalk board in the library help the children ascertain the importance of print in their lives.

Suggestions for interest centers in the classrooms are:

Tactile- Sensory Center

This should include a tactile/water table with material such as sand, rice or whatever material children can dig into or bury objects. The tactile table may be a different table from the sensory table. The tactile table is typically a sand/water table whereas the sensory table may have objects of different sizes, shapes and materials that help children access their senses in different ways

Literacy Corner

You may want to add earphones to plug into CD players for audio reading materials.

Safe Space

This can be a separate dedicated area or the safe space may be a part of the cozy corner together with the Literacy Center. Integration of these centers may be beneficial in limited space classrooms as being quiet areas where children can independently choose to be. The preference is to have more divisions and more center variety for children to choose when possible.

Gross Motor Center

This is the area for building and construction equipment and supplies. Building blocks are blocks that have smooth sides as opposed to interlocking blocks. Blocks without smooth sides are no longer considered building blocks for this area. The interlocking blocks are a favorite among teachers and children but must be in addition to the smooth sided blocks and may be more appropriate for the fine motor center.

Math/Science Fine Motor Center

This is the area you would have all your smaller fine motor manipulatives including counting materials, science supplies, puzzles, games that require fine motor exercise

Housekeeping/Domestic/Drama Center

Different centers decide on different names for this center. The goal of this center is for drama and role-play motivation. It is important to have a variety of mixed gender and multi-cultural materials and supplies. Dress up costumes, kitchen area with a variety of foods, cooking utensils, dishes, workbench section with a variety of tools, puppets and puppet theatre.

Computer Station

Art Center

It is important that the art materials are accessible to the children during the supervised interactive play times throughout the day. It is recommended to have accessible table areas in the art center for drawing and any other art projects. It is always good to have an easel in this area as well.

Storage

Storage is an important component in the effective classroom. Storage goals are for children to be able to locate the materials they wish to use and return them to the proper place. Interest center materials in use should be stored in clear containers on low, open shelves where children have access to and use them without teacher assistance. Some good containers are clear plastic sweater or shoe boxes, clear milk bottles or soft drink liter containers cut in half, plastic milk crates, silverware drawer dividers, and laundry baskets. Label each container with both a word and either a sample of the actual contents (a small block for example) or a picture of the contents (drawn by hand, a photo or cut from a magazine). Children enjoy making these labels and the job of making the labels helps the children learn what they stand for - and that's the whole purpose.

Classroom Equipment

You will need basic child-sized equipment such as tables and chairs. The standard preschool classroom should be equipped as follows.

Infants:

- One crib per child with enough linens for two changes per day
- Feeding table that seats many children or individual high chairs
- Diaper bag storage
- Changing table with sink

Competency VI: Educational Programming

- Diaper/personal article storage for each child
- Cubbies for toy display and storage
- Rug or carpeted area for crawling/floor play
- Adult rocking chair or hammock
- Developmentally-stimulating toys, mobiles, mirrors, wall decorations,
- Photographs of the children's families
- Small refrigerator for bottle and medicine storage

Toddlers through Age Four:

- Child-size tables and chairs - one space per child
- Personal items cubby storage units
- Toy/manipulative cubby storage
- Coat hooks or racks
- Large climbing piece - at least one per classroom

Learning Centers For:

- Dramatic play
- Homemaking
- Woodworking
- Science
- Quiet area
- Music
- Language arts
- Art
- Nutrition
- Blocks/construction
- Sand/water table
- Child size sink for hand washing and water fountain
- Cots or mats - one per child and sheets/blankets - one per child

Special Needs of Infants and Toddlers

Very young children need a safe environment to freely explore. When children feel safe in their environment they develop a sense of self-confidence that enables them to try new things and learn.

A safe environment where children can go wherever they please is most conducive to healthy development and certainly more relaxing for the teacher. Here are some ideas for interesting and safe exploration.

- Low risers (6" - 8") enable crawling children and toddlers to practice climbing. Children these ages need to move about so give them a place to do so.

- Low lofts with ramp access and walls or fences on the sides create a sense of coziness and offer the opportunity to climb and crawl.

- Louis Torrelli, MS. Ed., of the firm Space Designs, suggests hammocks are safer than traditional rocking chairs. Children cannot pinch fingers under a hammock, and the hammock can be taken down when not in use. A teacher can hold the child and rock in the hammock - a great place for reading storybooks too.

- Low windows, mirrors and pictures at the child's eye level are interesting to these very little ones.

(Note: Additional learning center information may be found in the interest centers section.)

Classroom Arrangement

Classroom arrangement depends on room design. Learning centers should be arranged in distinct areas and learning materials rotated periodically to keep the children's interest. Quiet areas should be some distance from active areas. As room arrangements are designed, consider the traffic flow in the room and how well the design will lend itself to being kept neat and orderly. Another important consideration is nap time. It may be necessary to move some equipment for naps and return them before the daily schedule resumes. When it is time to place the cots or mats for nap time, there must be spacing with an adequate aisle between each row for the teacher to walk down to observe each child.

Well designed classrooms result in happy, busily engaged children and relaxed teachers. Children come to school eager to participate in interesting learning activities where they can explore to their hearts' content. The classroom should give each child opportunities for both active and quiet play, group activities and individual time. The child in the well-designed classroom will be more likely to know what she wants to do, where the materials are for her work, will be able to get those materials for herself, use them, and know where to put them when finished. A well designed classroom encourages children to explore and experiment.

Consumable items in the preschool classroom such as toys, art supplies, hands-on books, etc., will have to be replenished on an as-needed basis. An annual supply fee should be included in the center budget to restock these materials from year to year. Standard equipment should not have to be replaced if the teachers will supervise carefully and keep the equipment in good repair.

You can promote good equipment care by assigning teachers specific responsibilities in maintaining their classrooms. Tables and chairs should be cleaned regularly to remove spills, paint, crayon marks, etc. Manipulatives should be inventoried and each piece accounted for after each use. Teachers should keep individual manipulative sets stored in sealed containers that are sturdy enough to withstand a lot of handling. Records and tapes should always be returned to cases for storage. Teacher resource materials should not be accessible to children. These materials should be stored in locked cabinets or on closet shelves. Dramatic play clothes should be replenished several times each year and laundered anytime they become soiled. Stuffed animals should be kept to a minimum and sanitized daily for children under three and weekly for those over three. Classrooms should be well organized with each item having its place, and children should participate in the clean-up process to the extent they can as they, too, learn to become accountable for taking care of the classroom materials.

Each classroom should have either a bulletin board or designated wall space for displaying children's work and posting parent information notes. Instruct the teachers what can and cannot be used on walls such as tape, nails, thumbtacks, etc. Tell parents of the parent information areas in the classroom and encourage them to check for daily news.

A Responsive Environment for Children

Environments that are responsive to learners' needs will greatly enhance learning.

- Safe (physical and emotional)
- Healthy
- Organized
- A learning environment
- Attractive
- Planned
- Providing meaningful experiences
- Providing an abundance of materials
- Encouraging children to explore and discover and experiment
- Interactive
- Building confidence and competence
- Providing opportunities for knowledge construction
- Supporting emergent literacy
- Offering a variety of means of self expression
- Respecting the child and her originality
- Supporting positive and supportive relationships
- Encouraging children to get along with each other
- Encouraging expression of feelings
- Teaching respect
- Promoting self discipline
- Supporting communication with families
- Providing opportunity for family participation
- Providing family support
- Developmentally and culturally responsive and appropriate
- About team building
- Assessed
- Guided by principles, values, and ethics
- Respecting the fact that we must all continue to learn together

Curriculum Implementation

Lesson Plans

Teachers' lesson plans should be prepared and reviewed weekly or according to your center policy and licensing requirements. Many Quality Rating Systems identify what must be included in these lesson plans and may include listing activities, educational objectives, books being read, free play opportunities both indoor and outdoor as well as recording special learning opportunities that were unplanned. Plans should reflect overall goals and learning programs. An effective administrator makes sure that there are both child-guided and adult-guided educational experiences for the children. When children get really excited about a particular subject, the lesson plans should allow the teacher the opportunity to go into greater depth or experiment.

Provide your teachers with some form of lesson plan book. Weekly activities should be put in writing and submitted to the director for evaluation for completeness and age appropriateness. Child activity times must be well planned and conducive to self discovery. Children with short attention spans cannot be expected to wait for a teacher to gather materials, choose a book, or plan an impromptu activity. Teachers should plan ahead and order any supplemental materials well in advance.

You may want to have teachers' lesson plan in a mind-map format. This format has the theme, learning unit or goals in the center of the page. Connecting areas to the theme of the lesson plan are in lists around the theme. This lesson plan format gives the director at a glance the opportunity to see that the teacher is integrating basic skill information into her lesson as well as teaching to the auditory, visual and kinesthetic learners. (See mind-map example)

Encourage your teachers, as they develop lesson plans, to use such verification as the anecdotal method or work sampling method as a part of their observations of each child as they play, interact with others, and express themselves. This information will help the teacher create and record an individualized plan for each child.

You are responsible for monitoring the staff for good program delivery. Successful teachers have good classroom management skills that include: following daily routines; writing good lesson plans; communicating clearly to the children; respecting the children by treating them fairly and consistently; maintaining a bright, organized, stimulating classroom; varying activities that interest the children; and being generous with praise and positive reinforcement.

Children Learn Through Experiences and Hands-on Activities

Developmentally appropriate practice identifies the domains of children's development as: Physical, Social, Emotional, and Cognitive. Learning involves eight elements which are: Interactive process, meaningful experiences, supportive context, scaffolding, independence, nurturing environment and relationships. Curriculum should incorporate the instructional component of the early education program into the whole scope of daily activities that routinely make up the daily schedule.

The daily schedule for each age group should be individualized to reflect staggered outdoor times in order to avoid mixing ages on the playground or having too many children in the play area at once. Morning activity times are primary for child response. It is during this period teachers introduce and reinforce concepts, give children opportunities to explore and make connections with these concepts through child initiated activities and undertake major projects. Afternoons should be used to reinforce morning activities and extended learning. It is vital to have closure with the children at the end of each day. Teachers should draw the children together, review the activities and concepts of the day, and make plans for the next day's activities.

In implementing the daily routine, children should be allowed to choose activities available in the classroom and enable them to pursue self discovery. The daily schedule is important for both teachers and children as it provides the structure for the flow of daily activity. It also gives teachers clear expectations of what is to happen in the classroom and when. Children develop a sense of security in knowing the daily routine stays the same, day in and day out. Time frames for the daily schedule may be flexible giving teachers control over the length of activity periods depending on the attention and energy levels of the children..

Exploring and Valuing Diversity

Our world seems to become smaller every year. With modern communications tools such as the internet, satellites, and cellular telephone service to nearly every spot on the globe, we are in greater need of understanding of others' cultures and languages. The corporate world has learned this and acted quickly to educate their employees who interface with persons from other countries and cultures. They know that conducting business effectively means understanding others customs and mores. They strive to learn new languages and understand others' attitudes to build relationships fostering mutual respect.

It is incumbent upon us to help equip young children with tools to magnify their relationships in the future. Encouraging interest in and respect for many cultures, paves the way for children to interact successfully throughout their lives. You can accomplish this by integrating an exploration of cultural diversity into your whole curriculum - from social studies to physical fitness. Start with the cultures represented within the classroom. Take advantage of parents and teachers from a variety of cultures. Sample their native dishes, display their native dress, learn bits of their language and music, look at pictures of their homelands, learn how they celebrate holidays, play their native games. These everyday activities which are already a part of school life can take on new and interesting flavors as we vary the materials or examples while we learn. For instance, learning a new song from India can be enhanced with examples of native musical instruments and pictures of Indian children in their classrooms. Or you might find that a cooking experiment is made new and different when you use a recipe from Mexico and show the children pictures of how and where the ingredients are grown and use the tools natives would use to prepare the recipe.

Fill your interest centers with multi-cultural items which will spark interest and understanding. For example, in the housekeeping area, provide clothing from a variety of cultures, many types of "canned and packaged food goods," and pictures of various types of houses and many types of families. In the art center have materials for children that will enable them to try their hands at art medium representing a number of cultures, such as tie-dying, block printing, origami. In the music center, offer as many types of instruments as possible and tapes or CD's along with pictures of various types of music such as pan drums, ukuleles, bagpipes, etc.

During story time, don't limit yourself to traditional North American stories. Search out children's books showing other cultures in a positive light and teach children tolerance and acceptance. Don't forget opportunities to learn about and discuss disabilities.

Even with the smallest children we can begin to teach the important principles of kindness and acceptance. In the infant room, use music from different cultures and photographs of every child's family hung low or even laminated to the floor so crawlers can see them. Use mirrors to teach self awareness. Encourage staff to use their native languages when talking to the children.

Meal times can be especially fun and enlightening when we vary our menus with dishes from many cultures and even different utensils and table settings. Lunch is also a great time to enjoy some soft music to complement the menu.

Always remember your attitudes about your children and their families influence their attitudes more than a clever curriculum or diverse learning centers. If you strive to respect each child and his individuality, that respect will give the child self confidence and will say to the other children that this is a person worthy of their attention and care.

We must value our differences. Every person is worthy regardless of his ethnic heritage, language, ability or disability, gender, family composition, religion, or color. The good teacher strives to eliminate his own preconceptions and stereotypes and treat each child as an individual. Be aware of the influence your own education and culture have had upon you and make an effort not to pass on any biases you may have inadvertently absorbed. For example, be aware of treating girls and boys (even infants) differently.

Remember children are born into families and cannot change their make-up. They will prosper if we respect their families regardless of how they are constituted. You may feel strongly that a child is best nurtured in a home with a mother and a father, but your respect and support for different types of families will only help all children lead healthy, happy lives.

Make a concerted effort to pronounce children's and parents' names correctly even if you have to have them repeated several times. One's name is tied inextricably to one's self image.

Find ways to make school life for children with disabilities as much like other children's as possible. Directors who have worked with children with disabilities soon forget the disability and see only another child with the same curiosity and humor of all children.

When we contemplate the opportunities diversity affords us to make a real contribution to peace in our world, we also recognize the enormous responsibility we have to teach our children compassion and understanding for all.

Guidance and Discipline

The word discipline means to teach. Discipline is a process which helps a child develop self-control and responsibility and expands self growth and learning. In early childhood education discipline may be considered an educational process by which staff assist children to develop the self-control and self-direction necessary to assume responsibilities, make daily living decisions, and learn to live within accepted levels of social behavior.

Competency VI: Educational Programming

When children make inappropriate choices, it is most likely because they are:
- Angry
- Scared
- Seeking attention
- Tired
- Frustrated
- Confused
- Troubled
- Have not been taught alternative behaviors or choices
- Bored

Teachers respond to inappropriate behaviors differently due to:
- Power struggle - needing to be in charge
- Childhood experience with conflict - how were we disciplined/role models
- Values - what do we consider appropriate and inappropriate and why?
- Cultural contexts - what is our cultural framework?

Relearning, or new learning, of appropriate and successful discipline techniques requires:
- Distraction - especially with little ones, engagement in something new may end the conflict
- Redirection - offer another activity
- Proximity - be nearby at eye level - sometimes a simple touch diffuses
- Talking - help children use their words to resolve conflict/attention
- Simple limits and rules - set limits that are necessary for individual and class safety, stress respect of others, self and the environment - be flexible
- Smooth transitions and no waiting - plan ahead, be organized, prepare the class for change, set a routine, limit waiting
- Interesting activities - long and short term activities that are appropriate, engaging and fun
- Choices – age appropriate, varied, child directed, purposeful, meaningful
- Reinforcement - notice the good
- Establishing relationships - with child and family

The above descriptions and suggestions for classroom management do not link discipline with a punishment such as time out or denying of a toy or activity, to harassment such as telling a child over and over again they behaved poorly, or to humiliation such as scolding a child in front of their friends. Rather discipline is positive reinforcement of good behaviors, good teacher instruction and guidance, redirection, and knowledge of the behaviors of young children.

Practicing good management skills helps preclude much misbehavior that occurs in the classroom. Good organization and clearly expressed expectations help children know what they should do. It is when children become confused and lack direction that problems occur.

This frequently happens during transition times when children are moving from one activity to the next. The teacher must plan transitions and tell the children specifically what he wants them to do. For example, preschoolers do not line up well and tend to get chaotic as they start grouping together. A teacher who plans for this event might place footprints, shape patterns, or even color squares on the floor for each child to stand on so he knows where he is supposed to be in line. Sometimes lining up is not really necessary.

Plan for success. Instead of telling children not to run in the hallway, tell them how to walk down the hall. Do not expect a group of toddlers to sit patiently at the lunch table while the meal is being served. Provide a story, sing songs or do finger plays to keep them entertained until they are ready to sit down and eat.

If the children are to be successful in meeting adult expectations, the adults must be clear in describing their expectations. Too often an adult will wait until a child does something inappropriate and has to be corrected before the adult will make clear the behavioral expectation. Children need to be reminded regularly so they can work towards success, not failure. And most important is telling children when they are doing something in an appropriate manner. Observe your staff to be sure each teacher has a clear understanding of how to be positive and lead the children to success.

Common behavior problems can be expected to occur within each age group as children progress through normal developmental stages. Children will often push behavior to extremes as they search for limits and boundaries of what is acceptable and what is not.

Teacher intervention becomes necessary when one child physically hurts another child. Common problems might be biting, unwillingness to share, hitting others and using bad language. These and other inappropriate behaviors should be addressed in the classroom with positive guidelines.

One method of curbing unwanted behavior is redirection. Explain in simple terms why the child's behavior is not acceptable, describe what the appropriate behavior looks like and then guide him to another activity. Time away where a child has a quiet place to calm himself and prepare to return to the group can be effective if the children are taught some skills in advance. The teacher can role model, tell stories about or describe how other children have used their time away to calm down and be ready to return to play with friends. A child is never to be spanked or punished in any physical manner for displaying inappropriate behavior at the center, nor should parents be allowed to hit or spank a child while he is at the center.

Children who display consistent inappropriate behaviors may have problems that go beyond normal developmental expectations. Keep abreast of any children in this category and work closely with the teacher to determine what actions need to be taken for the child.

Children with developmental delays, speech abnormalities, hyperactivity or symptoms of abuse may require more remediation and therapy than a particular early care and education program can offer. Assist parents in finding appropriate medical or social service agency needed to make a formal evaluation and suggest a means of treatment for the child. Unless you are a trained psychologist, you should not make a judgment call or diagnosis in these situations. Let parents and trained professionals make those decisions. Some of these children will be able to receive outside therapy and still remain in your program. Others will require more than the program is able to provide.

Children who exhibit abrupt changes in behavior are sending up red flags that something is out of order in their lives. These behaviors may signal the onset of illness or may be the result of an overly tired child. Other possibilities may include changes in the family situation or even the death of a family member or pet. Teachers should not over react to these situations rather do a bit of analysis to get to the root of the problem. A child's emotional state is often expressed more strongly through his behavior than through his verbal ability to tell an adult what is wrong.

School-age children require different disciplinary tactics than preschoolers. In some instances time away may be appropriate when an older child displays inappropriate behavior. In those situations when problems occur between two older children, the adults should act as facilitators in encouraging the children to resolve the conflict themselves. The adults working with the older children should serve as good role models by listening attentively and communicating positively. A child feels valued when he believes he is a valuable member of the group. If he has good self esteem he is much better equipped to handle conflicts with peers and adults.

Adults are products of their environments and as such their ideas of discipline reflect the way their parents treated them. You must monitor teachers to assure there are not inappropriate practices in action in the classroom, you are responsible to set the methods of discipline and training your staff to act accordingly. The early care and education center, the director and the teacher all become liable if a teacher strikes a child or becomes abusive in any way. You need to be sensitive and supportive of behavior problems in the classroom even to the extent of removing a problem child before his behavior leads to an explosive situation.

Directors, teachers and support staff serve as role models for the children in their care. Adults must use calm voices with children who display inappropriate behavior. Do not talk about a child in his presence or cause his self esteem to be diminished in any way. The process of growing up involves constant trial and error, and children need to be able to pattern themselves after adults who behave like adults, not adults who behave like children.

A few suggestions to consider:

- Teach children what to do rather than what not to do.
- Give children words to describe their feelings.

- Give children many opportunities to make choices appropriate to their age.
- Describe to the child what you want them to do or give to them positive options.
- Recognize that children and adults need to be noticed through a form of acknowledgment.

Intrinsic motivation plays a critical role in the degree to which children initiate interaction and become engaged in activities.

Characteristics of intrinsic motivation include:

- Enjoyment
- Control
- Interest
- Probability of success
- Feelings of competence

Extracurricular Programs

As teachers implement the program and plan activities, the core of the curriculum takes place at the center. Field trips giving children the opportunity for real-life experience may be scheduled as enrichment to the basic curriculum. Check with your licensing authority and insurance carrier for regulations regarding field trips, including the ages of children allowed to participate.

Planning a field trip includes:

- Scheduling the event with the site to be visited
- Educating the children about the activity
- Scheduling enough staff or parent volunteers to accompany the children
- Getting written permission from parents for each child in the class
- Scheduling vehicles to provide transportation

Be sure to follow your state law regarding seat belts and child safety seats. Teachers must check children onto the vehicles and off the vehicle when they return to the center. Emergency phone numbers for each child must be taken on the trip. It is also a good idea to have a copy of the parent's written permission with you in case medical attention is needed for a child on the field trip. Field trips are fun for the children and richly rewarding as long as they are well organized and staffed appropriately.

Outdoor Activities

Outdoor play is an integral part of any child care program. It allows for fresh air, physical activity and strong social interaction. It requires strict supervision to prevent unwarranted injuries.

Statistically the majority of accidents in early care and education occur on the playground, so outdoor time is not a time for staff to congregate in one area or socialize with one another in lieu of watching the children. Plan for playground safety by assigning teachers to visually inspect the play area daily before the children go outside. Look for removable debris, briars, mushrooms, defects on play equipment, problems with fences or gates, and check resilient surfaces under climbing pieces and swings to see that it is adequate to cushion possible falls. A playground safety checklist is a useful tool. (See the sample "Playground Safety Checklist in handout disc.")

The playground should be designed to include play equipment for all ages. Play pieces accommodating a number of children are more practical and economical than single child play pieces. Sand play equipment should be available for digging, sifting, and building. Riding toys and tricycles should be available with a riding path away from the other play equipment. Ropes should not be allowed unless teachers are supervising organized jump rope activities. Balls and outdoor games should also be available.

Playground activity should be structured to allow a combination of free choice play and teacher directed games or activities. Children enjoy having their teachers get involved in play activities, but teachers must remain vigilant of all children in their charge and not focus on a few. Teachers need to remember that if any child has to come inside for water or bathroom, he must be accompanied by a teacher. Never leave children on the playground unattended.

Early care and education centers with indoor or outdoor swimming pools must:

- Keep the pool area secure at all times.
- Keep pool water chemically balanced any time the pool is in use.
- Assure a certified lifeguard is on duty any time the children are in the pool.
- Maintain proper pupil/teacher ratios at all times for both swimmers and non-swimmers.

Center Enrollment

As families request entry to the center, you are responsible for accepting the enrollment and placing the children in the appropriate classes. In doing so you must predetermine each class configuration – how many children and how many teachers per class– based on your company policies, prescribed state or accreditation ratios and individual classroom capacity.

Programs that mix the ages of the children in a group must also adhere to state regulations for pupil/teacher ratios usually determined by the age of the majority of the children in the group. Remember grouping toilet trained and non-toilet trained children in the same class will require more extensive planning.

Enrollment procedures should include an interview with a prospective parent and child. At that time discuss program philosophy, parent/child policies, fees, and curriculum objectives. Give parents and children a tour of the facility and an opportunity to meet the staff. Allow the parent to ask questions and explore what he is seeking in terms of care and educational opportunities for the child. Once the child is officially enrolled, inform the classroom teacher about the new child and share background information parent's names, who has permission to pick up the child, family dynamics, food allergies, medical problems, and any other pertinent information for the safety of the child in the classroom.

Separation Anxiety

During the initial enrollment interview, advise the parent that some children adjust readily to new situations while others experience separation anxiety, the fear of a new situation and anxiety about parents not returning at the end of the day. It is difficult to predict how a child will react, so it is best to prepare the parent for the possibility. This anxiety may not appear for several days and is generally manifested by crying, clinging to the parent, and telling the parent not to leave. It can be an unnerving experience for both the parent and the child, and requires patience and understanding to overcome. Teachers should assist the parent in the mornings at arrival by physically taking the child and holding him until he can calm himself or be diverted to a classroom activity. Encourage staff and parent to have contact later in the day so that the parent may be reassured that the child is calm, happy, enjoying the day and has settled into the activities of the center.

You can help parents work with the child during this anxiety period by advising them to pick up the child at the same time each afternoon, and to leave expeditiously in the mornings. Explain to the parents how prolonging actual separation in the morning gives the child a false sense of control when separation is inevitable, and reassure the parents the child is easily distracted once the parents are out of sight. Once a child feels safe with the routine of the new environment, his anxiety will diminish. He will soon anticipate and trust in daily events, including knowing that his parents will return.

An Effective Administrator Understands and Implements Assessment Strategies In Order to Maintain a Proper Learning and Care Environment for Each Child

Placement and Assessment

Assessment is the process used to collect information about student abilities and progress.

At the beginning of each new school year and each time a new child enters the program, you are charged with grouping or placing children in new classes. Sometimes state regulations will determine how you must place children. For example, your state may require you to place children according to their chronological ages. If you have some discretion in placing children, you may want to use some type of evaluation tool. If you use a specific curriculum, you should use an assessment tool related to that curriculum.

Tynette Hills tells us that assessment in early childhood education is used to provide information to make educational decisions that affect a child. There are three basic purposes for assessment.

- To provide information for instructional planning and communicating with parents (This communication would discuss how the child is doing, what are the child's strengths, needs, and learning process, and how the center will plan the child's instruction and guidance.)

- Identifying children with special needs and identifying whether your program can meet the needs of the child
- To provide evaluation and accountability of your program

One of the best tools for placing children is anecdotal information gathered and recorded by the teacher on each child. Anecdotal information is simply the teacher's notes on observations of the child as he participates in activities in the program and interacts with others. These observations should include the health of the child and his physical and social development. Nap time is a good time for the teacher to record his observations of the morning activities.

Teachers must have some form of guidelines of expectations of behaviors, skills, and stages of development of children in order to know the significance of what they are observing. When assessment is done properly it has the following characteristics.

- It is free of cultural and gender bias.
- It provides information that may be shared with others.
- It occurs in a setting that is comfortable for children.
- It generates data or other information that is useful for instruction.
- It is on-going.

DAP Assessment

In DAP, assessment and curriculum are integrated. Teachers continually engage in assessment for the purpose of improving teaching and learning. The results of assessment are used to benefit children - in adapting curriculum, teaching to meet learning and developmental needs, communicating with families, and evaluating program effectiveness.

Most children develop at about the same rate and in the same way as other children of the same age and culture. For some children, however, the quality or rate of development may differ from that of their peers.

Differences in development may be due to differences in the opportunities to learn, differences in cultural expectations, or differences within the child.

Early care and education teachers typically have experience observing the range and variability of normal development in children of many different ages and backgrounds. This experience places teachers in key positions to identify those children who need additional help.

An assessment or evaluation is a systematic effort to gather information about a child's performance, ability, or development. It involves both formal and informal practices.

Informal assessments generally occur in the child's early care and education setting and are made by professionals who work with the child on a regular basis. These assessments occur over time and in a variety of circumstances.

Formal assessments are conducted by professionals with expertise in both typical and atypical development. Their expertise may include specialized training in psychology, special education, speech, etc.

Formal assessments are conducted to learn more about a child's strengths and needs, to determine eligibility for special services, and/or to make a diagnosis. They usually include observations in a variety of situations and settings, interviews with parents and teachers, and formal tests.

Children can be referred for assessment, and information about them can be shared with others, only with written parental consent by the parents or legal guardians.

Early care and education teachers should consider any cultural or linguistic differences that may influence how a child is perceived as well as ethnic, cultural, or linguistic differences that may enhance or interfere with communication between teacher and family.

When early care and education teachers approach parents with concerns about their children, it is important that they share all observations in a nonjudgmental manner.

Parents are vital members of the formal assessment team. Their participation will be enhanced if the process is explained to them and if they know how they can be involved and what they can expect following the assessment.

Early care and education teachers and professionals play a vital role by helping to identify those children who may benefit from in-depth assessment.

There are many evaluation tools for preschool assessment that can help you assess the child's development. Many of these assessments include check lists of skill sets for the teacher to observe and check off. The results indicate where the children are in terms of developmental skills, what they know, what they are ready to learn, and what skills are ready to be introduced later. This information helps you tailor the curriculum to meet specific developmental needs and place children in appropriate groups for learning experiences. The assessment tool also provides feedback and suggestions for parents on how to reinforce developmental learning skills at home.

The profoundly simple explanation of assessment given to us by Mary Conti of Creative Beginnings is "we assess so we can plan." We want to know how a child is progressing developmentally so our activities assist in strengthening weaknesses and implementing activities for skills still needing to be learned. It should be noted the term assessment is sometimes used for assessing the progress of children and sometimes used to judge the performance of a center. At this time we are discussing assessment as it relates to children only and discuss performance as it relates to the center as evaluation.

Choosing an Assessment Tool

There are many formal assessment tools available. Formal assessment tools have uniform procedures for administration and scoring. There are also informal ways to do assessment. This includes teacher observation checklists, portfolios and work samples, anecdotal records, narrative and diary descriptions, teacher made tests, and audio and video recordings. It is important to choose an assessment tool with which you and staff are comfortable, that corresponds to the philosophy of your center, and which is compatible with your curriculum approach so that it provides meaningful information for planning. It is always best to choose a variety of assessment tools for the most accurate evaluation of a child i.e. using anecdotal notes, running checklists, portfolios, work samplings for different times and different situations.

Child Outcome Assessment Tools for Early Childhood Education

NCCIC provides us with the following information about assessment. "Child outcome assessments are ongoing activities to measure a child's progress." The results inform program administrators, early childhood teachers and providers, policy-makers, parents, and the public about progress toward the broad goal of promoting children's learning and development over time by improving early childhood programs and services. More specific goals include identifying children eligible for special services, modifying curriculum to meet the needs of individual children, and easing the transition for children and families from home to school. What follows is a selected list of a federal system… and multi-domain assessment tools that measure child outcomes and that are designed for use by center and family child care educators.

Federal

The Head Start Bureau has prepared a procedure for use in all Head Start programs at the beginning and end of the program year to assess all four and five-year-olds on a limited set of language, literacy, and numeracy indicators. The Head Start Bureau plans to document Head Start's effectiveness nationally in a valid and reliable way by using the same set of tools to collect information from each Head Start program. The National Reporting System will not report or examine individual child progress: that will be managed in local programs and in partnership with parents.

Multi-Domain Assessment Tools

Teaching Strategies, Inc. offers curriculum materials, training programs, parenting resources, staff development services, and assessment tools that are practical, developmentally appropriate, and responsive to the needs of the field.

Strategies, Inc. has developed the following products to help programs assess children and report progress.

- Creative Curriculum Developmental Continuum Assessment Toolkit
- The Creative Curriculum Developmental Continuum Assessment Toolkit for ages 3-5 is a kit that includes all the forms needed to assess up to 25 children in programs that implement The Creative Curriculum. This resource is also available in Spanish.
- The Creative Curriculum Progress and Outcomes Reporting Tool (CC-PORT)
- The Creative Curriculum Progress and Outcomes Reporting Tool (CC-PORT) is a software teaching application to be used with the Creative Curriculum

Developmental Continuum Assessment Toolkit to produce reports on groups of children.

- Creative Curriculum.net
- Creative Curriculum.net is a secure interactive Web-based assessment system based on The Creative Curriculum Developmental Continuum for ages 3-5.
- Galileo Preschool
- Galileo is a comprehensive early childhood knowledge management system, which makes it possible to document, track, and report preferred information on children, staff, families, and volunteers.
- Galileo Online
- Galileo Online integrates assessment and the documentation of outcomes with eLesson Planning and eCurriculum features. Continuously evolving based on advances in research, the needs of educators, and innovations in software communications technology, Galileo offers an advanced approach for the electronic management of learning (EML), including Merlin, a child and family case management system; the Parent Center, which generates four individualized reports that tell parents about what a child has learned at preschool and about a child's readiness to learn new capabilities in a given developmental area, such as language and literacy or early math; and Storyteller Center, which provides learning opportunities and objective assessment directly articulated to instructional goals.
- Galileo G-2
- Galileo G-2 has stand-alone technology (available on CD-Rom) that connects assessment, screening, lesson planning, classroom activities, and outcome documentation. Galileo G-2 is an entire suite of tools that increases the availability of child outcome data and flexibility in analysis. Galileo G-2 comes with Online Reporter, a Web-based tool that allows programs to aggregate data and access reports online.
- The High/Scope Child Observation Record (COR)
- The High/Scope Foundation is an independent nonprofit research, development, training, and public advocacy organization. In a High/Scope program, students learn through active involvement with people, materials, events, and ideas. The High/Scope's Cognitively Oriented Preschool Curriculum represents an attempt to construct a developmentally valid educational framework for young children. The High/Scope COR for Ages 2-6 *is* an observational assessment tool that charts children's development and progress over time. *COR* assessment areas include language, mathematics, initiative, social relations, creative representation, and music and movement. The *COR* assesses the ways in which young children initiate their own activities as well as how they respond to teacher questions and demands.

It can be used in a variety of early childhood settings. Components of the *COR Assessment Kit* are the following items: COR Manual; COR Assessment Booklets; COR Anecdotal Notecards; COR Parent Report Forms; and COR poster.

- High/Scope COR for Infants and Toddlers

- The High/Scope COR for Infants and Toddlers looks at the whole child-highlighting broad areas of development for children from the ages of 6 weeks to 3 years. It can help caregivers gather, organize, document, and learn from observations of children within the context of everyday life at the center or home setting. This information can also be shared easily, accurately, and effectively with parents and others.

- Individual Growth and Development Indicators (IGDI)

- IGDIs are quick, efficient, and repeatable measures of components of developmental performance. They sample child performance in major developmental domains (i.e., language, social, cognitive, motor, and adaptive), with a special emphasis on assessment related to long-term developmental outcomes common across the early childhood years. They are functional and related to later competence in home, school, and community settings. These indicators measure young children's growth over time toward important developmental outcomes rather than their skill level at one point in time. Preschool IGDIs are intended for children between the ages of 30 months and 6 years of age. Early elementary IGDIs are intended for children between the ages of 5 and 8, or roughly from prior to kindergarten entry through the end of 2nd grade. IGDIs can be used by psychologists, teachers, and other program staff who want to measure, record, and act on information about young children's rate of growth and development toward long-term, developmentally important goals. This assessment may be completed to monitor children not receiving specialized intervention, to identify children who might benefit from such intervention, and to monitor the effects of such intervention.

- The Marazon Systems

- The Marazon Systems (Classroom System, Home Visitor System, Family Child Care System, Christian System, and Parent System) are developmentally appropriate planning and assessment systems designed for a variety of educational settings for children of all ages. The systems provide parents and professionals with the tools to support and challenge children's growth, development, and learning. It is focused on describing children's interests and developmental characteristics, and then using the everyday curriculum of the home, school, and the community to support and challenge their interests and promote development. The system celebrates 96 child development characteristics across six domains or areas of the child's growth. The six domains are Affective (relating to self), Social (relating to others), Creative (originating from self), Cognitive (thinking), Language

Competency VI: Educational Programming

(communicating), and Physical (doing). The four steps of the system-Plan, Environment, Assessment, and Partnership-assist practitioners in developing intentional plans to help children grow and develop as individuals. The comprehensive nature of the Marazon system enables teachers to observe children throughout the week to achieve the following tasks related to authentic assessment and individualized planning.

1. Record one-to-two anecdotes per day
2. Interpret the anecdotes according to the 96 target objectives that same day
3. Composite or summarize the target objectives onto the child assessment and planning tally that same day
4. Review each child's assessment and planning tally prior to planning each week
5. Develop individual and group domain plans based on data related to children's emerging needs and interests
6. Arrange the environment, interact with the children, and conference with families either formally or spontaneously

- The Ounce Scale
- The Ounce Scale is an observational assessment for evaluating infants' and toddlers' development from birth to age 3. Its purpose is to provide guidelines and standards for observing and interpreting young children's growth and behavior, and to provide information parents and caregivers can use in everyday interactions with their children. The Scale has three elements: the observation scale; the family album; and the developmental profile. It is organized around the following six major areas of development: personal connections; feelings about self; relationships with other children; understanding and communicating; exploration and problem-solving; and movement and coordination. The Ounce scale provides a way to evaluate children's accomplishments, areas of difficulty, and approaches to learning. The Ounce scale is available in Spanish.
- The Work Sampling System
- The work sampling system is an ongoing classroom performance assessment system that is used in preschool through 5th grade. Its purpose is to document children's skills, knowledge, behavior, and accomplishments across a wide variety of curriculum areas on multiple occasions in order to enhance teaching and learning. Curriculum areas include personal and social development, language and literacy, mathematical thinking, scientific thinking, social studies, the arts, and physical development.
- Work Sampling Observational Assessment

- Teachers using the work sampling observational assessment observe children with the Developmental Guidelines; record classroom observations efficiently using reproducible process note forms included in the *Using Work Sampling Guidelines and Checklists: An Observational Assessment* teacher's manual; document learning by completing a grade-level Developmental Checklist for each child three times per year; report to parents three times per year and maintain school records of student achievement with the optional *Work Sampling Report to Parents.*

Summary

Demonstrating competency in educational programming, an effective administrator:

- Understands that brain research has reaffirmed the importance of high quality early childhood education

- Implements curriculum reflecting the most accepted practices in child development and implements programs addressing all aspects of early childhood education

- Understands how children grow and develop, why children and parents experience separation anxiety, and is able to direct staff to productively work with children

- Ensures appropriate room and space arrangement and supports effective space design based on knowledge of environmental psychology and childhood development

- Understands and implements assessment strategies in order to maintain a proper learning and care environment for each child

If you feel you lack confidence in any of the skills listed above, please go back and review the appropriate section of this chapter.

Competency VII

Marketing, Advertising, and Public Relations

Competency VII

Marketing, Advertising, and Public Relations

Learning Objectives:

- To gain knowledge of the fundamentals of effective marketing, public relations, and community outreach including the understanding of the similarities and differences between marketing, advertising, and public relations

- To be able to lay out a yellow page advertisement

- To know how to respond to customer interest inquiries

- To be able to write a press release

- To develop professional telephone skills

- To know what steps to take to maintain optimum enrollment

- To be able to evaluate the cost-benefit of different marketing and promotional strategies

- To be able to communicate the philosophy of the program and to promote a positive public image to families, business leaders, public officials, and prospective funders

- To understand how to promote linkages with local schools

- To gain skill in developing effective promotional literature, handbooks, newsletters, and press releases

An Effective Administrator Maintains a Professional Program Image through Written, Verbal, and Visual Communication with Parents and the Community

A successful early childhood education program has a high quality program, great staff, a well maintained building, and an ability to promote the services of the center. Each of these goals can be met in part by using marketing, advertising, or public relations tools. Marketing, advertising, and public relations are interrelated disciplines with distinct differences that need to be understood, even though several of the tools outlined below can used for more than one purpose.

Marketing

Marketing allows the public to understand who you are by educating them about your curriculum, staff and staff qualifications, and the overall early childhood environment you maintain.

Name

Your name should be created to reflect your primary reason for doing business. Potential customers who see your center's sign, brochure or flyer should immediately associate your name with child care.

Image is the way your center, staff, and programs are viewed by the community. Your center's name is an image builder which conveys a statement or message about your profession. Therefore, caution should be used. Image is extremely important to project a positive attitude towards children and the child care profession.

When a center strives for uniqueness by using nondescript names such as *Alice in Wonderland,* many potential parents may fail to realize that *Alice in Wonderland* is an early care and education center and not a children's clothing store. Also, be careful about using too few words to describe your center. Until a director changed the center's name from Jan's Care Center to Jan's Early Care and Education Center, many thought the building belonged to a pediatrician! On the other hand, there are disadvantages in having a name very common to child care centers. Try to find a distinct, but appropriate, name.

Logo

The logo for your center is an important business tool. What companies or products do you think about when you see the golden arches, the little giggly dough boy, or Tony the Tiger? What child care companies do you think about when you see the soldier boy or the red bell?

Logos are graphic representations that convey the nature and image of your center. As with the golden arches example, the purpose of the logo is to equate the arches with McDonald's. Your logo should equate your center with the name of your center and the image (e.g., nurturing, educational) you wish to project. Do you think that, with the conception of the golden arches, hungry people immediately recognized the logo and flocked to McDonald's for a Big Mac? It took many years for this recognition to occur. Therefore, creating an effective logo and using it continuously is vital to the success of your business. Like McDonald's, you want to design and use a logo so that parents will immediately link your logo and the name of your center.

Your logo is the centerpiece of all your advertising efforts. The design of all other collateral materials (e.g., brochures flyers, stationery, business cards) material should pivot around your logo. It is such an integral part of your business that you might want to devote a portion of your advertising dollars to the development of this logo. Develop some ideas and put them on paper. If you have the funds, employ an experienced graphics artist who can design exactly what you want. An inexpensive, yet effective idea is to employ the local high school or college graphics class to develop your logo. Ask them to develop a few ideas and then work with the artists to develop a final product.

Some additional ideas in developing a logo include the following.

- Keep the graphics simple.
- Photographs for logos are not as effective as graphics.
- The logo should adapt to all forms of communication. It should work as well on a billboard as a piece of stationary.
- Do not design a logo which will outdate itself in a short period of time (e.g., cabbage patch dolls or care bear logos).
- Use fonts that are easily enlarged or reduced in size. An italic font, for example, may look good on stationery but may not be so effective on large billboards, signs or posters.
- Think about colors and their effectiveness in all applications (e.g. stationery, poster, outdoor sign). Consult with a sign maker to determine the best colors for an outdoor sign. For example, some colors (like black or red) can be seen from long distances. Some colors evoke certain feelings or moods. Blue, for instance, is considered serene and trustworthy, whereas green conveys an attitude of comfort.

Most importantly, before making a final decision on your new logo, evaluate it one last time. Enlist a few people to critique your logo before it goes to print and ask the following questions.

- Does it project the image of your center and adequately reflect your program and philosophy?
- Can parents easily link your logo with the name, by-line, or motto of your center?

By-Line (Motto)

A by-line (or motto) conveys in a few words what you feel is important to your client and what you consider the mission of your center. What company do you think of when you hear....

- "The quality goes in before the name goes on." (Zenith)
- "Better things for better living through chemistry." (DuPont)
- "We love to fly and it shows." (Delta)

- "You're in good hands with   …" (Allstate)
- "When you care enough to send the very best." (Hallmark)

When you are deciding on a by-line or motto, think about who your clients are and what they need from your early childhood program. Do they need a safe and secure center, a learning environment, a place for their infant or toddler, a fun program for their school-ager? Can you design the motto so it will transcend all age levels? For example, the motto for one center is "Caring for Your Most Precious Possession." This conveys the mission of the center yet is not age specific.

Staff and Management Appearance

Experts believe that, in order to be treated as a professional, you must look like a professional. Personal appearance is an important aspect of overall effectiveness and is a reflection of your success as a child care professional. As an administrator, you need to decide on your professional image comfort zone.

It is necessary to recognize the kind of work our staff does. They sit on floors or low chairs, hug children with spaghetti on their faces, play with children on the playground and change dirty diapers. This kind of work dictates the type of dress code we should have. Clothing should be clean and professional in appearance; however the dress code should allow teacher to be comfortable in working with children.

In addition, directors should consider the following.

- Learn What People Use to Form Their First Opinion
- When you meet someone face-to-face, 93% of how you are judged is based on non-verbal data--your appearance and your body language. Only 7% is influenced by the words that you speak.
- Choose Your First Twelve Words Carefully
- Express some form of thank you when you meet the prospective client.
- Ask the Person's Name and Use it Immediately
- Nothing gets other people's attention as effectively as calling them by name.
- Pay Attention to Hair--Very few people want to do business with someone who is unkempt or whose hairstyle does not look professional. Don't let a bad hair day cost you the connection.
- Keep Your Shoes in Mint Condition --People will look from your face to your feet. If your shoes aren't well maintained, the client will question whether you pay attention to other details.
- Walk Fast--Studies show that people who walk 10-20% faster than others are viewed as important and energetic – just the kind of person your clients want to do business with.

Competency VII: Marketing, Advertising, and Public Relations

- Fine Tune Your Handshake-- The first move you make when meeting your prospective client is to put out your hand. There isn't a businessperson anywhere who can't tell you that the good business handshake should be a firm one.

- Make Introductions with Style-- Say the client's name first and introduce other people to the client. The correct words to use are "I'd like to introduce..." or "I'd like to introduce to you..." followed by the name of the other person.

- Never Leave the Office without Your Business Cards-- Your business cards and how you handle them contribute to your total image. Keep your cards in a card case or holder where they are protected from wear and tear. That way you will be able to find them without a lot of fumbling around, and they will always be in pristine condition.

- Match Your Body Language to Your Verbal Message--A smile or pleasant expression tells your clients that you are glad to be with them. Eye contact says you are paying attention and are interested in what is being said. Leaning in toward the client makes you appear engaged and involved in the conversation.

Facility Appearance

There are two moments of truth experienced by visitors to your center. The first moment of truth is your curbside image. This is the impression given when the visitor first pulls into the parking lot of your center. Look critically at the outside of your center and ask yourself the following questions.

- Is the lawn mowed and manicured?
- Is the parking lot clean?
- Are the windows clean? (void of any dried masking/scotch tape)
- Is the front door clean? (void of children's finger prints)
- Look on the ground–are there weeds, cigarette butts, scattered trash?
- Are the items hanging in the windows current with the season/holiday?
- What do the drapes/blinds look like from outside the building? Are they neat and clean?

The second moment of truth is upon first entering the building. The foyer or entrance should be clean, bright and neat. In the first 11 seconds, your visitor's senses should be bombarded with positive images–from good smells, to pleasing sights, to happy sounds. Clean up your act if you think parents do not see messy desks, cobwebs in the corners, last week's corn kernel in the kitchen corner, dust balls behind the doors, faded construction paper on the bulletin board, think again. If your center is in a mess, potential parents will assume your business and the care for children is also in a mess.

Advertising

Advertising is an effort to let the public know that you have services to offer. Advertising may be done through yellow page in the phone book, brochures, flyers, promotional materials, newspapers, TV, the internet, signs etc. Here are some of the basics.

Advertisements and Yellow Pages

Advertising provides a direct link of communication between your center and the community. Effective advertising convinces the reader that your center provides the best child care available. Good advertising will draw clients to your center and informs readers of the benefits of doing business with you.

Benefits sell. Nothing you can put into your ad will sell your center better. Why? Because when people buy your service, they buy it for the benefit it brings to them. When they read your advertisement, they really ask only one question: "How will this benefit me?" So before you begin to write your advertisement, make a list of the benefits your center provides. Make sure you compile your list from the standpoint of your customer. Rank the benefits from the most important to the least. The benefit that comes out on top is the headline you should use in your advertising.

The headline is the most important part of your advertisement. If you do not have an attention getting headline, the main body of your ad will not be read. What is an attention getting headline? It is copy that communicates the biggest benefit your center provides. For example, the Wee-Wee Care at Work's Commuter Center is located conveniently next to the metro suburban train station. Wee Care can grab the attention of the reader in a headline like this: "Save Time and Eliminate the Hassle . . . Use Wee Care's Commuter Station Child Care Center!"

Effective advertisements always tell the basics of who, what, when, where, why and how. Here are a few more tips to improve your copy:

Keep It Short, Simple, and Friendly. Do not try to advertise too many things. Be informal and use a conversational style; think about your audience–the majority of your readers will not have a degree in early childhood education and, while you understand developmentally appropriate, it may mean nothing to your potential client. Write the advertisement as if you were talking to a friend; advertising experts believe strongly that friends do business with friends. Think about the essence of the advertisement for Motel 6': "This is Tom Bodette from Motel 6 . . . and we'll leave the light on for ya."

Use Headlines. Put the name of the market segment (e.g. parents, children) you are trying to reach in your headlines. Try to get the name of your center in your headlines. Studies show that five times more people read the headlines of an ad than the body copy.

Use Power Words. The most powerful word in advertising is free. The next most powerful word is new. Can you get these words in your ad?

Benefits Sell. Remember the list of benefits of your center? Put the most important benefit in your headline or (at least) in the first line of your copy.

Write for the Reader. Direct the words specifically to the reader. Focus on your customers' self-interests. They want to solve their own problems and satisfy their own needs. They are not so interested in the fact that you have been in business for ten years as they are interested in how they will benefit from those ten years of experience.

Is there anything which instantly grabs the attention of the reader? In order for your advertisement to be effective, you must first get her attention.

When you are traveling to other cities, take a minute to look at the Yellow Pages to see which child care ads catch your eye. Jot down ideas for your own ad if you see something unique and appealing.

Brochures

The brochure is another essential marketing tool. Since your brochure may be your first contact with a potential customer, it is a way of warming up her before she sees your center. A brochure should encourage prospective customers to visit your center. "Your brochure is one of the most inexpensive ways of adding heat," says Kim T. Gordon, author of *Growing Your Home Based Business*.

The brochure is, in effect, your salesperson making sales calls in the community. If it doesn't portray professionalism, the sale may be lost. The word professional does not necessarily equate to slick. Having a four color brochure isn't as important as creating a quality piece of information. Important factors for creating a quality brochure include professional writing, pleasant appearance, an understandable layout, and heavier weight paper (at least 60 to 80 lb).

Since most people do not like to read long, complex passages, your brochure should be short and simple. You have just a few seconds to grab your potential customer's attention. Therefore, stick to the following writing techniques.

- Keep your sentences short.
- Avoid educational jargon (e.g., age appropriate large muscle development) which may have meaning to you but not to a prospective parent. Simple words communicate your message better.
- Give basic information such as ages served, hours of operation, location (don't forget a map if you are off the beaten path), special programs offered, and a general statement about the mission of your center.
- Do not fill up the entire page with words; break up the words with plenty of white space. You do not want your reader to be overwhelmed with too much print.
- Do not include any information (such as tuition) which may become obsolete with the passage of time. This can be a separate advertising piece which can be changed as necessary and slipped into your marketing piece.
- Write the copy in the first person (with lots of personal pronouns); this makes the readers feel it was written just for them.

- Be sure to place your logo and motto on the front cover or at the top of the brochure. Remember when you were designing your slogan? Don't forget that conveying the benefits of your center is the most important goal in writing your brochure.

Prior to designing your brochure, it is a good idea to talk to several printers. You will want to discover what type of printing job fits your budget. It would be a waste of time for you to design a brochure which has four colors, tri-fold, and inserts that you cannot afford to print.

A professional printer can help you with the design of your brochure, and with the selection of graphics and fonts. It is also a good idea to obtain several estimates. You might be surprised at the wide range of printing prices. Be sure that each printer is quoting on the same product - the same paper, quantity, number of colors, etc. Also obtain a completion date for the print job; five to ten (working) days is an approximate length of time to expect a printer to complete a job.

Business Cards and Stationery

Some directors have a tendency to overlook the necessity for business cards or stationery. You may feel that you do not write enough letters to warrant this expense. Regardless of how little communication you feel you do, business cards and stationery are an important marketing tool for any child care center. Again, it is that image thing.

What you are really doing is creating a total marketing package. Business cards and stationery should not only communicate the essentials (e.g., name, address, phone, email address or web site, and logo), but should remain consistent with other vehicles of communication. Your logo, brochure, slogan or motto, business cards, flyers, and stationery should all fit together like pieces in a puzzle.

Stationary includes letterhead, thank you notes, and other printed forms you use to communicate information on behalf of your business. These should all follow the same style, format, and color. Always use the same font and color for the center name. Include your logo. If possible place you mission statement or byline at the bottom of your letterhead. Use a high quality paper for all stationary. This speaks of the quality of your program.

Marketing experts have recommended that you give out at least ten business cards a day. Each time you give out a business card, you are throwing out seeds of recognition and visibility. And, as Mark Twain once said, "If you throw out enough seeds, something is bound to grow."

Web Site

Many child care centers are now on-line. In other words, they have developed a web site on the Internet which can be used to promote their program and serve as an advertising tool. Most parents who work in offices have access to the Internet, and the public in general is increasingly turning to the Internet as a tool to find products and services.

There are lots of advantages of a web site over conventional advertising. One of the most important advantages is your ability to update the information as needed. Because you can put new information on the site whenever you wish, you can include information that would quickly become dated in other advertising media, items such as weekly menus, tuition fees, or your calendar of events. Web sites also give you more space, so you can tell more about your school.

And, best of all, on your web site you can accomplish several goals at one time. Your web site can be a bulletin board for parents announcing upcoming field trips, new teachers, special activities going on in each of the classrooms, recognition for individual children's accomplishments, or warnings about recalled products. If you include an email feature on your site, it can also be a great form of communication between center and parent, or even parent and child. One of the greatest benefits is that your web site can also be an advertising tool showing prospective parents the exciting programs that are happening in your center.

It is possible to design your own web site, and there are software packages that will help you do so; however, you must be prepared to spend lots of time completing this project. You might choose instead to have someone else design your site. Web site designers are proliferating, but not all are equal. You would be wise to spend some time on the Internet looking at web sites and noting the features you like. Look particularly at web sites of local businesses so that you can ask who designed the ones you like. Ask to see the work of several web site designers and discuss their ability to incorporate the features you want. The cost of developing web sites or virtual tours of your facility have become reasonably priced and therefore an option that should be considered. Be sure to hire a company that will maintain your site regularly by adding new information and one that can tell you how many hits (i.e., visits) your site has had in the past month.

Signs

A sign is one of the most direct forms of visual communication you have in marketing. Close your eyes for a moment; visualize yourself driving your car from your home to the child care center. Think of all the types of signs you see–railroad, stop, Dairy Queen, K-Mart, road construction, detour, ducks crossing–you see so many signs that you have a tendency to overlook their powerful impact. Signs help people find you and help you find people. They give information, create a mood, and set the stage. In many cases, you do not have to fully read the sign to understand the meaning. During the World Cup in Chicago, for example, all that was needed to direct fans to the stadium was a black and white soccer ball.

Signs can do three important things for your center.

i. They Can Direct Potential Parents to Your Front Door

ii. Signs can help with a poor location by providing effective communication direction to your front door. If your center is located off the busy thoroughfare, signs can help direct parents to your facility.

iii. They Can Give Constant Information about Your Center

Signs are always working for you; they are always on a sales call any time of the day, week or year. Signs do not sleep or take vacations. Every time parents pass your center, they see your sign. The more times they see your sign, the more chances they have of remembering your business. Working parents often drive at night (especially in the winter time) and, therefore, you might want to think about an electric sign. Having an electric sign will assure you of not missing any potential client who might be passing by your center in the evening.

Signs can build your image. The child care business is a mobile or transient business. A primary source of your center's customers are people who are new to the area or new to a job. Your sign is one of the most effective ways of reaching the ever-changing needs of a mobile, transient society.

Signs are relatively inexpensive when compared to other advertising costs. Some considerations for developing a road/billboard sign are the following.

- Rules and Ordinances
- The number one thing that you do is check on signage rules in your city ordinances. Some cities have strict rules and regulations regarding signs. Determine what the regulations are in your community before you discuss a design with a sign maker. Many sign companies are familiar with the regulations in any given community and can guide you in selecting a sign which is not in violation of the law.
- Traffic Patterns
- Determine your customers' traffic patterns. What roads do they travel to get to your center? Where are their main areas of residency and business? What are the primary arteries?
- Obtain a street profile (nearest large intersection) from the city's traffic engineer. They can tell you the intersection's traffic volume, where the motorists' travel originates and the destination, reasons for travel and when they travel (usually this information is available on an hour-by-hour basis).
- Noticeable, Readable, Legible
- The sign should be noticeable. This can be done with bright colors, moving parts (clock, temperature) and message signs. For example, a local restaurant recently put up a message sign which read, "Come in and eat before we both starve." This message sign ended up on the front page of the local newspaper.
- Be sure the sign is readable. Find the real traffic speed where your sign will be located. A professional sign maker will be able to use a formula to calculate the needed size for your sign.
- The sign should be legible. Select color combinations which are easily read. Your sign maker may be able to help you with your color selection. One also needs to check evening lighting and illumination since there may be problems due to the glares or shadows from the street lights, other signs or nearby business establishments. A well-designed sign is noticeable, has a message impact, and overcomes any viewing problems.
- Energy Costs

- Before you decide on a sign, determine the energy consumption. Inquire about energy-saving bulbs. Determine the type of bulb needed and how to replace bulbs or tubes in your sign.
- Insurance and Maintenance
- Determine if you need insurance. If you have an expensive sign you might want to insure your sign as part of your property and casualty coverage. Also, determine that you have proper liability coverage if your sign was blown down and someone was injured.
- Consider the sign maintenance. One thing you do not want is a dilapidated sign; this only sends a negative message to the community and your potential parents. If parents see a dilapidated sign, they wonder if you are going to take care of their child in the same way as you are taking care of your center's sign.

Promotional or Specialty Items

Specialty items may be used to help promote your center. Below are some specialty items that you might consider using.

Aprons	Insulated lunch totes	Pins
Balloons	Key chains	Plastic Cups
Bumper Stickers	Lunch Totes	Ribbons
Buttons	Magnets	Small stuffed toys
Calendars	Mugs	Sweat shirts
Caps	Ornaments	Tote bags
Certificates	Pencils	T-Shirts
Coffee Mugs	Pennants	Water Glasses
Diplomas	Picture Frames	

Public Relations

Public relations is the creation of good (or bad) will. We almost always know when something appears to be good public relations such as an early childhood education center receives a special award. We also know we want to avoid bad public relations, but what are bad public relations? It is anything that gives an unfavorable image about our facility or staff. It is created through communication that may be misunderstood, poorly executed policy, poor staff and facility appearance, poorly written documents and newsletters, and failure to keep children from harm just to name a few circumstances.

There is a distinct difference between marketing and public relations. Both strategies, however, help grow your business of early childhood education.

Public relations strategies include:

- Press releases
- Lecturing to a trade or civic audience
- Sponsoring a little league team
- Sponsoring a MDA Hop-a-Thon
- Active chamber & community participation
- Donating door prizes to the Cancer Society's fashion show
- Participating in the Fourth of July parade
- In-house community parent training seminars
- Hosting a community safety fair and inviting the community
- Adopting a grandparent in a nursing home
- Contracting with a children's author or musician to perform at the center and inviting the community to come listen.
- Writing parenting articles for the community newspaper or corporation newsletter

The purpose of marketing is to help the public know who you are and who you serve. The purpose of having good public relations is to develop a reputation so that when parents need child care, they will consider you because of your good reputation. Developing this kind of strategy means viewing all actions and events as windows of opportunities to spread the news about your center.

Steve Broe, Arizona child care consultant, illustrates the difference between marketing and public relations. When the circus comes to town, they put up flyers to advertise the date, time and place. On the first day of the circus, they have a parade with the lions, tigers, clowns and elephants. This is called marketing. When the elephant tramples the mayor's flower garden and you still get him to declare it Circus Week, that is public relations.

The advantage of public relations over marketing is you do not have to pay for public relations. The disadvantage is that you cannot control what the media says about you. If you do it right, public relations appears to have a much greater impact than marketing. Use public relations to reinforce positive messages not only about the quality of service you provide, but about early childhood education.

The Media and Public Support

The media can be your best ally or your worst enemy. To create an ally, take some time to cultivate contacts in the media. Send press releases about your center or about child care in general. Newspapers need to fill space, and child care is a topic of interest to many readers. Call your local newspaper to ask who covers community news, family topics, or children's pages. Contact this person and develop a relationship so that she will call you for information and publish the news releases you send. Try to become her official source for child care information. Make contacts with local radio or television stations as well.

Learning to write a good press release will serve you well. You should entice the reader to learn more about the person or event you are writing about but at the same time give enough information to enable a busy editor to write a filler piece from what you have provided. A good press release will answer the questions: who, what, when, where, and why?

Keep a mailing list of local newspaper, radio, and television contacts and send them press releases regularly about: special events at your center, special recognition a teacher or child has received, community service projects your center is involved in, new studies related to child development, or reviews of children's books and videos. If you have cultivated personal media contacts, you will be in a better position should a crisis occur. These contacts will be more likely to listen to you fairly and will be less intrusive and more accommodating.

During a crisis, either at or directly affecting your center, you must be prepared to deal with the questions and other pressures that intense media coverage causes. Here are some guidelines for such a situation.

- You are under no obligation to speak to the media.
- If you don't think you can handle the situation, remain silent.
- Do not allow yourself to be rushed. Think about what you are going to say. If time permits, prepare a statement in advance.
- Answer only those questions which you are certain do not breach confidentiality of either a child or employee. Do not be afraid to say you do not know or prefer not to comment.
- Restrict the use of all photographic equipment on your property and in your building. Remember that the reporters are just doing their job. They are not intentionally out to get you, but they will take every advantage that you allow.
- Above all, remain in control.

News Releases on Center Events

A news release is used to publicize events or tell of happenings in the community. There are many center events which seem ordinary and common to you, but would make interesting reading for your community. Write up a success story of something that happened in your center. Editors are always looking for fillers to use in their publication. Keep a camera nearby for pictures to accompany the article. Children involved in building a block structure, a cooking project or attending a field trip would all make excellent fillers. Or, write a letter to the editor on a pertinent topic regarding the child care industry. Another idea is to plan special activities and events for the Month of the Young Child. Invite a photographer from a local paper to attend the event. Special events like this can help bring your center to the attention of the community.

To get the attention of the local media, write a press release. It is important to direct the news release to the right person. With a small newspaper or TV station, it might be best to direct the news release to the editor. Large newspaper or TV station may have several editors, feature writers and correspondents who specialize in a particular geographical area or specific topic. After sending the one-page release, follow it up with a personal phone call.

A News Release should have the five W's (who, what, where, why and when). The five W's should appear in the first paragraph and, if possible, in the first two sentences. It should be written in correct format according to the following procedures.

- Typed and double spaced on one piece of plain white 81/2" by 11" paper
- Your organization's name and address in the upper left hand corner
- In the upper right hand corner, type: **FOR IMMEDIATE RELEASE**
- Directly below type: a contact name and phone number and e-mail address.
- At the top of the page and in the center should be typed, **NEWS RELEASE**
- Type the headline under News Release; the headline should be no longer than one line. It needs to be an attention grabber.
- Type the body of the News Release, remembering to put the Five W's and important facts in the first few lines of the article.
- Type # # # at the end of the article, centered on the page. This lets the editor know that it's the end of the article.

You might want to include a brochure and a photograph of you center along with your news release. If you wish to conserve your photographs, you could indicate on the news release that photographs are available upon request. If you use photographs of children in your center, be sure to have your parents sign a permission release form which allows the newspaper to print the picture. Some other hints:

- Use the correct information; be sure names are spelled correctly and that titles are right.
- Testimonials and quotes from professionals are very effective.
- Be concise and understandable. Have a friend or colleague read your news release for accuracy and readability.
- As a follow-up to the news release, call the editor a few days prior to the event. Don't pester the editor. Instead, let her know that you are there in case she has any questions or further comments about the press release you sent her.

Remember that, in the case of publishing, persistency is the key. What might strike an editor's eye one day might not catch it the next. Do not be discouraged if your news release doesn't get published. Instead, set yourself up as the child care expert by including two Rolodex cards (large and small) with the following:

Child Care and Early Education Expert – Your Name, Center's Phone Number/Home Phone Number, E-mail and Web Site address.

Most editors have a working rolodex by subject. They will put your card under "Child Care and Early Education," and the next time they have a child care question or a story they are writing, they may look on the Rolodex and find your name.

Developing a Niche

Webster's Dictionary defines niche as "a place or position particularly suitable for the person or thing in it." In defining your marketing niche, it is necessary to know your product – the kind of early care and education services that you offer your community–and to whom you target these services. The competition study defined in Competency II will also assist in determining your marketing niche. Understanding the differences in services, hours, curriculum, etc. will aid you in the development of your marketing plan.

"The aim of marketing is to know and understand the customer so well that the product or service fits him and sells itself. Ideally, marketing should result in a customer who is ready to buy. All that should be needed, then, is to make the product or service available." (Peter Drucker)

Choosing the Best Strategy

The purposes of marketing, advertising, and public relations are to increase enrollment at your center. Increasing your enrollment demands that you find a way to convince parents to select your center, and once they have selected your center, that they remain with you until they no longer need your services.

In-House Methods

So what marketing strategy is the most effective and least costly? In-house methods are the most cost effective; they are methods that increase your business because of the high quality services you offer. Word of mouth referrals are a complement to you and to your staff and say that are doing a very good job. You can encourage word of mouth by giving parents referral coupons or tuition discounts and, of course, providing good customer services and quality early childhood services.

If you have a web site, you may want to include a spot for the visitor to tell you how they found your site. If the visit is a result of a parent referral, arrange to give the referring parent a tuition credit if the new parent enrolls her child.

Other in-house methods include parent advisory boards, newsletters, suggestion boxes, and center evaluations. Special events can be a rewarding strategy that generates community awareness. For example, a safety fair or marionette show could be offered to the entire community. These events can create new interest in your center and educate the community about quality child care.

Out-of-House Methods

Out-of-house strategies can be more financially rewarding but also are typically more expensive to execute. For example, advertising in the Yellow Pages is costly but the return on investment is good. Other types of out-of-house marketing include bill board signs, internet, newspaper advertisements, press releases, TV, and radio advertising.

In evaluating your marketing, advertising, and public relations strategy options, it is beneficial to understand how parents select a center. *Child Care Information Exchange* magazine analyzed ten studies on the center selection process and discovered parents felt staff characteristics (e.g., loving, caring, patient, responsible) and logistics (cost, convenience of location, hours of service) were the most important factors in deciding on a center.

In Paul Haukens' book, *Growing a Business*, he contends that "To grow, your business (one) must earn the permission of the marketplace. . . the customer must give your business permission to sell to him." Mr. Haukens further espouses: "You should want to shop at the store you run or receive the services you offer. Every expression of the business–its ads, decor, service, packaging, pricing, and selling techniques–should be 100 percent credible, respectable and acceptable to you." It is only then that you will earn the permission of the marketplace; it is only then that your marketing program will become successful.

An Effective Administrator Manages the Response to Parental Inquiries Including Defining the Role of All Staff in Marketing, Handling Phone Calls and Tours, and Managing a Waiting List

"Sell service - Never Forget the Customer is our Employer." (Sam Walton, Founder of Wal-Mart)

If parents are going to do business with you, they must have confidence in every member of your team. When you are giving a prospective parent a tour of your center, you encourage the parent to think of the whole team rather than one individual staff member. Introduce the potential customer to all the members of the team (food service manager, transportation director, housekeeping, all staff). Then, when one member of the team is sick or leaves, there are many other people on the team who are familiar to the parent.

James B. Miller, in *The Corporate Coach,* contends that "what affects everyone can best be solved by everyone." Learning to work together and to strategize with other staff is a vital component for success. It is important to empower the front-line employees to make your parents happy. It is the teacher, not the director, who sees your clients on a twice- daily basis. They should be empowered to work, communicate and solve customers' complaints, problems and concerns. A director should assume the empowering viewpoint, which is a stance of delegation and enabling others to act. A successful center team will develop a bottom up game strategy.

The Tickler File: An Enrollment-Building System

The tickler file is a system which tickles your memory and reminds you to be persistent in enrolling new children into your center. A tickler file can be a three ring binder or a card file box. Inside the box or binder are inquiry or phone cards. Also inside are divisions of the 12 months of the year and 31 days of the month. When a parent calls, you record the information on the inquiry or phone card. If the telephone conversation occurred on September 19 and you have sent requested information, place the card after September 23. When you check the box on September 23, it will tickle your memory to follow up with that parent by inquiring if she has received the information you sent. You continue to make contact with that potential client and keep moving the card back in time. The card is a marketing wake up call reminding you to be persistent in obtaining that client. You could organize a marketing packet of letter mailers such as:

- Initial Inquiry Call: Inquiry letter informing parent of center (Includes brochure and director's business card)
- Tour Reminder: Note designed to remind parent of appointment
- Tour Follow Up Letter: Letter designed to send to parent after a tour
- New Parent Letter: Letter designed to welcome parent to the center

TOUR/ CALL Inquiry Cards

```
Date:_____ Time:_____
Person calling: _____
Names and ages of children:_____
Care needed beginning (approx date):_____
Phone # _____
Full or part time needs: _____
How they heard about our program: _____
Were they interested in a tour? _____
When they are coming by: _____ (date and time)

Are they interested in having information mailed to them? _____
Address: _____

Why are they looking for care? (just moved here, changing sites, new baby, etc.)
_____

Other: _____
Date of follow-up call: _____
Date of tour: _____
Enrollment date: _____
Reason for not enrolling: (circle one) cost  location  other: _____
```

Telephone Inquiries

The telephone is a valuable business-building tool. It is a vital link to enrolled parents, colleagues, vendors and, most importantly, prospective parents. By mastering and utilizing these telephone tips, you can become an effective telephone communicator. Julie Wassom, noted expert on marketing for early care and education makes the following suggestions.

Every Ring Counts

Callers want you to respect their time and value their business. The telephone should be picked up after the second, no later than the third ring.

No Second Chance

First impressions are powerful; you have fewer than ten seconds for parents to form a positive or negative impression about you and your center. Make every second count.

Put On a Good Phone Face

If you smile before you pick up the telephone, it reduces the chance that you will sound tired, short, or curt and increases the chance that you will have a positive conversation. Try putting a mirror or "smile note" by the phone to remind your staff.

Be Enthusiastic

Enthusiasm is contagious. Customer service experts indicate the telephone drains 30% of your energy through the transmission of the phone call. You will need to be 30% more energetic to recoup for this loss. Remember, all the caller has to evaluate us on is voice tone (enthusiastic or not?) and word choices (positive or not?).

Control the Conversation

The person who initiates the call is in control; therefore, when someone calls you, how do you get back in control? The person who asks the first question will be the person who is in control. "Thank you for calling ABC Child Care Center. How may I help you?"

Establish Rapport

Everyone has an invisible sign hanging around her neck that says, "I am important." Intersperse the caller's name in the conversation. Use "bridge building" language that conveys a message that the caller is important such as "I appreciate your phone call, Mrs. Jones".

100% Attention

Give the caller your undivided attention. If you must put your caller on hold, ask permission first. A Rule of Thumb is that you should get back to the person on hold within 30 to 45 seconds.

Listen With Both Ears

You are not going to be able to determine a caller's needs unless you know what they are. Listening is the key to success. As Irving Shapiro, past chairman of DuPont once said, "People who accomplish things do more listening than talking." Your caller needs to understand that you are not only in the business of providing care, but you are also in the business of solving a customer's problems and taking care of her needs.

Competency VII: Marketing, Advertising, and Public Relations

Take Notes

Make it a habit to take notes during the conversation (not after the conversation). Keep all of your notes in one place to avoid your desk looking like an organizational dumping-ground.

Convey Mutual Goals

Convey goals of quality care for all children and their parents.

Since a telephone call is often the first impression a prospective customer has of your center, you cannot afford sloppy telephone etiquette. Ask yourself whether any of these annoying telephone calls could have occurred in your center. The phone is answered by the infant teacher, and she cannot hear the caller because of the crying babies (and the caller wonders why the babies are crying). The caller wishes to leave a message for the director who is not available but she has to wait for the message taker to find a pencil and paper. The caller asks for the director and the answerer yells to another staff member, "Where's Ms. Jones?"

Your advertising dollars are spent for the purpose of getting potential clients to call or come into your center. If you take the total amount of money you spend in one month on advertising and divide that by the number of calls you receive in that month you will get an idea of how much that inquiry call has cost you. Don't waste your own money by missing the chance to increase your enrollment with every single call.

If any of these scenarios could be happening in your center (you might phone to find out), limit those who may answer the phone and be sure those who do are carefully trained in proper technique. You certainly don't want to lose a client before she ever visits the center.

Tours

The goal of the tour is to bond with the parent and to enroll the child at the end of the tour. Careful preparation should be given prior to the tour. For example, prepare name tags for the parent and the child or have the children make a welcome sign to hang on the classroom door.

The first step of the tour is to ascertain the parent's needs. Be ready for the parent at the front door. Greet the parent with "Good Morning. I am _____, the Director of the _____ center. I am so glad that you came to visit us today." Shake hands warmly and with a smile. The first question that you ask the parent is, "What are your needs?" Listen attentively to the answer as this will be your communication base for the entire tour. If, for example, the parent is looking for a new provider because the current provider isn't reliable, be sure to point out all the reliable features of the center. Or, if the parent is concerned about the safety of her babysitter's home, be sure to point out all the safety features including fire drills, multiple exits, wired-in smoke detectors, pull-handle fire alarms, panic hardware doors, locked medications and so forth.

Bonding with the child's teacher, classmates, and the classroom is an important part of the tour. If it is possible, take over the classroom while the teacher meets and talks with the parent and child. After all, it is the teacher who will be having the majority of interactions with the parent. It is, therefore, exceptionally important for the parent to have buy in with the person who will be providing care for her child.

An Effective Administrator Maintains Optimum Enrollment and Is Conscious of Good Customer Service

The business world has given a lot of thought to customer service. That is why we have words such as TQP (Total Quality Performance), TQM (Total Quality Measurements), PES (Performance Evaluation Systems) for the VIP (customer). Many times, in the child care industry, there is a tendency to overlook the importance of excellence in customer service.

In the child care business, where the profit margin is slim, losing even one customer can be lethal to a center's financial picture. The economics of poor service and dissatisfied customers therefore can conceivably make or break a center. Sam Walton, founder of Wal-Mart, once said, "The customer is our employer. There is only one boss–the Customer. And he can fire everybody in the company from the chairman on down, simply by spending his money somewhere else." Keeping the customer happy is not easy, but it can be done. How do you develop excellence in customer service?

Written Mission

We have already spent time discussing the importance of your mission statement. Missions are road maps and paths to success. Missions keep your corporation going in the right direction. They give you determination. Once you have a direction and dedicate yourself to it, you can go as far as you want to go. To offer quality care for children, you need a mission and the dedication to make your mission a reality.

Understanding the Needs of Parents

One way to deliver excellence in customer service is listening to your customers. Listen to what your customers want and then do your best to give it to them. When Charles Wang's family arrived in America in 1949, they had two suitcases. Now Wang, worth over $100 million in Computer Associates International stock, says that his company grew because they listened to their clients. Wang says that most computer companies sell people what they need; Wang decided to ask them what they wanted.

Wang followed the old theory of assume nothing and ask everything. Never assume that you know what your customers want. You have to ask constantly. One of the easiest ways to find out what your parents want is to ask them personally; you could conduct a parent satisfaction survey, develop a suggestion box, form a parent action council, assemble community focus groups, or develop a mail or a telephone survey.

What you want to discover is, "How are we doing? How well do we deliver what we promise? How flexible are we in meeting your individual needs? How courteous is our staff? How well do we make an effort to understand your special needs? Would you recommend us to your friends?

What difficulties do you have in reaching us with your concerns? Do you know about other services that we offer in our center?" One of the most important questions for you to ask is:

What are three changes that would make it easier for you to do business with us?

The purpose of all these questions is not just to find out what you did wrong. Of course, you want a chance to correct your mistakes. The real reason you ask these questions is to make sure you do not assume anything about what your parents want or need.

Consider the last question on the list. "What are three changes that would make it easier for you to do business with us?" You might be surprised how you could profit from the answer. One center installed phones in the infant classroom with a direct line so parents could dial immediately into the infant room. Parents are busy, working people with limited time during their work day. They do not have the time to wait for the director/secretary to make connections with the teacher and the teacher to make connections with the parent. They appreciate talking directly to the person who is responsible for taking care of their child. This also gives the teachers empowerment to deal with their clients.

Listening is the key to success. As Irving Shapiro, past chairman of DuPont said, "People who accomplish things do more listening than talking." We will be more successful if we listen more. If you understand that you are not in the business of providing care, but rather in the business of listening to the customer, solving the customer's problem and taking care of the customer's needs, you will be on the road to success.

One way to listen to parents is to conduct a parent evaluation. Barbara Batchelor, executive administrator of Day Nursery, developed a parent report card. The parents grade the child care center just like a child's report card. The report card results are used to improve existing programs, solve concerns, and generate innovative ideas.

Parent Communication Tools

It is important to understand that communication with our parents is part of our marketing endeavor and an important aspect of everyone's job. Professional communication either verbal or written conveys either positive or negative impressions. Not only do directors, teachers, and support staff communicate with parents, but the overall condition of the facility, the grounds, and vehicles communicate a message. Take a good hard look at yourself. Are you satisfied with how your communication tools may be perceived?

Below is a list of ways to communicate with parents.

Parent handbook	Weekly classroom activity notes
Mission statement	Daily classroom activity schedule
Daily schedule	Parent bulletin board
Written tuition/fee schedule	Written weekly menus
Student evaluations	Parent/teacher conferences
Parent newsletter	Open houses

Parenting classes

Community resources list

Parent Advisory Committee

Parent library

Posted notices

Children's art work

Staff Satisfaction Creates a Good Business Climate

It is important for staff to be happy with their jobs, since they are the first line of defense for our centers. One way is to develop a survey or questionnaire which asks staff to rate morale and job satisfaction. Michael Gilliland, founder of Libby Cook, developed an employee satisfaction survey which called for a number grade ranging from awful to wonderful or "remarkably bad to terrific." According to Gilliland, the language keeps the survey from being boring and encourages an upbeat attitude towards evaluations. The survey yields a Happiness Index which, according to Gilliland, shows whether the staff morale is giddy or suicidal.

Gilliland uses the information gleaned from the staff satisfaction survey to initiate new programs. In fact, Gilliland sets aside $200 for each employee as an annual wellness allowance which the employees can use for any form of mental or physical health. Gilliland and his company, Libby Cook, feel the surveys are successful since turnover has declined since their inception.

Ten Commandments of Good Business

Joe Griffin's book, *Speaker's Library of Business: Stories, Anecdotes & Humor*, outlines the ten commandments of good customer service. He notes that clients are:

1. The most important people in any business
2. Not dependent on us–we are dependent on them
3. Not interruptions of our work–they are the purpose of it
4. Doing us favors when they call–we are not doing them favors by serving them
5. Part of our business–not outsiders
6. Not cold statistics–they are flesh-and-blood, human beings with feelings and emotions like our own
7. Not someone with whom to match wits
8. People who bring us their wants–it is our job to fill those wants
9. Deserving of the most courteous and attentive treatment we can give them
10. The lifeblood of this and every other business

Summary

In order to show competency in marketing, advertising, and public relations, an effective administrator:

- Maintains optimum enrollment and is conscious of good customer service
- Manages the response to parental inquiries including defining the role of all staff in marketing, handling phone calls and tours, and managing a waiting list
- Maintains a professional program image through written, verbal, and visual communication with parents and the community

If you feel you lack confidence in any of the skills listed above, please go back and review the appropriate section of this chapter.

Competency VIII

Financial Management

Competency VIII

Financial Management

Learning Objectives:

- To gain confidence in understanding the differences between fixed and variable expenses, and between deviation analysis and break even analysis

- To be able to write a budget

- To understand how to accurately project, analyze, and report income and expenses

- To be able to manage payroll, benefit, and leave policies

- To be able to schedule your staff to assure adequate supervision

- To understand how to develop an employee compensation package

- To be able to provide incentives to attract and maintain quality staff

- To understand how to figure your true cost of providing care

- To be able to purchase effectively and efficiently

- To gain confidence in finding funding sources other than tuition fees

Competency VIII: Financial Management

An Effective Administrator Understands and Uses Financial Tools and Concepts Including Budget, Fixed and Variable Expense, Cash flow, Deviation Analysis, Staffing Plans and Breakeven Analysis

If you run a not for profit enterprise or a for profit enterprise, you must pay close attention to your finances. Inattention to financial detail may make or break you. This competency is to aid you in understanding budgeting and its importance in the overall operations of your center.

Definitions

The following definitions are a few of the financial or accounting terms listed in the glossary portion of the basic accounting text found in the reference CD handed out with this text.

- Balance sheet - a financial statement that presents a firm's assets, liabilities and owners' assets at a particular point in time
- Assets - the economic resources owned by an entity which have probable future benefit
- Accounts receivable - amounts due from customers for sale of services that have not yet been paid
- Liabilities - amounts owed by an entity to others
- Accounts payable - amounts due to suppliers relating to goods or services the company has purchased and not yet paid
- Net worth - the difference between the assets and liabilities
- Cash basis - an accounting approach where revenue is recorded when cash is received, no matter when earned, and expenses are recognized when paid, no matter when incurred
- Accrual basis - an accounting approach whereby revenues are measured and recorded as earned, not necessarily as received, and expenses are recorded as incurred not when paid
- Amortization - the process used to allocate costs of an intangible asset to the accounting periods being benefited (Good Will would be an example of this.)
- Depreciation - used to allocate the cost of property to the accounting periods being benefited
- Cash - items acceptable to a bank for deposit and free from restrictions to satisfying current debts; includes coins, currency and bank deposits
- Chart of accounts - a listing of all the accounts of an entity, along with any identification coding

- Expenses - costs incurred to produce revenues

- GAAP - generally accepted accounting principles-that is the rules, practices and procedures that define the proper execution of accounting

- General Ledger - a record of the accounts comprising financial statements and their respective balances

- Income statement - a financial statement that summarizes the revenues, expenses and results of operations for a specified period of time

- Working capital - the difference between current assets and current liabilities

Before we enter into an analysis of these financial tools and concepts, it will be helpful to have a sample financial statement to refer to as a part of the learning experience. On the next pages you will find two samples of income (profit and loss) statements. The second sample is set up for you to use in budgeting.

An income statement or profit and loss statement is a financial statement summarizing the revenues, expenses and results of operations over a specified period of time. Items such as tuition, grants, registration fees and fund raising represent potential sources of income.

The expense part of the statement similarly represents the current accounting period and the year-to-date expense for each category. The difference between the income the center has generated and the expenses that have been incurred to achieve this level of income is considered the profit (or loss) of the program. In a non-profit program, the same type of reporting would be important, but instead of considering the surplus of income over expense as a profit, it is considered a surplu*s*. Similarly, a loss for a private for-profit program would be equivalent to a defici*t* in a non-profit program. Let's look at several tools that are commonly utilized in the effective financial management of a child care center.

Budgets

On a personal level, most people set up a budget for themselves in which they balance the amount of money they earn versus the amount of money they need to spend. The same concept is important in an early care and education program.

Budgets for early care and education centers are forecasts of what is expected to be earned and spent over a certain period of time. Typically an annual budget, divided into the twelve monthly periods, is created for each category of income and expense appearing on the income statement. The monthly forecast of the revenue and expense budget lines, which occur on a monthly basis; such as tuition, payroll, rent, and utilities is relatively easy to project. Other expense and revenue budget lines require a forecast of budget lines which may occur on a quarterly, semiannual or annual basis. Various accounting software programs are available to allow the user to enter the amount in the appropriate spot while the program performs all of the mathematical functions.

The forecast of a twelve month budget plan of projected income and expenses lines allows for a comparison to the actual performance of the center to the amount that was budgeted. In fact, many formats of income statements actually show the current and year-to-date performance as compared to the amounts that were budgeted.

A properly prepared budget will provide a road map for the financial performance of the center. It will change as the year progresses if the previously forecasted amounts are no longer valid. In many businesses, budgets are revised every three months on a floating twelve-month basis. This allows the business managers a realistic comparison for the analysis of the business.

Budget 1/1 - 12/31, 2019
XYZ Child Care Center

INCOME		
	Monthly	*Annual*
Tuition	23,000	276,000
Registration	220	2640
CACFP	2,000	24,000
CCDBG	5,000	60,000
TOTAL	**30,220**	**362,640**
EXPENSES		
Salaries/Wages	16,500	198,000
Payroll Taxes	2,400	28,800
Fringe Benefits	300	3,600
Office Supplies	50	600
Educational Materials	200	2,400
Utilities	700	8,400
Refuse Collection	75	900
Rent	4,000	48,000
Repairs/Maintenance	850	10,200
Food	900	10,800
Insurance	400	4,800
Depreciation	420	5,040
Amortization	20	240
Advertising	375	4,500
Telephone	125	1,500
Dues/Subscriptions	225	2700
Permits/Fees	10	120
Postage	40	480
Payroll Preparation	45	540
Consulting	150	1,800
Legal/Accounting	75	900
Miscellaneous	100	1,200
TOTAL	**27,960**	**335,520**

Fixed and Variable Expenses

In the expense section of the income statement notice the categories of expenses.. Now challenge yourself to try to determine which of the expenses will remain the same regardless of the number of children for whom the center provides service that month. This type of expense would be considered a fixed expense. A classic fixed expense would be the rent the center owes on the facility it occupies. Take a moment to list all those expenses you believe are fixed expenses. As you are doing this exercise, keep asking yourself, "Will this expense vary based upon the amount of business the center does this month?"

Now perform the same type of analysis for those expenses which would vary depending on the number of children cared for in the month. This type of expense is called a variable expense. A simple type of variable expense would be the food cost of the program. If the center cares for ten more children this month, shouldn't the cost of providing food increase for the month?

Understanding the difference between fixed and variable costs is extremely important for the director of a center. As the program changes, you should constantly focus on controlling the costs of operating the program. The major area that you can impact is the area of variable expense where the correlations can be understood between the amount of service provided and the cost of providing this service.

The largest single area of expense in a program, and a variable cost, is payroll expense. Given the correlation between children and staff members (child/staff ratios), as the number of children increases to a level where more staff members are needed, the cost of payroll will increase. As this cost increases, the income of the center should also increase. Conversely, as children leave the center and openings occur, you will focus on payroll expense and evaluate methods of reducing this variable expense accordingly.

The bottom line... variable expenses will fluctuate depending on the level of service that is being provided. It's easy to increase expenses as revenue increases. The effective director is one who also understands the critical need to attack the variable expenses when revenue decreases.

Cash Flow

In various parts of this section, we have considered the income and expenses of a center. An important aspect of this equation is the consideration of the cash flow of the program. In simple terms, this means the timing of the cash (income) of the center versus the expenditures (expenses) of the center.

As you develop your personal budget that we mentioned earlier, it is easy to realize that you cannot spend your wages to purchase items until you receive your paycheck. You can't go out for lunch if you have no money in your wallet and don't get paid for another three days.

The finances of the center work in the same fashion. The center needs to receive the payments from the parents and any checks from any third-party payment sources before the money can be spent to meet the expenses of the center. The timing of the receipt of monies versus the expenditures of funds is the cash flow of the program. A typical example of this issue in early care and education is the frequent delay a center may incur in the receipt of monies from third-party payment sources, such as Child and Adult Care Food Program. Frequently these payments can take up to thirty days or more to be received after the provision of care for the child. In the meantime, the program must pay the staff members, feed the children, make the rent payments, and meet the other expenses of the program.

Many times in the American economy we see small business fail due to the problems of cash flow. The business may generate enough revenue to meet the expenses, but not enough cash at the right time to meet the expenses as they are due.

As the director is considering the budget for the center that we outlined earlier, she must consider the cash flow of the program. For instance, if a major piece of equipment is budgeted for the center, be sure that the cash at that point in time will be sufficient to meet the expenditure.

Deviation Analysis

Earlier we discussed the importance of comparing the income and expenses of the program with the budget for the center. Since the budget is the plan you expect for the center, it is important to evaluate how well the center is meeting the plan.

Areas where the center is not meeting the plan, thus deviating from the budget, are critical areas needing to be thoroughly evaluated. This process is typically called a deviation analysis.

Focus on the areas of deviation and determine the reasons for the variance from the plan. It is important to realize that deviations can be either positive or negative. It is possible the income will be greater than forecasted, and the expenses will be less than planned. The deviation analysis should still be performed so you can evaluate the cause(s) for this favorable variance.

Should your program be part of a multi-center operation, or should you be responsible for reporting on the financial condition to an owner or board of directors, an effective, on-going reporting tool is a deviation analysis report that is on the same schedule as the issuance of the financial statements for the center. This allows the responsible party a quick way of identifying how the center is operating relative to initial budget. A sample deviation analysis is on the next page.

Deviation Analysis for XYC Child Care Center

Date: January 31, 2019

INCOME

	Budget Amt. YTD	**YTD**	**Actual YTD Deviation**
Tuition	138,000	136,000	<2,000>
Registration	1,320	1,400	80
CACFP	12,000	12,600	600
CCDBF	30,000	31,200	1,200
TOTAL	**181,320**	**181,200**	**<120>**
EXPENSES			
Salaries/Wages	99,000	101,400	<2,400>
Payroll Taxes	14,400	14,703	<303>
Fringe Benefits	1,800	1,843	<43>
Office Supplies	300	225	75
Ed. Materials	1,200	1,175	25
Utilities	4,200	3,700	500
Refuse Collection	450	450	0
Rent	24,000	24,000	0
Repairs/Maint.	5,100	6,125	<1,025>
Food	3,600	3,800	<200>
Insurance	2,400	2,400	0
Depreciation	2,520	2,520	0
Amortization	120	120	0
Advertising	2,250	1,180	1070
Telephone	750	770	<20>
Dues/Subscript.	1,350	1,000	350
Permits/Fees	60	0	60
Postage	240	99	141
Payroll Prep.	270	276	<6>
Consulting	900	850	50
Legal/Acct.	450	700	<250>
Miscellaneous	600	430	170
TOTAL	**165,960**	**167,766**	**<1806**

Breakeven Analysis

An on-going challenge in child care is the calculation of the proper fees to charge for caring for the children. An important part of the determination of the fees should be the analysis of what the program needs to charge to cover the expense of operating the program.

This type of analysis is commonly referred to as a breakeven analysis. In this analysis you would look at the variable and fixed expenses of the program and determine the actual cost of providing care for a child in each age group. It is important to break this down by age group as the staffing levels, and therefore the labor costs, change depending on the age of the child.

Certain expenses of the program such as rent, management, and insurance may need to be assigned to each child based upon a calculation of the total cost divided by the number of children.

As you consider the various elements of the program and you consider the various levels of service the program can offer, you can quickly see that breakeven costs will change depending on the number of children in a room and the age of the child. For example, in any one room one additional child may necessitate an additional staff person.

Most breakeven analyses that are performed assign a standard cost to each child for many of the cost elements based upon an estimate of the total expense divided by the total capacity of the center. This allows you to determine the total number of children the center must care for in order to meet the expenses of the program, or the number of children necessary to break even.

The above tools and concepts are elements of your job that will allow you to effectively evaluate the on-going financial performance of the center. As much as quality early care is the goal of everyone in the early care and education profession, a center must be properly managed through effective financial management in order to allow the program to offer the resources necessary to provide quality early care services.

Competency VIII: Financial Management

XYZ Child Care Center Consolidated Income Statement

	–CURRENT PERIOD–		—YEAR TO DATE —	
—REVENUE—	*AMOUNT*	*% SALES*	*AMOUNT*	*% SALES*
GROSS REVENUE	33000.00	100.00	376000.00	100.00
TOTAL	33000.00	100.00	376000.00	100.00
NET SALES	33000.00	100.00	376000.00	100.00
COST OF SERVICES				
SALARIES AND WAGES	16500.00	50.00	190000.00	50.53
PAYROLL TAXES	2400.00	7.27	28800.00	7.66
FRINGE BENEFITS	300.00	0.91	3600.00	0.96
OFFICE SUPPLIES	50.00	0.15	600.00	0.16
EDUCATIONAL MATERIALS	200.00	0.61	2400.00	0.64
UTILITIES	700.00	2.12	8400.00	2.23
REFUSE COLLECTION	75.00	0.23	900.00	0.24
RENT	4000.00	12.12	48000.00	12.77
REPAIRS & MAINTENANCE	850.00	2.58	10200.00	2.71
FOOD	900.00	2.73	10000.00	2.66
INSURANCE	400.00	1.21	5000.00	1.33
DEPRECIATION	420.00	1.27	5000.00	1.33
AMORTIZATION	20.00	0.06	240.00	0.06
TOTAL	26815.00	81.28	313140.00	83.28
GROSS PROFIT	6185.00	18.72	62860.00	16.72
—EXPENSES—				
GENERAL & ADMINISTRATIVE				
ADVERTISING	200.00	0.61	4500.00	1.20
TRAVEL & ENTERTAINMENT	100.00	0.30	1200.00	0.32
TELEPHONE	125.00	0.38	1500.00	0.40
DUES & SUBSCRIPTIONS	10.00	0.03	120.00	0.03
PERMITS & FEES	10.00	0.03	120.00	0.03
POSTAGE	40.00	0.12	480.00	0.12
PAYROLL PREPARATION	25.00	0.08	300.00	0.08
CONSULTING SERVICES	150.00	0.45	1800.00	0.48
LEGAL & ACCOUNTING	50.00	0.15	600.00	0.16
MISCELLANEOUS	100.00	0.30	1200.00	0.32
TOTAL	810.00	2.45	11820.00	3.14
TOTAL OPERATING EXPENSES	810.00	16.29	11820.00	3.14
NET OPERATING INCOME	5375.00	16.29	51040.00	13.57
OTHER <INCOME>EXPENSE				
INTEREST	275.00	0.83	3300.00	0.88
INCOME TAXES	300.00	0.91	300.00	
TOTAL	575.00	1.74	3600.00	0.96
NET INCOME	4800.00	14.55	47440.00	12.62

An Effective Administrator Schedules Staff Consistent with Enrollment Patterns, Involves Staff in Scheduling Decisions, and Secures and Supervises Substitutes

Payroll

Payroll is the largest expense item in an early childhood education center's budget. Not only must the director spend his teaching man hours wisely, he must be very conscious of the proper group size for children allowed under state regulations or accrediting body. To staff successfully one must evaluate the number of children by age group and the time they will be at the center. It is then possible to ascertain the actual number of staff members needed at any one time. To help insure the center offers a quality program, a consistent, qualified staff should be your goal. Good staff are attracted and retained with competitive wages, benefits and professional working conditions.

As the annual budget is developed, you must calculate realistic salary projections to reflect current staff at present wages, new staff at entry level rates, and increases that will occur with annual staff reviews or in accordance with predetermined wage increase schedules. You can equate man hours with actual money to spend. If you spend more on a given day than you have been allotted, there will be less to spend in the future. Thus, a good director watches her man-hour expenditures very carefully, cutting back where it is feasible in order to add hours later when they are needed. Be prudent in order to maintain proper pupil/teacher ratios at all times while staying within your budget. Budgeted man-hour requirements may have to be adjusted if there is a dramatic shift in enrollment. At some point additional children will mean more hours needed to serve them, and if that occurs, the budget should be adjusted accordingly. A drop in enrollment will also require a budget adjustment.

Staffing

Maintaining a smooth operating early care and education program requires appropriate staffing, proper pupil/teacher ratios and careful budgeting. State licensing regulations establish minimum ratios of staff to child depending on children's age. These guidelines reflect the minimum requirements. The center may choose to provide a higher standard.

Staffing pattern work sheets should reflect the number of hours the center is open by classroom and the number of children coming, staying, and going within a time period. The coming and going of children is best calculated in either 30 or 60 minute intervals. By knowing the number of children present and staff needed, it is then easy to project budget expenditures for staff. Include in your budget auxiliary personnel such as the cook, bus driver, etc.

Scheduling

Developing a staff schedule depends on the number of children present at different times of the day. Children do not all come or leave at the same time, so the need for staff will vary equally. Conduct counts several times during the day to obtain an accurate accounting of the number of children present in each classroom at varying intervals to make a valid decision of the number of staff needed at a given time.

Each classroom must be covered from opening to closing unless multiple age groups are combined for short periods of time at the beginning or end of each day. Plan for adequate staff to come to work in the early morning and balance their departure times with staff coming in later in the morning and staying until closing. The goal is to staff according to center ratio requirements but not over staffed when fewer children are present. Plan for support personnel needed to relieve teachers for breaks and lunches.

When deciding on the number of staff persons needed, take into account the hours each person will work. Most centers are open 10 to 12 hours each day. Working with children is emotionally and physically demanding so it is wise to schedule breaks for the staff during the work day.

When hiring new employees, always check on their availability to work varying or altered schedules and make it clear that the employee is not hired for a particular class but may be asked to work with various age groups. Seek input from long-term staff on their continued availability and reward their tenure with first choice of work schedules. When hiring college or vocational students, be aware that their availability to work may vary due to their changing class schedules. Thus the master work schedule for the entire center may have to be revised every few months to accommodate changing staff availability.

Establish policies that require your employees to schedule vacations and planned absences well in advance to give time to secure substitute staff. Proper pupil/teacher ratios must be maintained regardless of absences or vacations. Keep a large monthly calendar in your office where you can record teacher's approved request for a planned absence. Vacations should be requested and approved on a seniority basis and should be listed on the calendar like planned absences. If there are certain days or weeks when the center cannot permit vacations, write those dates on the calendar as well. Typically, the week after public school ends and the week before public school resumes are times when enrollment is highest, and these are not good weeks to have the staff out for any reason.

There are times when illness and family emergencies may occur making scheduling staff a juggling act for the director. Teachers cannot always plan for these situations and notify you in advance. For this reason you have to cultivate and maintain an active substitute list of people who are willing to work on an as-needed basis. Treat substitutes as regular employees in terms of employee requirements. Keep a complete personnel file, including a criminal records check, on each substitute. All substitutes should go through the regular center orientation program and they should be required to complete necessary professional development training as required by state regulations. You will need to monitor substitute staff in the same manner as regular staff to insure compliance with company policy and procedure and to ensure quality delivery of the center's program.

Developing a substitute list can be difficult at times since most people who are interested in employment are seeking full-time positions. One possible way to have at least one guaranteed substitute available at all times is to employ a person to work as a floater - a staff member with no specific classroom assignment who works wherever he is needed in the center. This person would be hired knowing, however, he would be given a preference for the first full-time position that comes available. Then if he chooses to accept the full-time position, a new floater would be hired. This option does not always satisfy the need for substitutes, but it does make someone available for short-notice, emergency staff situations.

In addition to the teaching staff who work directly with the children, you will make decisions regarding other personnel necessary to maintain a smooth center operation. These people include food service personnel, a secretary/bookkeeper, and a custodian. Include these positions in planning the master center work schedule and include their man hours in budget considerations.

Sample Schedule

The following sample daily schedule is based on a center that is open from 6:00 a.m. to 6:00 p.m., Monday through Friday. This center maintains ratios in accordance with requirements set forth by hypothetical state regulations

INFANTS (8 children in the group)

State Ratio	Staffing Pattern
4 Children: 1 Teacher	Teacher A - 6:00 - 3:00
	Teacher B - 8:30 - 5:30
	Teacher C - 3:00 - 6:00 Part time

TODDLERS (1 Year Olds) (8 children in the group)

4 Children : 1 Teacher	Teacher A - 6:00 - 3:00
	Teacher B - 8:30 - 5:30
	Teacher C - 3:00 - 6:00 Part time

TWO'S (10 children in the group)

5 Children : 1 Teacher	Teacher A - 6:00 - 2:00
	Teacher B - 8:00 - 5:00
	Teacher C - 2:00 - 6:00 Part time

THREE'S (20 children in the group)

10 Children: 1 Teacher	Teacher A - 7:00 - 4:00
	Teacher B - 8:30 - 5:30

FOUR'S (20 children in the group)

10 Children : 1 Teacher	Teacher A - 7:00 - 4:00
	Teacher B - 8:30 - 5:30

SCHOOL AGERS (15 five-year-olds and 20 six-years-old and older)

15 Children : 1 Teacher (5's)	Teacher A - 2:30 - 6:00 – works with five-year-olds
20 Children : 1 Teacher (6+)	Teacher B - 2:30 - 5:30 – works with six-year-olds +

An Effective Administrator Manages Payroll, Benefit, and Leave Policies, and Develops a Compensation Structure that Rewards Retention and Increased Knowledge and Skills of Staff

A stable well trained staff has been closely correlated with high quality child care. It is to the center's benefit to retain excellent teachers. One way to do this is through the benefit and compensation structure of the center.

Benefits

Benefits have been traditionally lacking in the field of early childhood education; however, this should not prevent you from giving serious consideration to developing benefits for your staff. Benefits must be planned for in the budget process and may need to be implemented gradually. For example: If you do not give paid vacation or holidays, implement two or three in your next budget cycle. Implementation of paid holidays may be followed by a paid vacation or leave structure or medical insurance etc. All of these expenditures are part of your staff's compensation package and contribute to determining the true cost of care for children attending your center.

Paid holidays are benefits that generally include: New Year's Day, Independence Day (July 4th), Labor Day, Thanksgiving Day, and Christmas Day. Other possible paid holidays to consider are: Hanukkah, Friday after Thanksgiving, Christmas Eve, a floating birthday holiday or professional leave day. Vacations can be granted as the employer chooses. Possibilities include one week's paid vacation after one year employment; two weeks paid after two years; three weeks paid after ten years, etc. Offer vacations on a seniority and/or first come basis and allow them to be taken at a time that is mutually convenient for the employee and the center.

Free or reduced child care may be a benefit offered to eligible employees. Be sensitive to employees who do not have children and provide pay incentives or additional benefits of equal value to equalize the total benefit package for all employees. A cafeteria benefit plan is one way to do this. In a cafeteria plan all employees are given a dollar value for their benefits and they may select how they wish to use those dollars from a variety of possible benefits - child care, health care, life insurance, etc. Remember to calculate the cost of this benefit just as you calculate other costs.

Some programs give automatic raises based on years employed and then give merit raises on top of these. Others give bonuses or additional paid vacation for certain employment milestones such as one year, five years, ten years, etc. This encourages employee loyalty.

Earlier we discussed the importance of encouraging your teachers to seek on-going professional development and additional training, and we mentioned the incentive of a paid personal day off for completing certain training programs. You might also reward teachers who complete long-term, difficult programs such as the CCP or CDA credentials with pay raises.

Developing a career ladder for employees is another way to do this. As you develop your career ladder include increased responsibility with new titles and pay increases. Pay increases should be given on an annual or semi-annual basis to coincide with your employee reviews.

Compensation

Determine your pay scales for each year worked, education, degree or number of training hours and publish this information in your employee handbook or policies. This way, every employee will have their own focus and all will be treated the same.

When a new employee is hired by the program, you and the new employee should agree upon an entry-level pay rate. This pay rate should be written on the employment agreement, and both you and the employee should sign the agreement. Advise the employee of the program's procedure for recording time worked. This may be done by completing time cards, punching time clock, or simply checking on an attendance roster if the employee is salaried. Salaried personnel are paid at a set rate regardless of hours worked, although overtime rules may or may not apply. Hourly personnel should have their time indicators totaled each week and you clarify any discrepancies between time hours recorded and work hour assigned before submitting the time sheets for payroll processing. If time sheets are changed, both the employer and the employee should initial the changes.

Maintain payroll records on each employee to determine the tax liabilities of each individual. Regardless of the type of bookkeeping system used, the records must be permanent, accurate, compete and must clearly establish income, deductions, credits, employment information, and anything else specified by federal, state, and local regulations. The law does not specify any particular records, only that they be complete.

Income Tax Withholding Records

To help maintain an efficient bookkeeping system, the following guide to income tax withholding records required by federal law should be kept.

- Name, address, and social security number of each employee
- Amount an date of each payment of compensation
- Amount of wages subject to withholding in each payment
- Amount of withholding tax collected from each payment
- Reason that the taxable amount is less than the total payment
- Statements relating to employees' non-resident alien status
- Market value and date of non-cash compensation
- Information about payment made under sick-pay plans
- Withholding exemption certificates
- Agreements regarding the voluntary withholding of extra tax

Competency VIII: Financial Management

WEEKLY TIME SHEET

Name of Employee _____ For Week Ending _____,
20_____
Department _____ Exemptions
_____

Day of Week	Morning		Afternoon		Overtime		For Office Use Only	
	IN	OUT	IN	OUT	IN	OUT	REGULAR HOURS	OVERTIME HOURS
MONDAY								
TUESDAY								
WEDNESDAY								
THURSDAY								
FRIDAY								
SATURDAY								
SUNDAY								
TOTALS								

Employee Signature _____
    Date _____
Signature of Person
Authorizing Overtime _____

No person is permitted to work overtime without special authorization.

This time sheet must be personally completed and signed by employee.

Competency VIII: Financial Management

Payroll Recording Sheet

NAME:_____ PAYROLL:_____

SS NUMBER_____

ADDRESS:_____

DATE	GROSS	WAGES	TIPS	FICA	FED. TAX	ST. TAX	NET
1							
2							
3							
4							
5							
TOTAL							
1							
2							
3							
4							
5							
TOTAL							
1							
3							
4							
5							
TOTAL							
QTR. TOTAL							
1							
2							
3							
4							
5							
TOTAL							
1							
2							
3							
4							
5							
TOTAL							
1							
2							
3							
4							
5							
TOTAL							
QTR. TOT.							
YRLY TOT.							

An Effective Administrator Understands the Concepts of Income Projection and Pricing Strategies, the Effect of Discount Policies, and Full Time Equivalent Enrollment

In the previous section we discussed the importance of developing budgets for the program and projecting the income and expenses for the program on a monthly and annual basis.

As projections for the income of a center are developed, consideration must be given to the proper prices to be charged for the various levels of service. For example, should the charge for providing infant care at a staff level of four to one be the same as the care for a five year old at a staff level of ten to one? Granted, a number of other factors must be considered such as food consumption, the amount of space necessary to provide the care, the qualifications of the staff members, and so on, but the basic question remains ... what price should be charged for the provision of each level of service?

You must explore the various levels of service, and the effect on the total income of the center for each level of care. Other factors which must also be considered are the rates in the marketplace and the demand for certain levels of care. It is important to keep in mind the rate the other centers charge as a guideline. If your cost of operating is higher than the other centers, then you cannot afford to try to match the price. The prices your center charges must be based to a great degree on the income you need to generate to meet your financial needs.

Pricing Strategies

Following are some of the issues that must be considered in the establishment of prices for a center.

Cost of Providing Care

This should be the basic factor considered before any other elements are even contemplated. You must cover your cost of providing the care or your center will not be around for very long.

Competitor Rates

It is important to know what the approximate fees are in your demographic market. Consider whether your rates will be higher or lower than the rest of the market and whether you can justify this difference. Do not make the mistake many programs make of setting their fees by what others charge. Each center is unique with special circumstances and costs.

Age Groupings

This is the issue that we mentioned earlier relative to the need to vary prices depending on the age of the child. Your costs differ by age of the child, so your prices should also differ.

Market Demand

This is the age-old axiom of supply and demand. The prices of the center should be modified depending on the availability of the specific type of care in the immediate market. For example, if there is a shortage of infant care, your center should be able to increase the price for providing infant care because the market demand is greater than the supply of care.

Hours of Care

This refers both to the time care is provided, and the length of time care is provided. For example, if your center provides care for both first and second shift, the rates may change depending on the time service is provided. Also, the length of the care day must be determined as a part of the pricing calculation. A child receiving care for four hours should not necessarily be charged the same rate as a child receiving care for nine hours.

Frequency of Care

Should a child who receives care for five days per week pay the same daily rate as one who only attends the center for two days per week? Normally, centers charge increased rates for part-time attendance.

Special Services Provided

Many centers offer additional services to children which may or may not be included in the basic rate. Examples of this would be transportation services, special diets, music lessons, and so on. Consideration should be given to charging user fees to those children who avail themselves of the extra services.

Discount Policies

Many centers offer various discounts that may or may not be economically sound. For example, many centers offer discounts for multiple children from the same family. This policy may be economically sound for a center needing to attract children, but it is not economically sound for a center with a waiting list in the applicable age groups. The family discount simply reduces the revenue the center could receive by providing care to other children.

A similar discount policy also applies in many centers to children of staff members. Although this may be an excellent way to attract personnel for the program, it reduces the revenue of the center, especially if the program has waiting lists for the space the discounted child is filling.

Examine your policies regarding parent vacation. Some centers allow families up to two weeks a year without paying when parents take a vacation. Before implementing such a policy examine your expenses and determine if you can afford to have such a policy. How many of your costs continue whether the child is or is not at your center? Can you replace the missing revenue with revenue from another child? Is the vacationing parent being paid?

Discounts can be effective if directed to accomplish a specific goal (e.g., to attract additional children from the same family) or to entice employees from one employer to choose your center, or to attract the personnel you need to staff the center. The director should frequently evaluate the pricing policies to insure they logically meet a defined need.

Full-Time Equivalent Enrollment

Early care and education centers all deal with the issues of maximum licensed capacity, and therefore, a limit on the amount of revenue a center can generate. For example, suppose our Center has a licensed capacity of 100 children.

An enrollment audit to determines the actual enrollment for the center, they find that they are providing care to 25 children on a three-times-a-week basis. The full-time child is considered to be enrolled for five days each week, the part-time child represents three-fifths of a full-time student. On this basis, three-fifths of the 25 total part-time children are equivalent to 15 full-time children. This full-time equivalency is based upon the amount of time the children are enrolled.

Another way to look at the full-time equivalency of students is to consider the equivalency on an income basis. Let's assume a full-time child is charged $100 per week for care. There is a policy of charging part-time children a daily rate which has been established at $25 per day.

The 25 part-time children are each enrolled for three days per week. Therefore, each child pays $75 per week for child care. The total revenue for these part-time children is $1875 per week. Since a full-time child pays $100 per week for care, it would take 18.75 full-time children to generate this much revenue.

As you can see, on a basis of enrollment, the 25 part-time children are equivalent to 15 full-time children, while on an income basis they represent 18.75 children. It is important the director understands each of these concepts. The enrollment basis may be important for certain licensing requirements or insurance calculations, and the income equivalency should be used to develop budgets and projections.

Definitions:

Cost Per Child Analysis - Age group services divided by the number of children enrolled

Break-even Point - Number of children needing to be enrolled (per age group) in order to meet expenses

Tuition Setting - Expenses per room plus overhead divided by the number of children enrolled in room

---

An Effective Administrator Maintains Accurate and Complete Financial Expenditure Reports

An important part of the responsibility for financial control of the early care and education center is proper reporting and record keeping of deposits and expenditures. In the area of deposits, duplicate deposit receipts (or check listings) should be maintained allowing you to track deposits at a later date. For example, suppose a family pays the center by check, and disputes the balance in their account a month after the deposits were made. You need a way to verify the receipt of their check, and a record of the amount of the check.

Depending on the size of the program, consider maintaining two separate checking accounts - one for the accounts payable and one for payroll. This will give you a better audit trail for funds expended, while making the process of check reconciliation (account balancing) much easier.

As you perform the process of paying the bills owed, known as the accounts payable, keep a record of the amount paid on an annual basis to each vendor. If the vendor is not a corporation, the center has a legal obligation to provide the vendor with a Federal tax form (1099) if the payments to the vendor exceed $600 in a calendar year.

In addition to the tracking of payments to vendors, the bills should be coded (charged) to the proper expense accounts reflected on the financial statements of the center. If your program is new, or if proper financial controls are not in place, consult your accountant to establish proper accounting practices.

On a periodic basis, preferably monthly, the checking accounts need to be balanced - a process known as reconciliation. The person responsible for the accounts should verify the check amounts are the same as charged against the bank account. Deposits should be verified to insure they were credited to the bank account in the proper amount.

If one person at the center has the responsibility for making the deposits and writing the checks, that person should not be perform the reconciliation. By having a second person involved, produces a level of control or balance. This should not be considered an insult to either party, but simply a matter of proper financial management.

Should the program be fortunate enough to have excess cash not needed to meet current bills, consider the type of bank account used to gain interest on the money. Depending on the type of legal structure of the program, certain accounts may not be available. Consult your center's accountant and the bank manager for their recommendations for the arrangements that best meet the needs of the center.

Sample Statement: Early Education and Care Center–First and Main Streets–Anywhere, USA

INCOME AND EXPENSE STATEMENT

From   To

Budget Category	Budget Item	Formula	Amount
100	**Administrative and General Costs**		
101	Salaries plus fringe		
102	Director		
103	Book keeper		
104	Other		
105	Audit/Legal		
106	Office Equipment		
107	Office Furniture		
108	Postage		
109	Phone		
110	Insurance		
111	Travel		
112	Advertising/Marketing		
113	Office Supplies		
114	Printing		
200	**Facility Management**		
201	Rent/Mortgage		
202	Utilities		
203	Water		
204	Electricity/gas		
205	Trash		
206	Custodial services		
207	Cleaning supplies		
208	Grounds/landscaping		
209	Building Maintenance		
300	**Classroom/Programming Costs**		
301	Teacher Salaries plus fringe		
302	In service/professional development		

Competency VIII: Financial Management

303	Classroom supplies		
304	Classroom Furniture and equipment		
305	Field trips		
400	**Food and Nutrition**		
401	Cook salary/fringe		
402	Food supplies		
403	Kitchen equipment		
404	Food service equipment		
500	**Admissions and Parent Services**		
501	Newsletters		
502	Parent handbook		
503	Forms		
504	Parent Education		
505	Classroom meetings		
506	Family events		
600	**Transportation**		
601	Driver salaries/fringe		
602	Vehicle rentals/purchase		
603	Maintenance		
604	Insurance		
605	Operation (gas/oil)		
700	**Health and Safety**		
701	Health and safety supplies		
702	First aid kits		
703	Contracted services		
704	Screenings		
705	CPR/First Aid Classes		
800	**Miscellaneous/Other**		

Program Income

Source	Formula	Amount
Tuition		
Infants		
Toddlers		
Preschool		
School age		
Registration		
Supplemental fees (supplies/Curriculum)		
Tuition Supplements		
Grants		
Fundraising		
Donations		
Other		
Total		

Start-up Budget

Expense	Formula	Amount
Administrative Fees		
Director salary and fringe		
Other salary and fringe		
Attorney		
Licensing fees		
Business license fees		
Rent/ Mortgage		
Facilities		
Cleaning		
Renovation		

Building		
Equipment		
Lobby		
Offices		
Classrooms		
Kitchen		
Teacher work area		
Get well room		
Playground		
Cafeteria		
Other		
Supplies		
Lobby		
Offices		
Classrooms		
Kitchen		
Teacher work area		
Get well room		
Playground		
Cafeteria		
Other		
Utilities		
Gas		
Electric		
Phone		
Water		
Trash		
Recruitment and Hiring		
Advertising/ Marketing		
Printing		
Other		

Competency VIII: Financial Management

An Effective Administrator Sets and Collects Tuition Fees in an Efficient and Tactful Manner

The first challenge for a child care center is to develop an adequate customer base. The next challenge is to collect the fees the center is owed.

It is important for you are providing a valuable service and in return a family must pay the appropriate charges. To facilitate the collection of these fees, provide the parents with a consistent, well documented payment and collection policy. This policy should state clearly when the fees are due, and what penalties will occur if payment is not made on time. Notice that the word "will" has been underlined. In this sentence we specifically did not use the word "may". It is very important the center's policies be enforced in a consistent fashion in order to protect you from accusations of favoritism at a later date.

Many centers require payment for services at the beginning of the week or at the beginning of the month. Regardless of what policy you follow, the customers should know the penalty for non-payment. For example, if payment is not received on Monday, will they be allowed to use the center? How long can they go without paying before care will be suspended? Is there a late fee for not paying on time? These policies need to be clearly communicated to the families, in writing. In fact, the payment terms should be an integral part of the parent policies, and the customers should sign a receipt that they received a copy of the policies, have read, understand and agree to follow the policies. This will protect you from the excuse, "but I didn't know."

Although you have established a firm payment policy, you may have to collect past due payments. Keep in mind you are dealing with a customer, but the customer has not lived up to his end part of the contract. It is possible the customer has simply overlooked the payment, or perhaps one parent thinks the other has paid, or they might be experiencing serious financial difficulties.

An effective method of collection is a series of collection letters that become progressively stronger. These would be sent out on a time structured basis depending on the due date of the payment. For instance, the first letter may be on the first day the payment is late, the second letter on the third day, and the last letter one week after payment is due. This type of schedule needs to be modified to meet the particular needs and policies of your program.

If a family leaves your center owing you a large sum of money, you will need to pursue the matter through collection agencies or through the courts. However, we urge you to be very firm in your collection and payment procedures. Each day a child is with you and you have not been paid, continues to cost you in staff salaries, food, and consumable supplies. The child or children may be occupying space another child could fill from your waiting list or from a family needing immediate services.

An Effective Administrator Ensures the Cost Effective Purchase of Supplies and Equipment

One of the on-going responsibilities of a director is the purchasing of supplies and equipment for the center. An effective purchasing policy can result in the improvement of the quality of the items being purchased, and a reduction in the total cost of the purchases.

The first lesson for a director to understand is that many times the ultimate cost of the item(s) being purchased can be reduced. This may not be an easy task, and it may take some time, but the results of the director's efforts can be a lowering of the operating cost for the center.

Several aspects of the purchasing process should be reviewed. Let's look at each of these items and the way that the director handles the purchasing process for the center.

Use of Multiple Sources

The world of business that supplies early care and education centers with everything from food to games is expanding rapidly as the early care industry matures and becomes more sophisticated. Many suppliers have realized that early care and education is a relatively new market offering opportunities to expand. This is true for many firms who have sold to school districts over the years.

This more competitive environment can be a great benefit to child care directors who need to purchase a large variety of items, from food to educational materials to cleaning supplies to major equipment. This can be a benefit as long as the director opens up the purchasing process to look at the products and services of a number of suppliers.

Loyalty to one supplier can be an asset to a center as the supplier becomes familiar with the particular needs of the program. However, you should occasionally solicit prices from other firms to insure prices and services are competitive. By having more than one supplier for a type of product, especially ones which are purchased frequently, you can develop a type of insurance policy should the main supplier become unable to meet your needs.

Quotes

If you were considering buying an automobile, you would probably look at several different models from several dealers. This provides you with a good understanding of the features available, and the comfort of knowing you were getting a fair deal.

The same philosophy should be taken when purchasing for the child care center. For example, the director purchases educational materials for the center each month. On the average she spends about $200 per month. In a year, this amounts to $2400 out of the budget for the center.

The director has a policy of issuing a list of materials needed for the center and the projected quantities of each item to three different suppliers every six months. She asks the suppliers to quote their best price for each item. She then purchases these items from those suppliers, trying hard to make sure that she buys something from each supplier.

She has looked back on her purchasing costs and calculated she has saved almost 10% by using this process. That amounts to $240 in a year, or equivalent to receiving an entire month's supplies free. Not only has she saved money, the director has developed a roster of suppliers who continually offer special incentives and deals in an attempt to attract more business.

Negotiable Areas of Cost

There are several areas of cost to be considered as you negotiate the purchase price of any item. For example, once the absolute price of the item has been determined, there may be a charge for shipping. Frequently, this can be negotiated, reduced or eliminated. Alternatively, depending on the location of the supplier, you may pick up the supplies, saving the shipping charge altogether. This might offer one supplier a competitive advantage over another.

Another area to be considered is assembly. This is important on furniture, large equipment, and outdoor items. Occasionally the supplier may reduce or eliminate the assembly charge, or the sales representative may offer to assist with the assembly as an incentive to make the sale. The only way for you to know if the savings are possible is to ask.

Terms and Conditions of Payment

Before you commit to purchase from a specific vendor, find out when payment is expected. Will a deposit be required? Will the supplier allow you to pay for the purchase over 30 to 60 days?

These types of options are typically negotiable, and the result of your negotiations can have an impact on the center. For example, suppose you are purchasing new chairs for one classroom because you have four new children enrolled in the center. If the supplier requires you pay for the purchase at the time of delivery, you will need to have a sufficient amount of cash available to pay for the purchase. Conversely, if the supplier allowed you to pay for the purchase in 60 days, some of the increased revenue generated from the new children could help to pay for the new chairs.

An important lesson can be learned from the above scenario. Do not be afraid to explain to the supplier, or salesperson, your use of the materials you are purchasing and any limitations or concerns you may have. The sales person cannot be expected to assist your center if he doesn't have all the information about your particular needs.

Volume Discounts/Bulk Purchasing

The concept of volume discounts is a fairly well known procedure. Suppliers will reduce the cost of the items being purchased based upon the total volume of items being purchased.

It is important to keep in mind that volume discounts are not only available for large, single purchases, but may be available based upon the expected annual purchases of the program. For instance, the director explained to the paper products supplier the projected annual volume of paper towels, toilet tissue, and paper plates for the center would be substantial. Based upon this annual volume, and the director's commitment to purchase the paper from this one supplier for the year received a 7% discount and a six free bottles of liquid soap for each of the rooms. The savings covered the cost of some other materials the director needed to purchase, and the free soap saved the center an additional $25.

In addition to volume purchasing, similar savings can be realized through the effective use of bulk purchasing. Bulk purchasing is simply the acquisition of items in large quantities allowing the supplier to realize some savings in packaging, delivery, and inventory costs. Since the supplier is saving money, some of this savings is passed on to the bulk purchaser.

The director knows that over the next six months she will use 200 reams of construction paper. The director is also fortunate that the center has a large basement area allowing for storage of large quantities of materials. As part of purchasing efforts, she notifies the educational materials supplier she will accept one large delivery of construction paper, assuming she can receive a discount for the paper, and can pay for the paper in equal installments over the next three months. Since the supplier can make one large delivery and he can free up room in his own warehouse, he offers the center a 10% discount on the purchase and the payment terms the director requested.

Buying Groups

A spin-off of the bulk purchasing concept is the formation of buying groups. These are becoming more prevalent around the nation as early care centers pool their purchases to create much larger buyers. This size then allows the groups to negotiate more favorable prices, thereby saving the members money.

Probably the most effective use of buying groups is purchasing consumables, such as educational materials and general supplies. These items are characterized by a large number of suppliers, the products are easily stored, and the volumes can be large when the buying group services a number of members.

NCCA offers a comprehensive buying program : Member Plus Point. Or ask child care associations in your area, local resource and referral agencies, or area suppliers for the names of buying groups. Thoroughly review the terms and conditions of the group and check its references before making any commitment. Should the group require a contract, have it reviewed by your center's attorney.

Warranties

Remember the previous discussion of the purchase of the automobile? You wouldn't think of buying an automobile without some type of warranty. This warranty offers you peace of mind knowing you will have some level of protection if the product does not measure up to the expected standards and some assistance if further costs are incurred to make the product perform as expected.

With certain products, the manufacturers or suppliers may be willing to increase the warranty or offer other types of additional features. It never hurts to ask.

Purchasing Authority

Depending on the size of the program, you may not be the only person who purchases items for the center. Maybe the cook is responsible for purchasing the food, the janitor purchases the cleaning materials, or the teachers have the authority to purchase some of the educational materials. There should be clearly defined in policy as to who has the right to make purchases, types of purchases and the dollar limit on purchases.

If the center is managed by a board of directors, the board should establish purchasing parameters. If the center is privately owned, the owner should detail the responsibilities of individuals; limitations and procedures for purchasing. Extensive control should be exercised, and the centralization of the purchasing functions will allow greater opportunity for price negotiations.

An Effective Administrator Identifies Federal, State, and Local Funding Sources, both Public and Private

An important aspect of the financial management of an early care and education program is the generation of revenue from alternative funding sources, such as government grants, private and public foundations and agencies. The types of funds available change frequently, so you will need to be the look-out for information on the current programs.

One possible source for information on the types of funds available would be the resource and referral agency that services your market. These organizations typically have access to current government and private programs, and many resource and referral agencies have contracts to administer private grants in the local markets.

The licensing agency in your state may have information about grant or loan programs administered by the State. Communicate your interests and needs to these representatives and ask for their assistance.

A fairly recent trend you should investigate is the development of private funding programs supported by various large employers. In many cases, access to these programs is through the employee of the company who uses an eligible early education center. Take the opportunity to ask your customers through direct contact or through your newsletter to keep you informed on any information on funding programs.

Membership in professional organizations, such as the National Child Care Association, is an excellent resource for this type of information. Contact the offices of the organization and thoroughly read their web site and publication to become versed in the latest opportunities in the early childhood education field.

Another valuable information resource is early care and education industry magazines. These magazines typically run news articles on the latest development in new programs and many times mention funding programs while discussing other related issues. The internet is also a great resource when researching grant opportunities.

The legal structure of the child care center may impact the center's eligibility for certain programs. Check into the eligibility requirements of any program before you undertake the application process.

An Effective Administrator Mobilizes Needed Resources Including the Use of Fund Raising, Unrelated Business Income, Value-added Programs, and Government Grants or Purchase of Service Agreements

In order to provide quality child care and employ the quality staff you must constantly strive to maximize the income of the program. In addition to maintaining enrollments at their optimum level, other creative approaches may be necessary.

Fund Raising Programs

Fund raising activities take almost every form imaginable, including car washes, picnics, sale of merchandise, etc. Typically, the center receives a percentage of the revenue generated from the efforts, with the remainder of the money going to the fund raising organization.

Experience has shown it is important not to overdo the fund raising efforts. Parents and/or Boards of early care and education centers may be very active assisting in the operation of a fund raiser. However, should fund raisers become too frequent, interest will decrease and results will be unfavorable. Think about scheduling fund raising activities around certain events, such as the anniversary of the center or major holidays.

There are many reputable fund raising companies that can offer the center materials and programs designed to minimize the work load on the center while generating income. Should you decide to use one of these firms, thoroughly check out their references. Ask past customers questions such as: Did the company perform as you expected? How much work did it cause to operate the program? What was the reception from the parents and the community? Would you use this company, or program, again?

Unrelated Business Income

Do not overlook any reasonable opportunity to allow the program to generate income, even if the income may not be directly related to the provision of care for the children. For example, many child care centers are well located, with open areas which make the facilities attractive to firms, organizations, or businesses that have a part-time need to rent space. For example, why not rent out the center in the evening to an aerobic class, a karate club, a civic organization, or the like? The rent produced will be additional income the center has generated in a manner which is unrelated to the provision of child care. Renting out space may open up legal questions, such as rights of unions to rent same space for union organizational activities. The use of your space for additional revenue must be considered by an attorney so that you do not inadvertently create problematic situations.

Another excellent example of utilizing the assets the program may offer is the development of birthday parties on Saturdays. The center is ideally suited to providing resources designed for children, including the low tables, proper size chairs, playground areas, and kitchen facilities. Maybe the center actually operates the parties including the scheduling of entertainment and preparation of food, or maybe the center simply rents the space with the party responsible for making all the arrangements.

Additional Value Added Program Suggestions

Additional value added programs leading to unrelated business income may be a service you offer your customers to make use of your program as an additional value. The purpose of offering these programs is to generate additional income, while providing your customer with a service that makes your program even more important to them than just providing quality early care and education. The customers typically have the option of deciding whether to use the additional service or not, and normally are charged an extra fee for the service.

Some examples of value added programs that you may want to consider are:

- Dry cleaning drop-off and pick-up
- Friday night take-home dinners
- Video rentals or sales
- Children and family photos
- Extended or after-hours care
- Equipment rental

There are undoubtedly many other items that you can think of which you may want to consider. In some cases, (dry cleaning, for example) you would be facilitating the service with the assistance of an outside firm. In the case of the meals, you may want to prepare the meals, or you may want to establish a relationship with a local restaurant or catering firm. In all cases, you are providing a convenience for your customers which should allow you to generate extra income while reinforcing with your customers the image that your child care center is responsive to their family needs.

The options are endless. Consider a brainstorming session with your staff members to discuss the potential programs that could be established. In addition, read the industry magazines to see what other centers are doing in this area.

It is important to ascertain if you need addition property and casualty insurance for these endeavors or if the entity using your space will be required to have their own property and casualty insurance. Be sure to have your attorney help you draw up a contract which should free you of liability when your center is used by another group.

Government Grants or Purchase of Service Agreements

Many centers enter into agreements with government agencies, or large employers, to allocate slots in the center to provide care to a certain number of children in return for established payments or guarantees. This allows the center to better forecast the revenue that the program will generate. Frequently, in return for the security of payment for a specific service, the center will need to accept a slightly reduced fee as an incentive for the purchasing party to enter into the arrangement.

Borrowing Money

Many child care centers, especially privately owned centers, may find it necessary to borrow money for the center. This may be necessitated because of financing needs for the business, an opportunity for a real estate associated transaction, or making an equipment purchase. The legal structure, financial history and length of time in business of the center will have an effect on your ability to borrow money. Prior to undertaking any formal borrowing program, discuss the needs with your accountant. Regardless of the reason, certain basic elements of the process should be considered:

Collateral

The bank will need some security in knowing it will receive repayment of the money it lends to the business. In most cases, it will require the business, and/or the owner, to pledge collateral to secure the loan. In real estate, this is typically the real estate itself. In a business loan, this may be the personal guarantee of the owner with the bank having the right to collect the money from the owner if the business fails to make its payments on the loan.

In lieu of collateral, some loans may qualify for certain loan guarantee programs such as those offered by the Small Business Administration (SBA). In these instances, the SBA guarantees a percentage of the total loan to the bank (90%), which allows the bank greater security in knowing that they will collect their money.

Financial Statements

Banks will look at the financial history of the center in order to determine the likelihood that the loan will be successful. Prior to approaching the bank, you should have available three years' of financial statements (assuming that the center has been open for this long). These statements should be clear, concise, and accurately represent the financial performance of the center. The statements should include both an income statement and a balance sheet for the center.

Should any of the statements demonstrate a significant variation from the normal financial performance of the center, you should provide a written explanation for the variance.

Projections

The bank will want to know what you expect the center will generate in the future, especially detailing the impact of the money the center would like to borrow. The projections should be as detailed as possible, and must represent a reasonable expectation for the program. It does not help the center, or the bank, to develop a set of projections that are unrealistic.

If possible, the projections should be presented with a detailed explanation of forecast changes which may alter the present performance of the center. For example, if the center has historically seen the income rise each year by 5%, but the projections show a revenue increase of 10%, there will need to be a strong justification for this type of performance.

Ability to Repay

This may seem rather obvious, but the bank will want to know how the loan will be repaid. The applicant for the loan must present a very plausible explanation detailing the ability to repay the loan, including how sufficient cash will be generated to meet the scheduled loan payments.

For example, suppose you would like to borrow $25,000 to fund the development of a new playground. You are currently meeting all of its bills through the child care fees that it charges, but it does not generate any additional cash on a consistent basis. Even though the playground will be very nice for the children, and the existing playground does not quite meet current safety standards, the center is currently fully enrolled so the new playground will not generate any additional revenue to the center. In this case, you would not be able to demonstrate to the bank a plausible method of repaying the loan.

Alternative Funding Sources

Banks are not the only source of outside funding to assist businesses with growth needs. Ask your accountant or attorney for suggestions. Sources such as mortgage brokers, private lenders, venture capital firms, sale/lease-back arrangements on real estate, and government-backed loan programs may be directions the center should pursue.

Summary

To demonstrate competency in financial management, an effective administrator:

- Understands and uses financial tools and concepts including budget, fixed and variable expense, cash flow, deviation analysis, staffing plans and breakeven analysis

- Schedules staff consistent with enrollment patterns, involves staff in scheduling decisions, and secures and supervises substitutes

- Manages payroll, benefit, and leave policies, and develops a compensation structure that rewards retention and increased knowledge and skills of staff

- Understands the concepts of income projection and pricing strategies, the effect of discount policies, and full time equivalent enrollment

- Maintains accurate and complete financial expenditure reports

- Sets and collects tuition fees in an efficient and tactful manner

- Ensures the cost effective purchase of supplies and equipment

- Identifies federal, state, and local funding sources, both public and private

- Mobilizes needed resources including the use of fund raising, unrelated business income, value-added programs, and government grants or purchase of service agreements

If you feel you lack confidence in any of the skills listed above, please go back and review the appropriate section in this chapter.

Competency IX

Operational Planning and Evaluation

Competency IX

Operational Planning and Evaluation

Learning Objectives:

- To know the essential elements of a business plan
- To be able to conduct an operational and financial evaluation of a program
- To understand that there are internal and external influences on early childhood education programs
- To grasp strategic planning techniques
- To understand risk management techniques

An Effective Administrator Understands and Uses Business Planning Techniques to Ensure Long Term Success of the Program and to Ensure Its Ability to Adapt to Changing Conditions

A business plan is a detailed description of your business with the added aspect of including projections and descriptions of where the business will be in the future. It should include financial information about the center and an analysis of the "outside" factors that affect the center such as regulations, competition, etc. Other necessary information is to give specific plans for the short-term and long-term operation of the center, how these plans will be achieved, current management structure including key individuals, marketing material, and any other information that will help the reader understand your business.

Therefore, your business plan defines your business, identifies your goals, and serves as your organization's resume. Frequently requested by banks and lending organizations, a business plan demonstrates that the service or product you intend to offer is needed and is realistic, and that you have the skills and knowledge necessary to carry it out. You may be seeking a loan to start a business, or expand your program. The lending institution must be convinced you will be successful enough to pay back the loan in a reasonable amount of time. Your plan must be carefully prepared and reliable. The budget you propose must reflect consistency with the narrative portion of your plan. Before you begin writing your business plan, consider four core questions:

- What service or product does your business provide and what needs does it fill?
- Who are the potential customers for your product or service and why will they purchase it from you?
- How will you reach your potential customers?
- What resources do you currently have and where will you secure other financial resources to start, expand, or operate your business?

Business Plans should include the following:

Executive Summary

This should be a brief description of your business, the market, your management team, a summary of financial projections, the amount of investment requested and how the money will be used.

A Section That Provides a Thorough Description of the Services You Will Provide

This may include history of the industry, major influences affecting the industry, short and long term goals, and your legal structure.

Marketing Plan

This should be something that shows how you will market your services including your competitive advantage.

Description of the Facilities and Equipment Required

This should include the ages and number of children you will serve, and curriculum.

Resumés

The resumés of key personnel are necessary as well as information on the anticipated needs for additional personnel.

Funding Request and How the Funds Will Be Used

This includes a projected pro-forma P & L (profit and loss statement). If you are an existing entity you may also be requested to provide a current P & L, a balance sheet, a projection of cash flow, and a personal financial statement.

An Effective Administrator Evaluates the Program and Its Components, and Uses This Evaluation to Change and Improve the Program

One proven way for any program or business to eventually fail is to rest on its laurels. Every program must continually look into itself to assess its performance and insure that it continually meets the needs of its customers.

There are basically two types of self-evaluations that a program should conduct on a periodic basis - operational and financial. In other sections of this credential process, extensive insights are provided that deal with the multitude of operational issues that are critically important to a successful program. In this section, we will deal with some tools for evaluating the program and the financial and management elements that should be considered in a thorough analysis of a center's performance.

The importance of setting goals for a center and asking every staff person to work towards those goals was discussed previously. In order to assess whether the goals are actually being met and whether the program's quality is what you want it to be, valid measurement tools can be used. There are evaluation tools which you design yourself and others that are available from outside sources.

Program Evaluation Techniques and Performance Measurements

There are five steps to choosing an evaluation tool:

- Step One: Start with a Strategy
- Step Two: Identify Your Options
- Step Three: Select the Most Appropriate

- Step Four: Plan and Implement
- Step Five: Adjust as Needed

Step One: Start with a Strategy

Total company agreement on the basics is critical. What is your mission (overall purpose); What are your goals? (desired results supporting the mission); What are your objectives? (things or tasks to accomplish in order to achieve a goal).

An overall organizational consensus on your mission, goals, and objectives are integral and mandatory to reaching your goals. Once these have been determined, they need to be articulated, written, and able to be quantitatively measured.

Step Two: Identify Your Options

In order to find your best performance measurement, discussed later in this competency, look at your options. What are your resources and your staff workload? What is the efficiency of this performance measurement? In other words, what is the amount of output (financial/time) related to the cost of producing it–and what will be the impact of it? Last, what is the time frame involved? Are you developing performance measurements for the short-term, intermediate or long term goals?

In identifying your options, it is best to seek ideas from both inside as well as outside your organization. Community Advisory Boards, parents who are experts in particular fields and association/chamber members can help you collect options and ideas.

When determining your options, answer the following questions:

- Can the performance be measured?
- What is the time frame?
- How often should the measurement be taken?
- Is the help of outside people needed?
- How feasible is the implementation?

Step Three: Select the Most Appropriate

When you are selecting your option for a performance measurement, think about reliability, simplicity and cost effectiveness. Try to choose performance measurements that let you know exactly what progress you are making and if you are working towards your objectives. Decide upon a relatively small number of measurements as too many can result in confusion and overload of information.

Before selecting an option check to see if the measurement is objective- linked or directly related to your written objectives. Is the measurement responsibility-linked? Is there someone who will be directly responsible for the project? Is the measurement organizationally acceptable? Is the measurement valued by all the staff and is there ownership in the project? Is it cost effective? Is the measurement acceptable in terms of the cost invested in the project as well as the return on the investment? Is the performance measurement easy to integrate? Is it easy to implement and will the results be easy to understand by all those involved with the project?

Step Four: Plan and Implement

The important thing in performance measurements is to take action. For example, if you decide to work toward accreditation, then plan the steps you will take and get started.

Step Five: Adjust as Needed

Frequently reevaluate your performance measurement. Remember, success is a journey, not a destination. Success in performance measurements requires calibration of the idea to be sure that the ideas you implement continue to work over time.

Financial Health

It goes without saying that the financial health of the center is of crucial concern. If the center is in debt or short of funds, both the operation and the goals must be reworked to accommodate the challenge of reduced ability to purchase supplies and provide services. If this is not done center may find itself unable to function at all.

The director must have a clear understanding of the opportunities and restrictions confronting the organization. She must monitor both external and internal factors that affect the program and know where attention needs to be directed at any one time. The new center must pay particular attention to external factors, but no center can grow and prosper without paying attention to internal issues. The well-organized director will set aside time for a monthly review of internal and external factors in order to assess priorities for the coming month.

Financial and Operational Performance Measurements

Evaluation of the center's financial and operational performance needs to be done on a regular basis. In order to allow an honest appraisal of a center, you will need to develop the skills to step back from the program and conduct an extensive, critical review of the key elements of running the center. One proven method of accomplishing this review is to complete a business profile on your own center, as if you were evaluating the program with the intention of attempting to acquire the child care business.

Imagine for a second that you were provided the opportunity to purchase a child care center. There would be a number of areas that you would want to review to make sure that the center was a good purchase and that the program had the potential of meeting the short and long term goals that you would need to establish to justify the purchase of the center. Following are some of the financial and management areas that you would undoubtedly consider as you looked at the possible center acquisition:

Detailed Analysis of the Expenses of the Center

One good way to evaluate the expenses of a program is to state the expenses as a percentage of the operating revenue. In other words, maybe payroll expense represents 52% of the operating revenue of the center. By stating the expenses in this way, it then becomes easy to compare one month versus another, or one year versus another.

Sample Profit and Loss Statement

In Section VIII there is a sample profit and loss statement which demonstrates the method of showing expenses as a percentage of revenue. By following this example, you can lay out the expenses for your own center and compare each month and/or year of your operation. Once the financial statements are developed, it is easy to see any major changes or deviations by comparing the percentages. By performing this type of analysis, you will be able to determine areas where expenses are fluctuating and perform a further evaluation to determine the reasons. In addition the percentage shown, based upon the revenue of the center, will demonstrate those areas where the expenses fluctuate based upon the enrollment (revenue) of the center.

Revenue Analysis

Any business analysis that a person would perform would always include an analysis of the revenue, or income, of the business and determining the true cost per child to operate the business. In child care, this type of income analysis is best performed by looking at a detailed enrollment analysis of the center by classroom, age, billing category, and associated costs to operate the center. This analysis will not only demonstrate what part of the program is producing the revenue, but it will show any areas where there may be a greater potential to increase enrollment.

Vacancies

As a part of this analysis, develop a detailed listing of vacancies by classroom and age grouping. It is important when doing this to remember that every hour that the center is open is potential revenue, so determine the openings in the rooms by the half-hour or whole hour. In other words, if the center opens at 6:00 am, and a specific child does not come into a particular classroom until 9:00 am, then there are three hours of child care in that classroom that may be sold to generate extra revenue for the program.

Hourly Enrollment

Once this type of analysis has been performed (demonstrating the enrollment by the hour) compare this enrollment to the staff members who are scheduled to work in each classroom for the same periods of time. In child care, the cost of labor is normally the largest expense in operating a program. A comparative analysis of this type may demonstrate areas where staff members are scheduled to work, but where they are not needed to meet the desired staffing ratios of the center. Conversely, this type of analysis may show a classroom where the enrollment justifies additional staff support. In either case, the enrollment analysis and subsequent staffing analysis will help you improve the overall financial and operational performance of the center.

Staff Stability

Child care experts agree that stability in the staff of the child care center will improve the quality of care provided to the children. In order to evaluate the amount of turnover that a center has realized, you should analyze the staff turnover for the past twelve (12) months by job title and position.

When performing this type of analysis, it is very important not to simply perform a numerical analysis of the number of employees that the program has had over the past year. The accurate analysis must look at the positions that each employee held to determine the turnover by position. For example, a center with 10 employees which during the year may have lost two employees may be said to have a 20% turnover, but if the two employees both held the same position, in the same classroom, for parts of the year, is this equivalent to a center who lost two employees but each one worked in a different room? If the evaluation demonstrates what you feel is a higher than acceptable rate of turnover, this analysis can then point the director to an area that should receive some attention.

Staff Credentials

One other area of analysis that should be performed, relative to the staff members, is the evaluation of the credentials of each person including detail on any staff members who have received recognition from a nationally recognized credentialing program such as the Certified Childcare Professional Program (CCP) of the NCAA.

Staff Cost

As was mentioned previously, one of the largest expenses in operating a child care center is the cost of the staff members. Any program review should contain a review of the wage and benefit program to insure that it is fair and continues to meet the goals of the organization.

Classroom Asset List

An excellent process for a center to undertake as a part of this self-evaluation is the development of an asset list by classroom, which details the physical assets (furniture, equipment, etc.) and the condition of the asset. Not only is this information valuable for insurance purposes, the detail by classroom may demonstrate areas where purchases may be needed in the next year to supplement existing assets or to replace certain assets that have deteriorated over time.

Policies

Be sure to review all the policies of the center including personnel, parent, and various operating policies. Look at each policy to insure it still meets the operating needs of the center and remains consistent with the center's goals. Every day new guidelines and laws are established that can impact the legality of certain policies. When reviewing staff and parent policies, seek input from your attorney or a human resources consultant to be certain you have no mistakes that could make you the subject of a suit and assure you have incorporated all new legal requirements.

Be sure the parent policies are consistent with your current services and accurately reflect the level and nature of services you provide. The employee policies of the center must be consistent with current regulations and must reflect the level of wages, benefits and employment guidelines the center provides. The operating policies of the center must be consistent with the method of operation currently in existence at the center and must comply with any regulatory requirements that may be a part of the center's licensing requirements.

Marketing

Other areas of this text have provided detailed information on the marketing of a center and the importance of understanding the competition a center may encounter. As a part of a program review, a director should develop information on any competing programs within a five mile radius, including a description of their program, ages served in the center, and various fee structures.

A self-study of a program is one of the best ways for center management to improve and prosper. As a part of this program review, insure the center continues to meet each aspect of the state's licensing requirements. If your program is accredited, your self-evaluation should include a review of the critical items considered part of the accreditation process.

We've all heard the expression, it's difficult to see the forest for the trees. A self-evaluation can be a difficult process, but one which can provide substantial rewards to the individuals and to the center. Develop a checklist for those areas of the program needing review, and conduct a critical review of the program at least once per year. Think of yourself as an outsider and look at the center the way you would if it were your money buying the center.

Once the evaluation is performed, develop action plans in those areas where changes need to be made.

SWOT

A vital step in analyzing your business plan is to perform a SWOT analysis. In this process you look at your organization in terms of its Strengths, Weaknesses, Opportunities, and Threats (SWOT). As part of your routine environmental scanning, once a year take a hard look at the opportunities and threats confronting your center. You may want to do this over a night or two at the center, or better yet, by finding a retreat location where you can do this over a series of days. Pull together a diverse group of parents, teachers, and friends who are committed to the success of your center and who bring to the table a wide variety of perspectives and skills.

Start by brainstorming long lists of trends and events occurring in the nation and in your community (don't worry at this point whether they will have an impact on your center). After you have compiled a long list, go through the list and cross off those that will not have the remotest impact on your center.

For those that remain, whether they will represent a threat or an opportunity (some may be both). Next, by whatever means works for your group, identify the five threats and the five opportunities which are likely to have the biggest impact on your center.

Now comes the fun part. Take each of the five threats and brainstorm strategies for heading them off. Then look at the five opportunities and brainstorm strategies for taking advantage of them. The resulting compilations of strategies should give you, the director, a springboard for ongoing planning.

Below is an example of a SWOT analysis.

Mission Statement

The ABC Early Age Care and Education schools strive to maintain the highest standard in Early Age Care and Education for children from six weeks to six years old. We provide a safe, loving, educational environment that is intellectually stimulating with a uniquely innovative Early Age interactive learning curriculum.

SWOT Analysis:

Marketing
Strengths
Weaknesses
Opportunities
Threats

Facilities
Strengths
Weaknesses
Opportunities
Threats

Capacity
Strengths
Weaknesses
Opportunities
Threats

Human Resources
Strengths
Weaknesses
Opportunities
Threats

Finance
Strengths
Weaknesses
Opportunities
Threats

Quality
Strengths
Weaknesses
Opportunities
Threats

Government Regulations
Strengths
Weaknesses
Opportunities
Threats

Risk Management
Strengths

Weaknesses
Opportunities
Threats

Created Strategies to Support the Future Vision of the Program
(capitalize on strengths –overall themes and strategies- not how and when)
314

Implementing Action Plans
1. Time Table
2. Responsible Person
3. Staff Qualifications
   a. By the year 2010 100% of supervising staff will have an ECE or related field BA degree with a minimum of 30 ECE credits.
   b. By the year 2010 100% of assistant staff will have an AA in ECE or related field with 18 credits in ECE.
   Staff Development
   Supervising staff will join, attend or become involved in a professional growth and development activity
Child Observation/Curriculum/Assessment
   a. Continue and complete by 8-08 the professional development workshops on Conscious Discipline and full implementation into the classrooms
   b. ERS professional development for supervising teachers within 3years
   c. Child tracking for 2 years past graduation from ACW
   d. Differentiating instruction for ongoing child assessment
Community Resources and Family Involvement
Parent forums 3-4 times per year
Director Development
Director Credential by 2008

An Effective Administrator Understands and Uses Strategic Planning Techniques to Ensure the Long Term Success of the Program, and to Ensure Its Ability to Adapt to Changing Conditions

Strategic Planning

Strategic planning can be used to determine mission, vision, values, goals, objectives, roles and responsibilities, timelines, etc. The plans you put into place to insure the long-term viability of the center should encompass all operating and financial areas of the program. Taking time to develop a strategic plan will give members of management a:

- Tool to help an organization do a better job

- Formulation of the organization's future mission in light of changing external factors such as regulation, competition, technology, and customers

- Competitive strategy to achieve the mission

- Creation of an organizational structure which will deploy resources to successfully carry out its competitive strategy

For instance, you may develop short and long term plans for:

- Reinvestment in the on-going operation of the center to replace necessary equipment and supplies
- Training programs for the staff members to insure that the program continues to meet the demands of quality child care
- On-going surveys of the customers to guarantee that the program continues to meet the needs of the client base
- Performance reviews of the programs, similar to those that are the basis for any of the nationally recognized accreditation programs
- On-going demographic surveys of the potential client base

Strategies for the future should capitalize on the strengths of the program and strengths that need to be developed–not just how and when.

Implementing Action Plans

You will need :

- A time table
- A Responsible person
- Staff qualifications (e.g., for the year 2010, 100% of supervising staff will have an ECE or related field BA degree with a minimum of 30 ECE credits.)
- Staff Development (e.g., Supervising staff will join, attend or become involved in a professional growth and development activity.)
- Child observation/curriculum/assessment (e.g., Continue and complete by 8-10 the professional development workshops on conscious discipline and full implementation into the classrooms.)
- Community resources and family involvement (e.g., parent forums 3-4 times per year)
- Director development (e.g., director credential by 2010)

There are numerous other types of plans that should be in place in an effective program. As a way of illustrating the concept of strategic planning in a child care setting, let's look at the XYZ Child Care Center, and their strategic planning process.

Competency IX: Operational Planning and Evaluation

> The director of XYZ, Mary Jones, has a goal of becoming the leader in child care in the community. There are three other centers in the immediate market that directly compete with XYZ. Mary, after participating in the National Administrator Credentialing program, has determined that she needs to develop a strategic plan to accomplish her goal.
>
> She has identified what she believes to be the effective strategy to accomplish the goal of becoming the market leader. That strategy is one of offering unique services to the customers at no additional basic expense. Now she needs to develop plans to put this strategy into place.
>
> After talking to her staff members, and informally surveying many of the parents who already use the center, Mary now plans to implement a new service each month. As a part of the new service, she will publicize the new service to the parents and issue press releases to the local paper. She believes that this strategy will create the appearance in the marketplace that the XYZ Child Care Center is a leader in providing quality programs that meet the customers' needs. Once this image is in place, the XYZ Child Care Center will have plenty of enrollments and may even be able to raise the rates.
>
> Speaking of rates: Mary has determined that her strategy will allow her to keep her market position over the long term because the increased rates will allow her to retain her staff and constantly invest in new programs and new equipment. These new programs and equipment will keep XYZ ahead of the rest of the market.
>
> Mary begins her plan by introducing a new service each month, with the cost of the service paid for by only those parents who use it. In the first few months the center begins to offer drop-off of dry cleaning, then take-out meals on Friday nights, then child care on Saturday nights so the parents can have a night out, then video rentals of popular children's tapes, and so forth.
>
> As the plans are implemented, Mary continually assesses the success of the strategy by closely watching the enrollments. An important aspect of the evaluation of the strategy is the on-going surveying of all new families to ascertain why they chose XYZ over the other child care centers.
>
> Mary has done an excellent job of understanding the importance and effectiveness of strategic planning. She has put into place plans which allow the on-going evaluation of the program. She has developed a strategy to achieve her goal of becoming the market leader in child care services. And she has utilized the process as a method of achieving long-term success for the program.

As a director, you need to establish and/or understand the goals of the center. In order to reach those goals, you will have to put into place an effective strategy to meet those goals. Once the strategy has been devised, develop and implement short and long-term plans that will allow the center to successfully reach the goals you've established.

It is extremely important throughout this process to understand the importance of being able to modify the plans in order to adapt to outside changes and demands. Do not become so rigid in your planning process that you lose site of the ultimate goal in favor of trying to meet a pre-determined plan that no longer suits the needs of the center.

As a part of the strategic planning process, periodic formal reviews of the overall program and the strategic plan should be scheduled to allow you an opportunity to refine and redirect the plans as needed to reach the ultimate goals.

Strategic plans should not be confused with business or operational plans. Strategic plans review strengths, weaknesses, threats, and opportunities in an effort to devise good business strategies. A simple way to outline a strategic plan is to make a chart that examines key strengths and key weaknesses as well as key opportunities verses key threats. All of the above components are affected by both internal and external strengths and weakness and external threats and opportunities. Examine all of these factors carefully when doing strategic planning.

An Effective Administrator Understands the Value of National Accreditations and Standards as Effective Evaluation Tools to Ensure High Quality Early Childhood Education

Performance Measurements and Program Evaluation

Perhaps you will develop your own standards and methods of evaluating whether you are meeting your standards or perhaps you will use outside standards such as the following program accreditations.

NECPA (National Early Childhood Program Accreditation)

This is a center accreditation offered through The NECPA Commission, Inc. Evaluation measures are program description, classroom observation form, staff surveys, parent surveys, AAIS (Automated Accreditation Indicator System) review, and National Accreditation Council Review.

CAP (Center Accreditation Project)

This is a center accreditation offered through the National Academy of Early Childhood Programs. The evaluation measures are program description, classroom observation form, staff questionnaire, parent questionnaire and Accreditation Commission Review.

NAEYC (National Association for the Education of Young Children)

Established in 1985, NAEYC accreditation is a voluntary system by which programs measure themselves against a national set of standards. In 1999, the NAEYC Governing Board created a National Commission on Accreditation Reinvention. For two years, the Reinvention Commission solicited extensive input from the early childhood field and other stakeholders; consulted specialists in the fields of accreditation, law and other related areas; and tested innovative accreditation practices. The result was ten recommendations to strengthen the reliability and accountability of NAEYC Accreditation for children and families, for early childhood educators and programs, and for employers, foundations, facilitation projects and others who support the system.

Accreditation is a seal of approval, a Good Housekeeping award for child care programs. It is awarded to programs that excel in all areas. As you complete the process, you will be assessing all aspects of your program and discovering weaknesses and ways to improve. Accreditation is an excellent assessment tool.

To become accredited a child care program first completes a self-assessment. This is a time-consuming process which requires the cooperation and enthusiasm of your staff. You will be evaluating every aspect of your program and making changes (some small and some major changes) where indicated. If you are serious about accreditation, the self-assessment can take several months or a year, because you will want to comply to the letter with every indicator.

After you are satisfied that you are in compliance, you will request a "Verifier" or "Validator" visit your program. This person's duty is to observe your program, interview your staff, and look at documentation to verify that your responses to the self-assessment questions are accurate.

Following the verification, all the information is sent to a committee who studies it and makes a recommendation regarding accreditation for your program.

If you are serious about having the very best program you possibly can have and about having public recognition for excellence, you should seek accreditation. However, even if you are not ready to invest the time and money in full accreditation, completing the self-assessments will give you valuable feedback about potential areas for improvement in your program.

Published performance measurement or evaluation tools for quality in an early childhood program include the:

- *Early Childhood Work Environment Scale* (Dr. Paula Jorde Bloom)
- *Early Childhood Environmental Rating Scale* (Thelma Harms, Debby Cryer, and Richard M. Clifford)
- *Infant Environment Rating Scale* (Thelma Harms, Debby Cryer, and Richard M. Clifford)
- *School-Age Environmental Rating Scale* (Thelma Harms, Ellen Vineberg Jacobs, and Donna Romano White)
- *COR: Child Observation Record* (High Scope Foundation)
- *Blueprint For Action* (Dr. Paula Jorde Bloom)

The Survey

Another type of performance measurement is the survey. Parent and staff surveys are excellent tools for learning about your performance. But the information derived from a survey is only as good as the questions you ask, and the quantity and quality of responses you receive.

Designing a good survey is more difficult than you might think. First you must determine exactly what information you want to gather and then you need to create questions that, when answered, will give you that information. And you must make sure that your questions cannot be misunderstood. You may want to hire a professional researcher to create your surveys. At the very least ask for input from someone who is objective, detailed, and analytical. Then revise your survey until you are satisfied that it will give you the data you need.

Remember that you are seeking objective information that will help you improve your program - not pats on the back. Be prepared to receive criticism and design your survey so that the criticism will be useful.

You will need to receive feedback from enough of your parents or staff to make the information statistically valid. Explain the importance of returning the completed surveys. complete anonymity. Even offer an incentive for those who return surveys promptly.

Read every survey carefully, tabulating the various questions and making note of comments and suggestions. Have a trusted friend or colleague study the surveys as well and together develop a list of actions you can take to make improvements based on this feedback.

While performance measures are powerful tools, they are only tools. They are no more likely to guarantee quality child care than an accurate speedometer is likely to prevent speeding tickets. If properly developed and used, they can reveal problems, point to solutions, and be a check on the effectiveness of solutions once implemented. In the end, performance measures are only as good as the decisions they support. And to be effective, they must continually respond to new issues.

In defining and executing a mission of the center, it is wise to build quality in - not to just add it. It is also wise to think of quality as a process. Revisit your choices of performance measurements of quality frequently to see if they continue to provide clear, consistent pictures of the program results. Good performance measures are rarely created in a single undertaking. They evolve over time.

They say that a frog can sit in a pot of hot water and not notice the temperature rise. Administrators can be that way too. They can ignore indicators that the program needs a change until it is too late. Do not put off necessary changes.

Some ways to be sure you don't ignore changes in the environment that may indicate the need for changes in the center are: (1) conduct parent satisfaction surveys, (2) have a suggestion box, (3) form parent councils, (4) conduct a telephone or mail survey, or (5) use follow-up evaluations after special events.

One final way to detect changes occurring in the environment is to conduct bench marking studies. Bench marking studies are comparing your program's performance to those of organizations which are leaders in the early childhood education industry.

An Effective Administrator Understands and Uses the Risk Management Process and Planning Techniques to Ensure Long Term Success of the Program and to Ensure Its Ability to Adapt to Changing Conditions

Risk Management

Risk management is a structured assessment of risk, the development of strategies to manage and plan for risk by using normal managerial resources.

The strategies include transferring the risk to another party, avoiding the risk, reducing the negative effect of the risk, and accepting some or all of the consequences of a particular risk.

The objective of risk management is to reduce different risks to a selected level normally accepted by society. This includes types of threats caused by environment, technology, humans, organizations and politics. It focuses on risks from physical or legal causes (e.g. natural disasters or fires, accidents, death and lawsuits). It involves all means available for the management entity; person, staff, organization.

Common Risk Identification Methods

Objectives-based Risk Identification

Organization has objectives. Any event that may endanger achieving an objective partly or completely is identified as risk.

Scenario-based Risk Identification

Different future scenarios are created to plan alternative ways to achieve an objective. Any event that may trigger an undesired scenario alternative is identified as risk.

Taxonomy-based Risk Identification

The taxonomy in taxonomy-based risk identification is a breakdown of possible risk sources. Based on the taxonomy and knowledge of best practices, a questionnaire is compiled. The answers to the questions reveal risks.

Common-risk Checking

Industries common lists of known risks are created. Each risk in the list can be checked for application to a particular situation or company.

Risk Charting

This method combines the above approaches by listing resources at risk, the threats to those resources, the factors which may increase or reduce the risk and the consequences to avoid. Risk charting creates a matrix under these headings. Management can begin with resources and consider the threats and the consequences of each or start with the threats and examine which resources they would affect, or begin with the consequences and determine which combination of threats and resources would be involved.

Once risks have been identified, they must be evaluated as to the potential severity of loss and to the probability of occurrence. This can be either simple to measure, in the case of the value of a lost building, or impossible to know for sure in the case of the probability of an unlikely event occurring. Therefore, in the evaluation process it is critical to make the best educated guesses possible in order to properly prioritize the implementation of the risk management plan.

The fundamental difficulty in risk evaluation is determining the rate of occurrence since statistical information often may not be available. Evaluating the severity of the consequences is often quite difficult for non-material assets. Risk evaluation should produce information for the management of the organization so that the primary risks are easy to understand and that the risk management decisions may be prioritized whereby the risks with the greatest loss and the greatest probability of occurring are handled first, and risks with lower probability of occurrence and lower loss are handled in descending order.

Intangible risks are those risks which directly reduce the productivity of knowledge workers, decrease cost effectiveness, profitability, service, quality, reputation, brand value, and earnings quality. Intangible risk management allows risk management to create immediate value from the identification and reduction of risks that reduce productivity.

Risk management also faces difficulties allocating resources. This is the idea of opportunity cost. Resources spent on risk management could have been spent on more profitable activities. Ideally one should minimize spending while maximizing the reduction of the negative effects of risks.

Steps in the Risk Management Process

Identification

After establishing the context, the next step in the process of managing risk is to identify potential risks. Risks are about events that, when triggered, cause problems. Risk identification can start with the source of problems, or with the problem itself.

Source Analysis

Risk sources may be internal or external to the system that is the target of risk management. Examples of risk sources are: stakeholders, employees of a company or the weather.

Problem Analysis

Risks are related to identifiable threats. For example: the threat of losing money, the threat of abuse of privacy information or the threat of accidents and casualties. The threats may exist with various entities, most important with shareholders, customers and legislative bodies such as the government.

Risk Treatment

Management knows that an ideal use of these four major strategies may not be possible. Each strategy may involve a trade-off that is not acceptable to the organization or person making the risk management decisions.

Avoidance

This means not performing an activity that could cause risk. An example would be not buying a property or business in order to not take on the liability that comes with it. Another would not be flying in order to avoid the risk of being hijacked. Avoidance may seem the answer to all risks, but avoiding risks also means losing out on the potential gain.

Reduction

This involves incorporating methods that reduce the severity of the loss or the likelihood of the loss. Examples include sprinklers designed to put out a fire to reduce the risk of loss by fire. This method may cause a greater loss by water damage and therefore may not be suitable. Halon fire suppression systems may mitigate that risk, but the cost may be prohibitive as a strategy.

Outsourcing could be an example of risk reduction if the outsourcer can demonstrate higher capability at managing or reducing risks. Examples include: contracting with a service or other company to provide housekeeping, meal service or maintenance.

Retention

This involves accepting the loss when it occurs. Self insurance falls into this category. Risk retention is a viable strategy for small risks where the cost of insuring against the risk would be greater over time than the total losses sustained. All risks that are not avoided or transferred are retained by default. This includes risks that are so large or catastrophic that they either cannot be insured against or the premiums would be infeasible. War is an example since most property and risks are not insured against war, so the loss attributed by war is retained by the insured. Also any mounts of potential loss above the amount insured is retained risk. This may also be acceptable if the chance of a very large loss is small or if the cost to insure for greater coverage amounts is so great it would hinder the goals of the organization.

Transfer

This involves causing another party to accept the risk. Insurance is one type of risk transfer that uses contracts. It may involve contract language that transfers a risk to another party without the payment of an insurance premium. Liability among construction or other contractors is very often transferred this way.

Creating a Risk Management Plan

A risk management plan should document the decisions about how each of the identified risks should be handled. Mitigation of risks often means selection of controls or a responsible individual. This documents and identifies which particular control objectives and controls from the standard have been selected, and why.

Implementation

Follow all of the planned methods for mitigating the effect of the risks. Purchase insurance policies for the risks that have been decided to be transferred to an insurer, avoid all risks that can be avoided without sacrificing the entity's goals, reduce others, and retain the rest.

Review and Evaluation

Practice, experience, and actual loss results will necessitate changes in the plan and contribute information to allow possible different decisions to be made in dealing with the risks being faced.

Risk analysis results and management plans should be updated periodically. There are two principle reasons for this:

- To evaluate whether the previously selected security controls are still applicable and effective
- To evaluate possible risk level changes in the business environment

Limitations

Improperly assessed and prioritized risks waste time resources in dealing with risk of losses that are not likely to occur. If the risk is unlikely to occur it may be better to retain the risk and deal with the result if the loss does in fact occur.

Prioritizing the risk management processes too highly could keep an organization from completing a project or even getting started. This is especially true if other work is suspended until the risk management process is considered complete. Therefore it is important to keep in mind the distinction between risk and uncertainty.

Risk Management and Business Continuity

Risk management is the practice of systematically selecting cost effective approaches to minimize threats to the organization. No risks can ever be fully avoided or mitigated simply because of financial and practical limitations. Therefore all organizations have to accept some level of residual risk.

Markel Insurance has provided the following essential facts checklist to help document any crisis incidents.

- What happened?
- Who was involved?
- What is their present condition?
- Where are they now?
- Where did the incident occur?
- What internal resources are available?
- Who was supervising?
- Who is in charge?
- What action has been taken so far?
- What outside resources are needed?
- How will assistance be delivered?

Summary

In order to demonstrate competency in operational planning and evaluation, an effective administrator:

- Understands and uses business planning techniques designed to insure long term success of the program and its ability to adapt to changing conditions
- Evaluates the program and all its components, and uses this evaluation to change and improve the program
- Understands and responds to factors, both internal and external, which influence the program and its goals
- Understands and uses strategic planning techniques designed to insure long term success of the program and its ability to adapt to changing conditions
- Understands and uses the risk management process and planning techniques designed to insure long term success of the program and its ability to adapt to changing conditions

If you feel you lack confidence in any of the skills listed above, please go back and review the appropriate section in this chapter.

Competency X

Leadership and Advocacy

Competency X

Leadership and Advocacy

Learning Objectives:

- To understand organizational theory and leadership styles as they relate to early childhood work environments

- To gain knowledge of the legislative processes, social issues, and public policies as they relate to young children and their families

- To know how to articulate a vision, clarify and affirm values, and create a culture built on norms of continuous improvement and ethical conduct

- To be able to evaluate program effectiveness

- To understand how to define organizational problems, to gather data to generate alternative solutions, and to effectively apply analytical skills

- To be able to advocate on behalf of young children, their families, and the child care profession

- To gain an understanding of different family systems and different parenting styles

- To be able to implement programs that support families of diverse cultural, ethnic, linguistic, and socio-economic backgrounds

- To understand how to support families as valued partners in the educational process

- To understand the communication process and the importance of developing relationships

- To gain knowledge of communication methods and plans

- To be able to practice two-way communication techniques

- To understand how to combine technology and paper as it relates to management of communication processes

- To be able to listen to parents and identify referral needs

- To gain skills required for public speaking, oral communication, and written communication

- To understand the difference between a leader and a manage

An Effective Administrator Works with and Contributes to the Development of a Board of Directors and Advisory Groups Where Applicable

If you are the administrator of a child care program overseen by a board of directors, you can be influential in the board's involvement in and knowledge of the program. This is important, as an active, informed board will be more likely to make wise decisions regarding the program and to support your efforts as director.

Ask to speak at regular intervals at board of directors' meetings. Come well prepared with information on changes in the program, recent staff changes, trends you see that will affect the program in the future, financial data, etc. Speak briefly and have the details of each topic on a hand-out the board can review later.

Issue a standing invitation for board members to visit the program at their convenience and be sure to invite them to all programs, parent/teacher meetings, and special events. When your program uses facilities under the purview of another group such as a church or a school building a good working relationship is valuable. It is vital to maintain open and frank communications with your host.

When two different groups use the same space, some conflicts may result - conflicts over the use of equipment or materials, disagreements over room arrangements, disputes over storage space, etc... To lessen these conflicts and foster a good relationship between the child care program and the host organization, shared information is again of critical importance. The more your host knows about your program and the more you understand the host's needs, the easier it will be for you both to seek mutually acceptable solutions.

Take every opportunity to share information about your program. Include your host in any program mailings - newsletters, parent notices, etc... Invite your host organization to participate in your special events. Prepare a written report at least annually to inform your host of changes that have occurred in the program, highlights of major events since your last update, and give a brief financial review.

One of the best ways to encourage interest in your program from boards of directors and host organizations is to request their assistance in appointing an advisory group or liaison to meet with you regularly. These meetings can avert disagreements by candid discussions concerning expectations. An advisory group is a valuable source of guidance and will likely be enthusiastic supporters of your program.

Recruit a Board of Advisors

To help you get a better fix on the environment in which your center is operating as well as to gain some valuable insights into the operation of your program, you might want to set up an advisory board. Recruit experts in your community who can fill in some of the gaps in your own expertise to serve on this board. Maybe you will want a lawyer, a CPA, an economist, an early childhood educator, a pediatrician, a business planner, a marketing specialist, a work/family consultant, a sociologist, a computer expert, or an engineer as well as parents. Invite four or five of the key advisors you need to attend two or three meetings a year and to be available for an occasional phone call. When you meet, do so in a pleasant environment and keep the meeting focused on picking their brains; do not bore them with lengthy reports that are difficult to follow. Keep it as short and simple as possible. Thank them frequently and publicly.

Tap Your Parents' Expertise

The parents served by your center are likely to possess a wide range of talents. Take advantage of their unique perspectives by questioning them about trends they feel will impact your center. Either approach parents in person one-on-one, or send out a quick survey asking parents to list and describe three trends they feel will have the most impact on the center and why.

An Effective Administrator Facilitates the Development of Community Spirit among Staff, Parents, the Board of Directors, Advisory Groups, and Children

The first step in building a sense of community within any group is to share your vision and your goals. Your staff, your Board of Directors or advisory group, and your parents must clearly understand your philosophy and vision of your early care and education program. Then each individual must understand how she fits into the vision.

You communicate your vision in a variety of ways. The most effective way is through your actions - where you place your personal priorities, the manner in which you relate to others, your interest in continued learning. Everything you do on a day-to-day basis reveals your attitude about your work and what you value. Set an example of courtesy and honesty.

While your staff and your children are involved in the program on a daily basis, parents and Board members may be less involved than you would like. They cannot share the vision or advance the vision if they are not a part of the program, so it is important to get them more involved in order to develop their sense of community.

We have all seen how working together on a project that benefits someone else has a way of bringing out the best in all of us and building relationships with one another. Offer this type of opportunity to your parents or Board members - a service project that is really needed, can be accomplished in one day, and utilizes the talents and abilities of every person. Then follow up with other opportunities for group interaction such as social gatherings, all-center picnics, P.T.A. meetings, Board retreats, lunch with the children, etc.

Help the individuals get to know one another by publishing a directory or a newsletter with articles featuring families, Board members, and teachers; ask small groups to help you with special projects such as designing a brochure or speaking to civic groups. This interaction will enable individuals to get better acquainted and foster cooperation in the future.

Communicate regularly with each group. Be concise, select important topics, and be positive. Make a real effort to get good press coverage for your early care and education program. Everyone likes to be a part of something that is well-known and well-respected.

Say thank you often and sincerely. Write thank you notes.

See your staff, Board of Directors, Advisory Groups, liaisons and parents as partners. Work at developing their sense of partnership. Be a partner yourself. This sense of community and commitment to a common goal will be invaluable in helping you attain your goals and building a better program for children.

An Effective Administrator Understands the Educational, Social, Political, and Cultural Context of Her Community and Keeps Up to Date with Events and Public Policy Decisions

Environmental Scanning

Early care and education would appear to be a straightforward endeavor, well insulated from the noisy turmoil of the outside world. It's just taking care of kids, isn't it? Anyone who has worked in the early childhood education in the past five years knows life inside the center is not immune from the realities of the outside world.

What center in recent years has not seen the effect of drugs, the AIDS crisis, media reports about sexual predators, parent and societal concerns about school readiness, and the growing diversity of the population?

To ensure your center is properly prepared for changes in its environment and to help you keep your concerns in their proper perspective, you need to establish some simple ongoing environmental scanning practices. Practices such as the following should enable you to (1) spot events and trends that may impact your center, (2) evaluate what that impact might be, and (3) take appropriate measures in response.

Read Widely

If you focus your attention too narrowly on early childhood topics, you may miss the forest for the trees. Try to set aside 30 minutes two to three times a week to expand your reading horizons. Scan through publications such as your local newspaper, the Wall Street Journal, American Demographics, Time, Newsweek, and Working Mother. Read whatever catches your interest; don't analyze and screen your reading choices. After you have read an article, take a few moments to ponder the implications for the field and for your center. Don't feel guilty if you enjoy these breaks from reality. This is important work.

Get Others Thinking

If you belong to a state association or local directors' group, involve them in discussions beyond reimbursement rates and licensing regulations. Encourage them to bring in an outside speaker to address a key social, demographic, or business trends. If there is no local group in your area, invite peers to your center for a stimulating evening speaker, and then encourage them to take turns hosting such events.

Get Involved in Your Community

An effective administrator is acquainted with the local environment and is a participating member of the local community. If you belong to an association of early care and education centers, you know the value of sharing ideas and concerns with others who have the same interests. Networking in your own community can be just as valuable. There are a variety of entities that should be your good neighbors.

What organizations in your community seem to have their fingers on the pulse of developments? Is it the Chamber of Commerce, the Junior League, the Lions Club or other significant community organizations? Find time to participate in a non-child care organization that is doing something about issues and trends impacting your community. The best way to be prepared for changes in your community is to take part in helping to shape them.

You need not take on all these activities and you need not do this by yourself. Pick the approaches that appeal to you and recruit others on your staff to be part of your environmental scanning team.

An Effective Administrator Has Knowledge of Local, State, and National Public Policy Efforts Relating to Early Childhood Education, and Is Able to Use this Knowledge to Build Community Networks and Coalitions

This knowledge includes understanding:

- The differences and similarities of child care programs
- Child care resource and referral organizations
- Auxiliary services for both the center and parents
- Regulatory policies
- Federal, state, and local funding policies and their systems
- Legislative processes and how to participate in them
- Public relations, media techniques, and methods to develop public support

Other Child Care Programs

While centers within a community are in competition with one another, the benefit of working together will invariably prove more valuable than each center working alone. Take the lead in getting local center owners and/or directors together on a regular basis. Centers can share the expense of a training program, a guest performer for the children, or benefit from volume purchasing. They can share their substitute lists and their vendor contacts. Working together center directors can:

- Inform and influence their local Boards of Education, County Commissions, federal and state legislators
- Inform and influence public policy makers
- Pool buying resources, organize a buying club

Do not isolate yourself. Make it a point to contact other center directors in your community regularly. Invite other directors to your center to discuss issues of interest to all, to see a demonstration of a new product, to share ideas for summer field trips, to learn what skills each director has that can be shared with the group.

Child Care Resource and Referral Agencies (CCR&R)

Resource and referral agencies (CCR&R or just R&R) can be a wonderful source of new customers. One of their functions is to field calls from parents looking for child care and to steer those parents to programs that will meet their needs. Often these organizations work directly with businesses to offer their employees child care. Get to know every CCR&R agency in your area as well as the national ones. Register with them. Send them detailed information about your program. Ask what training opportunities they offer. If you have expertise in a particular area, volunteer to teach a workshop or to help in some other way.

The National Association of Child Care Resource and Referral Agencies (NACCRRA) can be contacted at 202-393-5501 or at their web site, www.NACCRRA.org.

Vendors and Providers of Services

Tapping hidden resources with your suppliers can be a profitable and easy way to provide extra training or special events for the community. Your supplier wants to keep you happy. If you offer her the chance to showcase products, she will benefit as well. Ask your suppliers if they have educators on their staff who can provide workshops. For example, ask your food purveyor to sponsor a workshop on nutrition for center personnel in your area. In return you might offer the vendor time at the end of the program to tell about her products and services. Many manufacturers offer this service, and your supplier can ask her supplier, the manufacturer, to provide a workshop for you.

Many providers of early childhood education products have daily, weekly, or monthly newsletters or newsflashes over the internet you can access. The spectrum of information varies widely but will help keep you up-to-date on the latest happenings in the field as well as provide information to assist you in care and education functions.

Many vendors are often willing to contribute materials for special community events because of the publicity these occasions generate. If you are putting on a Saturday carnival, ask one of your vendors to provide balloons or hot dogs or prizes. In return, you will want to put the vendor's name in the program or on signs acknowledging the contribution.

You might organize a holiday (Christmas) buying program with a toy and equipment supplier and allow your parents to purchase through your center (at a discounted price) the gifts they want to get for their children. The supplier makes one delivery to your school, and you distribute the products to the parents. Your parents will like the convenience, and your supplier will love the business, plus give you a percentage of the sales in free merchandise for your center.

Policies and Rules Affecting Early Childhood Education Programs

The financial success of an early childhood education program is directly affected by regulatory policy, funding policy, and educational policy. You must be aware of changes in these areas; be active and involved in changes and issues which affect either your business or your ability to deliver high quality child care.

The best way to stay on top of proposed policy changes is to join an organization involved in policy making. Examples might be state child care associations and their local chapters, the National Child Care Association and the National Association for the Education of Young Children. These organizations usually have representatives on important committees and task forces which help set policy. Members of these groups receive information about proposed policy and policy changes and have an opportunity to express their opinions before changes are finalized. Members are notified of hearings at which they have an opportunity to speak or offer written testimony. Just knowing what changes are coming can help you prepare for them rather than being surprised when they are implemented.

Legislative Processes

It is important to know your legislators at both the state and federal levels and for them to know of you. Frequently, political persons will respond to opportunities to have "photo ops" with children. Invite your representatives to speak at special events at your center; they may bring staff and the press with them to visit and participate in planned activities with the children. Or, you may send out press releases yourself. A "hands on" good impression of your important role in the early education of young children goes a long way toward developing a sense of your contributions to your community – educationally and economically.

You may also ask for meetings at their offices that allow time for you to bring forth information about the variety of services provided by the private early childhood sector both non-profit and for profit providers. In such meetings you may discuss proposed legislation and public policy and the implications. The protocols for accomplishing these tasks include being tempered by good manners, being well versed on topics, timeliness in arriving and in departing, flexibility, and responsiveness to requests for further or clarifying information.

State and national early childhood organizations also inform their members on public policy issues. These groups offer a means for their members to express their viewpoints and the offices of these organizations strive to develop relationships that enable constituency opinions to be voiced. Such local and national groups may assist in strategic planning, build coalitions, organize testimony before legislative committees, write op ed pieces for newspapers, and arrange critical meetings. Most groups use volunteers interested in public policy to augment limited budgets and welcome new participants.

The national and state public policy makers consider legislation and policies that affect early childhood education. Therefore, it is very important you get to know your federal and state legislators. Your legislators are not experts on early care and education. They likely know very little about this industry. This is your opportunity to make a difference in the lives of children all over your state by offering information, statistics and your expert opinion to your legislator. He will not have time to do extensive research into early childhood issues and will likely welcome the advice and assistance from someone entrenched in the field. Just remember that professionalism always comes first.

Other Community Resources

In addition to the community groups mentioned above, you should also make an effort to develop a relationship with representatives of your local schools. The information you obtain about their programs will assist as you assess the success of your program's educational component. Look for ways to initiate and develop a positive relationship with local schools.

Get to know something about community clubs and organizations. Form partnerships with these groups for service projects. For example, your center might be a drop-off point for a holiday (Christmas) toy collection for underprivileged children sponsored by the local Rotary Club. Or you might join with the local garden club in a fundraiser for a city beautification project. These groups are full of talented individuals who will come to your center and offer programs, read stories, or teach the children a unit on a particular topic.

Local businesses are usually happy to give tours to children. Sometimes a private business will donate materials they produce for craft projects. Take an inventory of your local business community. Think of ways you can help them as well as ways they can help you and ways you can work together to help someone else.

The director who makes a genuine effort to develop a network of other center directors, child care resource and referral agencies, vendors, child care associations, legislators, policy-makers, media contacts, schools, and businesses will find excellent resources for learning and accomplishing goals. This director will expand her professional skills, find opportunities for sharing, and make a greater contribution to the community, the center, and the children and families she serves.

Relationships

As stated, there are many government entities that impact your program, and the children and the families you serve. Since laws and regulations change, it is important for you to build good relationships with the lawmakers and regulators and be a part of rule changing decisions when they occur. Here are some other reasons to build good relationships:

Players Will Change

Licensing/regulatory staff will change as will elected officials. You can impact the nature of those changes if you have good ongoing relationships with those agencies.

Resources Will Change

Government agency's funding changes and at some point they may not be able to hire adequate staff to assure that children are safe in licensed programs. And you may find if rule requirements for staff increases, your pool of qualified applicants will diminish.

Environments Will Change

The welfare reform changes of the mid-1990's are an example of major policy changes dramatically changing the discussion of services for children and the role of government in families' lives. The move to create programs for younger and younger children in our public schools known as Universal Pre-K or Voluntary Pre-K are examples of a changing environment.

Technology Will Change

These changes, both literally (e.g., computers, Internet) and figuratively (e.g., new information on early brain development), impact government decisions about how child care should be offered.

With all these reasons to build a great relationship with your regulatory agencies and lawmakers, here are some things you can do as the administrator to build a positive relationship with them:

Establish Individual Relationships with Regulators

Governmental agency officials visiting your program should be treated respectfully. Always be pleasant and professional. When you are found out of compliance with a rule, establish your good faith by making changes promptly and agreeably. Regulators can be great resources for information. You might ask them to provide training to your staff or to make a presentation to your parent council.

Develop Good Relationships with Regulatory Supervisors

Don't be afraid to ask why a decision was made including the rule reference. If you feel a mistake has been made, ask to speak with the supervisor for clarification. If you have previously demonstrated your professional commitment to abiding by the rules and regulations, your request will be honored openly.

Have Periodic Meetings with Regulators

These meetings (either on your own or with a committee) establish a tradition of communication that will remain even when the players change.

Find Opportunities to Communicate with Regulators

Invite your licensor to a holiday party. Tell them about new equipment you are purchasing. Put them on your newsletter mailing list. Ask their advice on policies and procedure changes.

Volunteer to Be on Committees and Task Forces

This work is important because it is not done frequently. You will have to abide by the results for a number of years. If you have demonstrated your interest in high quality early care and education through your program and your participation in committees and organizations that promote quality, you may be sought after to serve in this capacity.

Participate In an Association that Represents Business Interests

This is a great opportunity for pooling expertise and resources to impact the working of government agencies. Associations can speak forcefully for private early childhood educators and can reduce fears of government retaliation towards an individual person or program.

Budget Time for Government Relations

Just as you budget time for center activities. If you don't plan for it you will likely not have time to do this important work (and it is work). Government regulations and officials can have a significant impact on the educational and financial viability of your center. You need to stay in touch.

Keep in Mind that Ideally We All Have the Same Goal

The goal for all of us is a high quality, safe, nurturing places for children while their parents work. If you and your regulator focus on this goal, you can work to overcome any differences of opinion with a little diplomacy and a lot of good humor.

An Effective Administrator Demonstrates Communication Skills

There are many types of communication skills. These skills include:

- Public speaking
- Giving media interviews, and maintaining media contacts
- Dealing with the media in crisis situations
- Writing (proposals, business plans)
- Supervising the production of brochures, fliers, parent handbooks

Public Speaking

You will have many occasions to speak to groups. Certainly you will need to speak before your staff on a regular basis and to parent groups at center programs, graduations, etc. If you want to be a particularly effective director or to take advantage of opportunities to advance your center or early care and education in general, you will need to cultivate public speaking ability. If you are uncomfortable speaking before groups, you should take a public speaking course or study courses online. This will help you practice in a non-threatening environment. You will learn tips to be more at ease and effective speaking to groups.

Media

You may have to draw on your public-speaking skills for media interviews. These can be tricky, because you may not know the questions ahead of time. If you are asked to give an interview, be sure you know exactly what the topic will be and be sure you know the subject matter thoroughly.

Ask the interviewer to stick to the topic agreed upon and even what questions he will be asking, and then be prepared to turn the interview back to the topic should the interviewer stray.

Crises Situations

In the advertising, marketing, and public relations section we look to the media to be our friend. But there are those occasions when we wish the media did not exist. If you have a crisis at your center, here are some helpful hints for managing the media:

1. ***Designate One Spokesperson.*** Do not allow the media to interview just any staff person.
2. ***Inform Your Staff.*** Do so immediately and thoroughly of any incident which may create a crisis.
3. ***Think Before You Speak.*** Make a few notes of the facts of the case and stick to these facts. Do not presume something happened. Be sure it happened.
4. ***Do Not Over Respond.*** Do not try to spin your comments.
5. ***Be Honest.*** You may not know the answers to many of the questions initially. Do not speculate. Say you do not know and that you will have to investigate. Do not feel compelled to answer every question.
6. ***Be Available.*** If you refuse to speak to the media, the assumption is that you have something to hide. Giving an honest statement and making an honest effort to get the facts will make you more credible with the public. It is advisable—as part of risk management—to prepare a generic statement that could be used in many different situations to assist you when a statement is needed and you do not have many facts.
7. ***Make Sure Your Face Can Be Seen.*** Sun glasses or hats do not allow the public to see your face and may give the impression you have something to hide.

Writing

A center director also needs to write well. Your duties include writing letters, center policies, parent handbooks, curriculum guides, etc. Keep a good dictionary and grammar guide handy and use them when you write anything. Always ask several people you trust to proofread and edit your material. When you proofread your materials read the page out loud. This helps your brain read what is on the page and not what you think you wrote. Many times what we write is the first impression we make upon others. If you write well and precisely, your readers will assume you are just as careful and skilled in other areas. Conversely, if your writing is sloppy, the reader may assume you are sloppy in all you do.

Brochures, Fliers, Parent Handbooks

Though child care center directors are masters at many tasks, they cannot be expected to be experts at everything. You may need to hire someone else to do many of your writing tasks such as developing brochures, posters, fliers, larger handbooks, manuals, etc. Become knowledgeable about printing terms. Learn something about paper quality and ink. Be able to describe a concept to an artist. And, above all, prepare well in advance of a deadline. Find a reputable printing company able to do simple to sophisticated projects with a graphic artist on staff. If you use one company for all your printing needs, they will give you good service in a crunch.

Having great communication skills is not worth much if you don't use them. You can be a terrific public speaker, write a very persuasive proposal, and give great interviews, but unless you do these things, you have not benefited from your abilities. Always be on the lookout for opportunities to promote your center, your employees, and excellent early care and education. Then use these opportunities to your best advantage.

In a major city, the biggest newspaper in town once sponsored a neediest children's fund during the Christmas season. Knowing this, an alert center director organized her after-school children to hold a bake sale. The children publicized their bake sale by making posters; contacting neighbors, friends and relatives; writing news releases; and telephoning reporters at the newspaper. The children baked the cookies, pies, and cakes and on a Saturday morning the center was the scene of a mad shopping spree. The proceeds were donated to the children's fund. The newspaper gave the project great coverage, complete with photographs of the sale and the presentation of the donation check. The children learned about budgeting, making change, measuring ingredients, cooking, publicity, writing, etc. and they had the pleasure of doing something meaningful for someone less fortunate. The center received great publicity. And the newspaper received a nice donation for its children's fund. This became a win-win situation because the director was alert to possibilities and opportunities to interact within the community.

An Effective Administrator Understands the Principles of Leadership, Management, and Accountability

Organizations are always searching for the best techniques to manage and motivate their employees. There is a difference between being a manager and being a leader although at times the two are closely related. Good management is an art and demands an understanding that problem-solving and setting a clear and defined direction are key characteristics of the job.

Many management experts believe that organizations that work hard to get employee input and ultimately buy in to the goals and tasks at hand will be more successful than organizations that have a more authoritarian approach.

As an effective administrator you must develop and implement management strategies that build teamwork and staff participation, that make effective use of time and resources, and that allow you the opportunity to incorporate short term problem solving with long-term planning.

Teamwork

> **Coming together is a beginning,**
> **Staying together is progress,**
> **But working together is success!**

The word teamwork has become a business buzz-word. You hear the word teamwork on every corporate tongue. And, sooner or later, the word shows up in the commitment, vision, or mission statements of most companies.

Yet when a closer look is given to the daily interactions and workings of many businesses, one finds teamwork is often more lip service than action. In other words, there is a "Talk ten, Do Two" mentality to the teamwork concept. Early care and education centers are no exception.

So why don't child care centers do this thing called teamwork? One of the biggest obstacles is the multitude of facets inherent in the structure of the business. Often these facets become opponents in the operation of the center.

For example, there are:

- The morning staff and the afternoon staff
- The two year old room and the toddler room
- The preschool personnel and the child care personnel
- The administration and the staff

Getting these different interest groups to operate as an effective, functioning team can be, at times, overwhelming for the administrator. Let us look back at the proven strategies in creating a "brain friendly" (Seidman, 2008) environment where administrators, staff, parents and children feel happy and safe. The more people of all ages and roles feel emotionally safe the more effective the learning experience and teamwork becomes.

Leadership requires vision as well as an ability to define the vision to others. It requires holding others accountable and an ability to focus on the mission, goals, and objectives at hand. Leadership creates a challenging climate within which to work, and creates committed employees. Leadership ensures that employees have a sense of direction and strives to create a work environment that allows employees an opportunity to be creative and to take pride in their work. Leadership does not overstress employees and does not condone amoebic managers. Below is a reprint of a Leadership Assessment Guide. How do you assess your skills at this time? Remember, we are always growing and developing. The purpose of doing your leadership assessment is to learn and grow.

Competency X: LEADERSHIP AND ADVOCACY

Leadership Assessment Guide

Rate your center on this scale for each of the 14 leadership elements listed below. Select the statement which most accurately describes the situation in your center, and place an "X" in the box next to the number.

		1. Clarity of Objectives
	9	The center has clear objectives which are understood by all staff members.
	6	The center has fairly clear objectives which are understood by most staff members.
	3	The center has objectives, but few staff members are aware of them.
	0	The center does not have any established objectives.
		2. Communications
	9	Communications flow both ways between director and teachers and are extremely frank and open.
	6	Communications flow both ways and are moderately frank and open.
	3	Communications flow primarily down from the director and are somewhat guarded and cautious.
	0	Communications flow only downward and are extremely guarded and cautious.
		3. Ongoing Planning
	9	Staff members engage in planning on a weekly basis to insure that the daily curriculum promotes the center's objective.
	6	Staff members engage in planning on a monthly basis to promote the center's objectives.
	3	Staff members engage in occasional planning with little emphasis on objective.
	0	Staff members do not engage in planning on a regular basis.
		4. Creativity

	9	Staff members are encouraged to be creative, to take risks, and to explore their own interests.
	6	Staff members are allowed to be creative, to take risks, and to explore their own interests.
	3	Creativity, risk taking, and the exploration of one's own interests are discouraged.
	0	Creativity, risk taking, and the exploration of one's own interests are forbidden.
		5. Evaluation
	9	Center objectives, curriculum results, and staff performance are continuously evaluated.
	6	Evaluation occurs on a frequent basis.
	3	Evaluation occurs on a sporadic basis.
	0	Evaluation seldom, if ever, takes place.
		6. Decision making
	9	The director seeks input from all staff members in making major center decisions.
	6	The director seeks advice from most teachers before making major center decisions.
	3	The director seeks advice from a few teachers before making major center decisions.
	0	The director makes all decisions with no teacher input.
		7. Problem Solving
	9	Problems confronting the center are always addressed promptly and decisively.
	6	Problems confronting the center are usually addressed promptly and decisively.
	3	Problems confronting the center are occasionally addressed promptly and decisively.
	0	Problems confronting the center are never addressed promptly and decisively.

Competency X: Leadership and Advocacy

	\multicolumn{2}{c}{**8. Policy Implementation**}
	9	Center policies and procedures are enforced with extreme consistency and fairness.
	6	Center policies and procedures are enforced with moderate consistency and fairness.
	3	Center policies and procedures are enforced with moderate inconsistency and unfairness.
	0	Center policies and procedures are enforced with extreme inconsistency and unfairness.
	\multicolumn{2}{c}{**9. Feedback**}
	9	Staff members are given constructive feedback on their performance on nearly a daily basis.
	6	Staff members are given constructive feedback on a weekly basis.
	3	Staff members are given constructive feedback about once a month.
	0	Staff members are seldom if ever given constructive feedback.
	\multicolumn{2}{c}{**10. Discipline**}
	9	Discipline is totally self-imposed; staff is fully responsible for controlling their own behavior.
	6	Discipline is mostly self-imposed.
	3	Discipline is mostly imposed from above; control is exerted mostly through close supervision.
	0	Discipline is totally imposed from above.
	\multicolumn{2}{c}{**11. Staff Development**}
	9	Continuous efforts are made to upgrade staff members' skills and knowledge.
	6	Frequent efforts are made to upgrade staff members' skills and knowledge.
	3	Sporadic efforts are made to upgrade staff members' skills and knowledge.

	0	Staff development seldom, if ever, takes place at the center.
	12. Staff Motivation	
	9	Staff members are highly motivated to perform to the best of their ability.
	6	Staff members are moderately motivated.
	3	Staff members are moderately frustrated with their work or the center.
	0	Staff members are highly frustrated.
	13. Director Motivation	
	9	The director is extremely enthusiastic and productive in her performance.
	6	The director is moderately enthusiastic and productive in her performance.
	3	The director is slightly enthusiastic and productive in her performance.
	0	The director is not at all enthusiastic and productive in her performance.
	14. Staff-Director Relationship	
	9	The director is on warm, personal terms with all teachers.
	6	The director is friendly with all teachers.
	3	The director is friendly with some teachers.
	0	The director is personally isolated from the teachers.

Reprinted with permission from *Child Care Information Exchange*, November 1985

Scoring: Place your ratings for all **odd** numbered elements on the **Results** line, and place all ratings for the **even** numbered elements on the **Relations** line. Add the ratings on each line. This will provide your center's overall rating for the leadership dimensions of results and relations.

Results: (odd numbered items) ___+___+___+___+___+___+___ =

Relations: (even numbered items) ___+___+___+___+___+___+___ =

Sample Forms

ADMINISTRATOR JOB DESCRIPTION:
Directs the daily activities of the Child Care Center. Responsible for developing and planning operational procedures to ensure a safe and healthy learning environment for children.

Duties and Responsibilities:
- Establishes and implements short- and long-range organizational goals, objectives, policies, and operating procedures; monitors and evaluates program effectiveness; effects changes required for improvement
- Designs, establishes, and maintains an organizational structure and staffing to effectively accomplish the organization's goals and objectives; recruits, employs, trains, supervises, and evaluates unit staff
- Develops and manages annual budgets for the organization and performs periodic cost and productivity analyses
- Develops and implements operational procedures and practices to ensure a safe and healthy environment for children
- Serves as a liaison between teachers, families, and the community for information, counseling, referrals, and problem resolution
- Represents the Center to various ECE forums as well as externally to media, government agencies, funding agencies, clients, and/or the general public/local community
- Recommends and participates in the development of policies and procedures; may serve on the planning and policy-making committees of the Board
- Plans, develops, and implements strategies for generating resources and/or revenues for the Center

Minimum Requirements: Bachelor's degree in ECE with minimum of 5 years experience directly related to the duties and responsibilities specified. CPR and First Aid Certified

Desired Knowledge, Skills, and Abilities:
- Ability to supervise and train staff, including organizing, prioritizing, and scheduling work assignments. Skill in examining and re-engineering operations and procedures, formulating policy, and developing and implementing new strategies and procedures
- Strong interpersonal and communication skills and the ability to work effectively with a wide range of constituencies in a diverse community
- Knowledge of customer service standards and procedures
- Outstanding interpersonal and community relations skills and the ability to communicate and work effectively within a diverse community
- Counseling and behavior management skills
- Assessment and referral skills
- Ability to foster a cooperative work environment
- Employee development and performance management skills
- Knowledge of accreditation, certification, and regulatory requirements and standards
- Knowledge of staff hiring procedures
- Ability to analyze and solve problems
- Ability to identify and secure alternative funding/revenue sources

- Knowledge of applicable legislation, standards, and policies and procedures within specialty area
- Knowledge of child development theory and practice
- Ability to use independent judgment and manage and impart information to a range of clientele and/or media sources
- Ability to provide a supportive and caring environment for children

Summary

Showing competency in leadership and advocacy, an effective administrator:

- Works with and contributes to the development of a board of directors and advisory groups where applicable

- Facilitates the development of community spirit among staff, parents, the board of directors, advisory groups, and children

- Understands the educational, social, political, and cultural context of her community and keeps up to date with policy efforts relating to early childhood education, and is able to use this knowledge to build community networks and coalitions

- Demonstrates communication skills

- Understands the principles of leadership, management, and accountability and public policy decisions

- Has knowledge of community services, is able to refer families and staff to social services, to health services and education, and to training appropriate to their individual needs

- Has knowledge of local, state, and national public

If you feel you lack confidence in any of the skills listed above, please go back and review the appropriate section in this chapter.

List of Competencies and Supporting Statements

The National Administrator Credential is designed to meet the highest standards of professional development for early care and education administrators. This composite list of competencies and learning objectives is presented as evidence of that quality. They will also serve to assist you in understanding and evaluating your progress toward a successful and fulfilling career as a child care professional.

I

History of Early Childhood Education, and Personal and Professional Development of the Child Care Professional

An effective administrator understands that early childhood education operates within an ever changing environment. She is able to recognize the primary purposes of early childhood education in the United States. She understands that political, social, and economic factors influence early childhood education.

An effective administrator knows the history and key milestones of the early childhood education industry. She understands that she works in a dynamic and evolving profession that serves three major purposes of society. She understands the historical perspective, the milestones, and the key national organizations involved in early childhood education.

She is able to list and describe the various types of early childhood care and education available to families in the community.

An effective administrator is capable of self review and assessment and can identify stages of development. She reflects on, evaluates, and strengthens her skills and career goals.

II

An Effective Organization

An effective administrator develops a management philosophy which includes a clear mission statement and clear objectives based on the values of the program and understanding of child care needs in the community being served. He understands why an organization needs a mission statement. He is able to write a clear and concise mission statement that supports organizational values and understanding of child care needs in the community. (This includes a review and critique of organizational mission statements.)

An effective administrator understands the legal structure of organizations and how this structure effects his operations. He is able to distinguish between the six types of legal structures that an organization can adopt.

And effective administrator assesses the supply and demand characteristics of the area served, and positions the program to respond to those needs. He understands how to define and write goals and objectives to accomplish the mission of your organization. He understands how to conduct a demographic study, and how to conduct a needs assessment and competition study. He is able to determine relative market share.

III

Internal and External Systems

An effective administrator develops systems to keep the center running smoothly and to comply with applicable laws, rules, and regulations, and keeps these systems up to date to ensure the safety of staff and children. She is able to develop systems to ensure compliance with local, state, and national codes.

An effective administrator understands the importance of communication and develops communication systems for staff, parents, and the community. She has mastered the development of staff and parent communication systems.

An effective administrator communicates both formally and informally with parents regarding their child's development.

An effective administrator establishes and maintains security practices. She understands the development of facility security and safety systems.

An effective administrator manages the program efficiently using an organized system which may include the use of computers combined with a paper system. She is able to create business practices and communications to maintain financial stability.

An effective administrator provides a nutritious, sanitary, cost effective food service that is responsive to the scheduling needs of the center. She creates and manages an efficient and nutritious food service

An effective administrator oversees janitorial and maintenance needs of the building, grounds, and vehicles to ensure safety and proper repair. She develops and uses management systems regarding maintenance and janitorial needs that ensure health and safety of the center.

An effective administrator manages shared space by negotiating and maintaining a positive relationship with the host and any other users. she grasps the essential elements of sharing space,

IV

Laws and Regulations

An effective administrator understands and complies with applicable federal, state, and local regulations. He identifies local, state, and federal rules and regulations that effect early education programs. He adheres to state licensing rules and regulations, and to local fire and health standards.

An effective administrator works with legal counsel and demonstrates general knowledge of legal issues concerning child care. He understands important legal information regarding child abuse and neglect, confidentiality, labor laws, health occupational safety laws, contracts, and anti-discrimination laws.

V

Staff Management and Human Resources

An effective administrator provides a mechanism that defines tasks, job roles, the distribution of authority, quality standards, and concepts of teamwork and decision making within the program. She creates effective personnel policies and job descriptions.

An effective administrator develops and manages personnel policies and job descriptions and maintains and safeguards personnel records. She understands how to safeguard and maintain staff records.

An effective administrator recruits, selects, and retains staff. She knows how to recruit, hire, provide incentives, and keep good employees. She is able to conduct an effective interview process for prospective employees.

An effective administrator provides staff development which includes orientation, in-service and career development training, and understands concepts of adult learning and motivates staff to participate in training. She understands how to ensure that her staff continues to develop professionally.

An effective administrator provides guidance and supervision for each employee. She is able to develop a formal staff evaluation procedure. She uses staff evaluations to promote high quality early childhood education.

An effective administrator develops and manages a formal staff evaluation process which is based on observation and opportunities for regular and continuous self-evaluation. She has confidence in providing her staff with guidance and leadership in order to encourage personal and professional growth.

VI

Educational Programming

An effective administrator understands that brain research has reaffirmed the importance of high quality early childhood education. He has confidence in the understanding of basic information regarding the development of the brain.

An effective administrator implements curriculum reflecting the most accepted practices in child development, and implements programs addressing all aspects of early childhood education. He understands that contemporary learning concepts are based on theories developed over time. He has an understanding of the value of national accreditation, standards, and evaluation tools

An effective administrator understands how children grow and develop, why children and parents experience separation anxiety, and is able to direct staff to productively work with children. He understands developmentally and culturally appropriate practices.

An effective administrator ensures appropriate room and space arrangement and supports effective space design based on knowledge of environmental psychology and childhood development. He selects and uses curriculum, materials, and equipment for the best early childhood education practices.

An effective administrator understands and implements assessment strategies in order to maintain a proper learning and care environment for each child. He selects and uses assessment tools and strategies.

VII

Marketing, Advertising, and Public Relations

An effective administrator maintains optimum enrollment and is conscious of good customer service. She has knowledge of the fundamentals of effective marketing, public relations, and community outreach including the understanding of the similarities and differences between marketing, advertising, and public relations. She possesses professional telephone skills. She knows what steps to take to maintain optimum enrollment. She understands how to promote linkages with local schools.

An effective administrator manages the response to parental inquiries including defining the role of all staff in marketing, handling phone calls and tours, and managing a waiting list. She knows how to respond to customer interest inquiries. She is able to communicate the philosophy of the program and to promote a positive public image to families, business leaders, public officials, and prospective funders.

An effective administrator maintains a professional program image through written, verbal, and visual communication with parents and the community. She is able to lay out a yellow page advertisement. She is able to write a press release. She is skilled in developing effective promotional literature, handbooks, newsletters, and press releases. She is able to evaluate the cost-benefit of different marketing and promotional strategies.

VIII

Financial Management

An effective administrator understands and uses financial tools and concepts including budget, fixed and variable expense, cash flow, deviation analysis, staffing plans and breakeven analysis. He understands the differences between fixed and variable expenses, and between deviation analysis and break even analysis.

An effective administrator schedules staff consistent with enrollment patterns, involves staff in scheduling decisions, and secures and supervises substitutes. He is able to schedule staff to assure adequate supervision.

An effective administrator manages payroll, benefit, and leave policies, and develops a compensation structure that rewards retention and increased knowledge and skills of staff. He is able to manage payroll, benefit, and leave policies. He understands how to develop an employee compensation package. He is able to provide incentives to attract and maintain quality staff.

An effective administrator understands the concepts of income projection and pricing strategies, the effect of discount policies, and full time equivalent enrollment. He is able to write a budget. He understands how to accurately project, analyze, and report income and expenses.

An effective administrator maintains accurate and complete financial expenditure reports.

An effective administrator sets and collects tuition fees in an efficient and tactful manner He understands how to figure the true cost of providing care. He has confidence in finding funding sources other than tuition fees.

An effective administrator ensures the cost effective purchase of supplies and equipment. He purchases effectively and efficiently.

An effective administrator identifies federal, state, and local funding sources, both public and private.

An effective administrator mobilizes needed resources including the use of fund raising, unrelated business income, value-added programs, and government grants or purchase of service agreements.

IX

Operational Planning and Evaluation

An effective administrator understands and uses business planning techniques designed to insure long term success of the program and its ability to adapt to changing conditions. She knows the essential elements of a business plan.

An effective administrator evaluates the program and all its components, and uses this evaluation to change and improve the program. She is able to conduct an operational and financial evaluation of a program.

An effective administrator understands and responds to factors, both internal and external, which influence the program and its goals. She understands that there are internal and external influences on early childhood education programs.

An effective administrator understands and uses strategic planning techniques designed to insure long term success of the program and its ability to adapt to changing conditions. She grasps strategic planning techniques.

An effective administrator understands and uses the risk management process and planning techniques designed to insure long term success of the program and its ability to adapt to changing conditions. She understands risk management techniques.

X

Leadership and Advocacy

An effective administrator works with and contributes to the development of a board of directors and advisory groups where applicable. He understands organizational theory and leadership styles as they relate to early childhood work environments. He understands how to define organizational problems, to gather data to generate alternative solutions, and to effectively apply analytical skills.

An effective administrator facilitates the development of community spirit among staff, parents, the board of directors, advisory groups, and children. He is able to evaluate program effectiveness. He understands how to support families as valued partners in the educational process.

An effective administrator understands the educational, social, political, and cultural context of her community and keeps up to date with events and public policy decisions. He has knowledge of the legislative processes, social issues, and public policies as they relate to young children and their families. He has an understanding of different family systems and different parenting styles.

An effective administrator has knowledge of community services, is able to refer families and staff to social services, to health services and education, and to training appropriate to their individual needs. He is able to implement programs that support families of diverse cultural, ethnic, linguistic, and socio-economic backgrounds.

An effective administrator has knowledge of local, state, and national public policy efforts relating to early childhood education, and is able to use this knowledge to build community networks and coalitions. He is able to advocate on behalf of young children, their families, and the child care profession.

An effective administrator demonstrates communication skills. He knows how to articulate a vision, clarify and affirm values, and create a culture built on norms of continuous improvement and ethical conduct. He understands the communication process and the importance of developing relationships. He possesses knowledge of communication methods and plans. He is able to practice two-way communication techniques. He understands how to combine technology and paper as it relates to management of communication processes. He is able to listen to parents and identify referral needs. He possesses the skills required for public speaking, oral communication, and written communication.

An effective administrator understands the principles of leadership, management, and accountability. He understands the difference between a leader and a manager.

APPENDIX

Periodical Resources

Child Care Information Exchange
Box 2890
Redmond, WA 98073
206-883-9394
Magazine

Early Childhood News
330 Progress Road
Dayton, OH 45449
Magazine

Early Childhood Today
Scholastic, Inc.
555 Broadway
New York, NY 10012
800-544-2917

Totline Newsletter
Warren Publishing House, Inc.
Box 2255
Everett, WA 98203
Newsletter

Parenting Information News
2399 Rolandale
West Bloomfield, MI 48324
810-363-5030
Magazine

Journal of Child-Care Administration
202 Cirrus Road
Holbrook, NY 11741
516-472-8009
(16-page journal, published quarterly)

Child Care Related Websites

American Academy of Pediatrics
www.aap.org

American Public Human Services Association
www.aphsa.org

Bureau of Labor Statistics
www.bls.gov

Center for the Child Care Workforce
www.ccw.org

Child Welfare League of America
www.cwla.org

Children's Defense Fund
www.childrensfoundation.net

Consumer Product Safety Commission
www.cpsc.gov

Department of Education
www.ed.gov

Department of Labor
www.dol.gov

Empowerment Zone/Enterprise Communities
www.ezec.gov

Families and Work Institute
www.familiesandworkinst.org

The Finance Project
www.financeproject.org

Indian Health Service
www.ihs.gov

Military Child Development Program
www.military-childrenandyouth.calib.com

National Black Child Development Institute
www.nbcdi.org

National Center for Children in Poverty
http://cpmcnet.columbia.edu/dept/nccp

National Child Care Association
www.NCCAnet.org

National Clearinghouse on Child Abuse and Neglect
www.calib.com/nccanch

National Conference of State Legislatures
www.ncsl.org

National Early Childhood Program Accreditation

www.necpa.net

National Head Start Association
www.nhsa.org

NEC*TAS
http://www.nectas.unc.edu

National School Age Care Alliance
www.nsaca.org

The ARC
www.TheArc.org

Zero to Three
http://www.zerotothree.org

Historical and Philosophic Context

High Scope Foundation
www.highscope.org

Bankstreet College of Education
Main Campus Location
610 West 112th Street
New York, NY 10025-1898
www.bnkst.edu

Montessori International
www.montessori-ami.org

Teaching Strategies
www.teachingstrategies.com

Head Start Bureau
www2.acf.dhhs.gov/programs/hsb/

National Membership Organizations

National Child Care Association (NCCA)
www.nationalchildcare.org

National Association for the Education of the Young Child (NAEYC)
www.naeyc.org

National Association of Child Care Professionals (NACCP)
www.naccp.org

National Association for Family Child Care
www.nafcc.org

National Organizations of Interest

National Association for Child Care Resource and Referral Agencies
www.naccrra.org

Child Care Law Center (CCLC)
221 Pine Street, Third Floor
San Francisco, CA 94104
Phone: 415-394-7144
http://www.childcarelaw.org

Child Welfare League of America, Inc.
440 First Street NW, Suite 310
Washington, DC 20001-2085
Phone: 202-638-2952
http://www.cwla.org

Children's Defense Fund
25 E Street NW
Washington, DC 20001
Phone: 202-662-3545
http://www.childrensdefense.org

The Children's Foundation
725 Fifteenth Street NW, Suite 505
Washington, DC 20005-2109
Phone: 202-347-3300
http://www.childrensfoundation.net/

National Network for Child Care (Extension services)
www.nncc.org

Families and Work Institute
330 Seventh Avenue
New York, NY 10001
Phone: 212-465-2044
http://www.familiesandworkinst.org/

National Association for Regulatory Administration
1016 Rosser St.
Conyers, GA 30012
770-388-7771
http://www.nara-licensing.org

National Resource Center for Health and Safety in Child Care
University of Colorado Health Sciences Center
School of Nursing
4200 E. Ninth Avenue
Campus Box C287
Denver, CO 80262
Phone: 800-598-5437
http://nrc.uchsc.edu

Small Business Administration
www.sba.gov

U. S. Department of Labor
www.dol.gov

Links to Other Information

National Child Care Information Center (NCCIC)
www.nccic.org

The Children's Foundation
www.childrensfoundation.net

Directory of State Child Care Regulatory Offices:
http://nccic.org/dirs/regoffic.html

Individual States' Child Care Licensure Regulations
National Resource Center for Health and Safety in Child Care
http://nrc.uchsc.edu

Indicators of Quality Child Care: Research Update (2002) Richard Fiene, Ph.D.
http://aspe.hhs.gov/hsp/ccquality-ind02/index.htm

2002 Child Care Center Licensing Study
The Children's Foundation
http://www.childrensfoundation.net/publications.htm

2002 Family Child Care Licensing Study
The Children's Foundation
http://www.childrensfoundation.net/publications.htm

Caring for Our Children: National Health and Safety Performance Standards: Guidelines for Out-of-Home Child Care Programs, Second Edition (2002)

National Resource Center for Health and Safety in Child Care
http://nrc.uchsc.edu/CFOC/index.html

Family Child Care: What's in a Name? (June 2001)
Gwen Morgan, Sheri Azer and Sarah LeMoine
http://nccic.org/pubs/fccname.pdf

Non-licensed Forms of Child Care in Homes: Issues and Recommendations for State Support (June 2001)
Gwen Morgan, Kim Elliott, Christine Beaudette, Sheri Azer and Sarah LeMoine
http://nccic.org/pubs/nonlic-wheelock.pdf

Regulation of Child Care (Winter 2002)
Sheri L. Azer, Sarah LeMoine, Gwen Morgan, Richard M. Clifford, and Gisele M. Crawford
National Center for Early Development and Learning
http://www.fpg.unc.edu/~ncedl/PDFs/RegBrief.pdf

State Efforts to Enforce Safety and Health Regulations (January 2000) General Accounting Office (GAO)
http://www.gao.gov/new.items/he00028.pdf

Stepping Stones to Using Caring for Our Children
National Resource Center for Health and Safety in Child Care
http://nrc.uchsc.edu/national/stepping.html

National Resources

Child Care Information Exchange
P.O. Box 3249
Redmond, WA 98073
800-221-2864
http://www.ccie.com

The Exchange is a bi-monthly magazine primarily for child care administrators and managers. In the past, it has featured assessment in the "Beginnings Workshop" section of the magazine. The following selected articles address assessment:
"Assessment Tools in the 21st Century" (July/August 2002); and
"Needing to Assess and Assessing Needs" (September/October 1998).

The Early Childhood Education Assessment (ECEA) Consortium
Council of Chief State School Officers (CCSSO)
One Massachusetts Avenue NW, Suite 700
Washington, DC 20001-1431
202-336-7000
http://www.ccsso.org/Projects/scass/projects/early_childhood_education_assessment_consortium

ECEA was initiated in 2000 to provide guidance to decision-makers on appropriate assessment systems in order to promote and ensure high-quality learning opportunities for young children. The consortium's focus is on early childhood learning and developmental outcomes, appropriate assessment, program evaluation, and using data for system accountability.

Early Childhood Outcomes (ECO) Center
785-395-0829
http://www.fpg.unc.edu/~eco/index.cfm

The ECO Center seeks to promote the development and implementation of child and family outcome measures for infants, toddlers, and preschoolers with disabilities. These measures can be used in local, State, and national accountability systems. The ECO Center actively pursues their goals by collaborating with stakeholders and other groups concerned with outcomes measurement; researching issues related to the development and implementation of outcome measures; and providing technical assistance to support States in developing and implementing outcome measurement systems. The ECO Center is a five-year project funded by the Office of Special Education Programs (OSEP) in the U.S. Department of Education. It is a collaborative effort of SRI International, Frank

Porter Graham Child Development Institute at UNC-Chapel Hill, Juniper Gardens Children's Project, the National Association of State Directors of Special Education, and the University of Connecticut Health Center. The following publications relate to measuring outcomes:

Uses and Misuses of Data on Outcomes for Young Children with Disabilities: Draft (July 2004), by Kathleen Hebbler, produced by the Early Childhood Outcomes Center, identifies in table format the ways that data can be used effectively (or misused) – at the national, State, and local level – to determine outcomes for young children with disabilities. The tables are designed to help policy-makers clearly delineate the various purposes and limitations of specific measurement approaches and alert them to possible interpretations of results made by the public. This resource is available on the Web at http://www.fpg.unc.edu/~eco/pdfs/ECO_Outcomes_Uses.pdf.

Considerations Related to Developing a System for Measuring Outcomes for Young Children With Disabilities and Their Families (revised April 2004), by the Early Childhood Outcomes Center, presents a framework for thinking about the key considerations related to the development of a system for measuring outcomes. Examples of key decisions that must be made are presented. This resource is available on the Web at http://www.fpg.unc.edu/~eco/pdfs/considerations.pdf.

"Beyond Outcomes: How Ongoing Assessment Supports Children's Learning and Leads to Meaningful Curriculum," by Diane Dodge, Cate Heroman, Julia Charles, and Jessica Maiorca, discusses how ongoing assessment can be a manageable and dynamic process, directly linked to planning curriculum and supporting each child's learning and development. They describe effective assessment methods such as mapping children's progress on a continuum. Additional information is available on the Web at http://www.naeyc.org/resources/journal/item-detail.asp?page=1&docID=2891&sesID=1096561428710.

"Ensuring Culturally and Linguistically Appropriate Assessment of Young Children," by Rosa Santos, discusses useful tools accessible through the Early Childhood Research Institute on Culturally and Linguistically Appropriate Services (CLAS), which offers information on numerous Internet-based resources to assist professionals, families, and others in ensuring that assessments are culturally and linguistically appropriate. The article includes a list of considerations for appropriate assessment. Additional information is available on the Web at http://www.naeyc.org/resources/journal/item-detail.asp?page=1&docID=2895&sesID=1096561428710.

"Who Goes to Pre-K and How Are They Doing?" (Spring 2005), in "NCEDL Pre-kindergarten Study," Early Developments Vol. 9, No. 1, published by the FPG Child Development Institute at the University of North Carolina at Chapel Hill, describes research by the National Center for Early Development & Learning (NCEDL) on public pre-K classrooms, teachers, and children in their study, Multi-State Study of Pre-Kindergarten. Measures used by NCEDL in their assessment of 240 prekindergarten classrooms in six States include the following:

Classroom Observations

Early Childhood Environment Rating Scale – Revised (ECERS-R), (Harms, Clifford, Cryer, 1998).

Classroom Assessment Scoring System (CLASS), (Pianta, La Paro, & Hamre, 2004).

Emerging Academic Snapshot, (Ritchie, Howes, Kraft-Sayre, & Weiser, 2001).

Direct Assessments of Children's Skills

Peabody Picture Vocabulary Test 3rd edition (PPVT-III), (Dunn & Dunn, 1997).

Oral & Written Language Scales (OWLS) (Oral Expression Scale), (Carrow-Woolfolk, 1995).

Woodcock-Johnson III Tests of Achievement, (Woodcock, McGrew, & Mather, 2001).

Applied Problems Subtest.

Sound Awareness-Rhyming Subtest.

Identifying Letters, Numbers, Counting and Writing, (NCEDL, 2001).

Color Bears, (Zill & Resnick, Head Start Family and Child Experiences Survey, 1998).

Teacher Reports

Teacher-Child Rating Scale, (Hightower et al., 1986).

Language and Literacy Skills, (National Center for Education Statistics, 1999).

Teacher Attitudes and Beliefs, (Schaefer & Edgerton, 1985).

Student Teacher Relationship Scale, (STRS; Pianta, 2001). (page 14)

This resource is available at http://www.fpg.unc.edu/%7ENCEDL/PDFs/ED9_1.pdf.

The Early Language and Literacy Observation and Assessment Tools document under the Literacy topic of NCCIC's Web site in the Popular Topics section at http://nccic.org/pubs/goodstart/assessment-literacy.html includes information on research of selected State prekindergarten initiatives.

Resources on Diversity

Alike and Different, Exploring Our Humanity with Young Children, Bonnie Neugebauer, Editor, 1992, National Association for The Education of Young Children, 1509 16th Street, NW, Washington, DC 20036-1426.

Passages To Inclusion, Creating Systems of Care for All Children, Monograph for State, Territorial and Tribal Child Care Administrators, U.S. Department of Health and Human Services. Available from the National Child Care Information Center, 243 Church St., NW, 2nd Floor, Vienna, VA 22180, 800-616-2242, www.nccic.org.

Valuing Diversity: The Primary Years, Janet Brown McCracken, 1993, National Association for The Education of Young Children, 1509 16th Street, NW, Washington, DC 20036-1426.

The following publications are available through the Educational Resources Information Center at www.accesseric.org:

The Anti-Bias Approach in Early Childhood, Barbara Creaser, Elizabeth Dau.

Diversity & Developmentally Appropriate Practices: Challenges for Early Childhood Education, Bruce L. Mallory, Editor.

Diversity in the Classroom: New Approaches to the Education of Young Children, Second Edition, Frances E. Kendall.

"Early Childhood Educators'Beliefs and Practices of Anti-Bias Curriculum in Rural Areas", Janis R. Bullock, *Early Child Development and Care*, Volume 126, pp 1-13, December 1996.

Early Childhood Reform: Innovative Approaches to Cultural and Racial Diversity among Families, Carol Brunson Phillips.

"The Education of Hispanics in Early Childhood: of Roots and Wings", Eugene E. Garcia, *Peabody Journal of Education*, Volume 70, pp 112-124, Spring 1995.

"A Few Words about Diversity and Rigidity: One Director's Perspective", Lori D'Entrmont, *Young Children*, Volume 53, pp 72-73, January 1998.

"Include Me too! Human Diversity in Early Childhood", Gyda Chud, Book review, *Canadian Journal of Research in Early Childhood Education*, Volume 7, pp. 91-93, June 1988.

"Look to the East to Gain a New Perspective, Understand Cultural Differences, and Appreciate Cultural Diversity", Nancy K. Freeman, *Early Childhood Education Journal*, Volume 26, pp 79- 82, Winter 1998.

"Meeting the Challenge of Linguistic and Cultural Diversity in Early Childhood Education," Eugene E. Garcia et. al., *Yearbook in Early Childhood Education Series*, Volume 6.

Meeting Family and Community Needs: The Three C's of Early Childhood Education, Sharon L. Kagan.

"Multicultural Education in Early Childhood Classrooms," NEA Early Childhood Education Series.

"Recognizing Diversity in the Early Childhood Classroom: Getting Started," *Teaching Exceptional Children*, Volume 28, pp 22-25, Summer 1996.

The Role of Play in Inclusive Early Childhood Settings, Catherine Marchant, Cheryl Render. *Special Children, Special Care: Early Childhood Education for Children with Disabilities*.

The Young Black Exceptional Child: providing Programs and Services, Elouise Jackson, Editor.

Abbreviations

ACCESS	Architectural and Transportation Barriers Compliance
ADA	Americans with Disabilities Act
ADEA	Age Discrimination in Employment Act
B & A	Before and After (School Care)
CAP	Center Accreditation Project
CCDBG	Child Care Development Block Grant
CCP	Certified Child Care Professional
CC-PORT	Creative Curriculum Progress and Outcomes Reporting Tool
CCR&R	Child Care Resource and Referral Agencies
CDA	Child Development Associate
COBRA	Consolidated Omnibus Budget Reconciliation Act
COR	Child Observation Record
D.B.A.	Doing Business As
DAP	Developmentally Appropriate Practice
EML	Electronic Management of Learning
EPA	Environmental Protection Agency
FLSA	Fair Labor Standards Act
GAAP	Generally Accepted Accounting Principles
HIV	Human Immunodeficiency Virus
IGDI	Individual Growth and Development Indicators
NAC	National Administrator Credential
NACCP	National Association of Child Care Professionals
NACCRRA	National Association of Child Care Resource & Referral Agencies

NAEYC	National Association for the Education of Young Children
NANE	National Association for Nursery Education
NBCDI	National Black Child Development Institute
NCCA	National Child Care Association
NCCIC	National Child Care Information Center
NCLB	No Child Left Behind
NECPA	National Early Childhood Program Accreditation
NICHDT	National Institute of Child Health and Human Development
NLRA	National Labor Relations Act
NLRB	National Labor Relations Board
OSHA	Occupational Safety and Health Administration
R & R	Resource and Referral Agency
SWOT	Strengths, Weaknesses, Opportunities, and Threats
TANF	Temporary Assistance to Needy Families
UPK	Universal Pre-kindergarten
VPK	Voluntary Universal Pre-kindergarten
ZDP	Zone of Proximal Development

Glossary

Abstract: a summary of a proposal providing an overview of the proposal to the reader

Accessibility: safe, easy access to and throughout the building

Accreditation: a form of official recognition. This means that the program meets certain established standards of quality. The program has also gone through a specified evaluation by an organization that represents the professional field.

Administrative staff: those employees with organizational and planning skills who provide direction for the total program. They seek funds, pursue licensing, recruit and enroll children, and manage personnel needs and professional development. They do not usually work directly in the classroom.

Adult to child ratio: the number of adults who must be in the classroom with the children. This may be established by your organization, state regulatory agencies, or an accrediting agency.

Advisory board: a board of individuals who can study issues and make recommendations, but cannot require that those recommendations be carried out.

Anecdotal notes/records: a common form of observation where teachers or others write down brief descriptions of children's activities, actions, and or behaviors.

Assets: things that represent some value to the center (e.g. cash in bank, money people owe you, furniture, fixtures)

Audit: a verification undertaken to examine the accuracy of records and verify expenses and income.

Behaviorist: developed from the psychological theory known as the scientific analysis of behavior which focuses on observable behavior and does not identify stages of development. Child development programs that follow this philosophy might be referred to as "behaviorist programs."

Break-even analysis: an analysis of what the program needs to charge to cover the expenses of operating the program

Budget: projected spending plan based on expected income, often projected on a yearly basis.

Business plan: a plan written to convince a bank or lending agency that the program you want to start or expand is needed, realistic, and you have the skills necessary to carry it out. This is sometimes referred to as an organization's resume.

By-laws: a set of rules that identify the official structure and makeup of the board and decision making processes. They also specify the rules by which the board will conduct business.

Cash flow: the movement of money into and out of a bank account/timing of income (cash) versus the expenditures (expenses).

Cash reserve: money set aside to cover times when money is not flowing into the program.

Center based care: care for groups of children in settings that have been organized specifically for their use.

Center profile: a brief overall description of the program.

Code of ethics: a guide for behavior

Corporation: an entity that employs workers, pays bills, files tax returns, and has liability should debt or obligations be incurred.

Contract: a legal agreement between two or more parties committing each party to the terms specified in the agreement.

Co-pay: when an organization or agency subsidizes or pays a portion of tuition fees, the amount that remains to be paid by the family is the "co-pay."

Curriculum: a plan of instruction that details what students are to know, how they are to learn it, what the teacher's role is, and the context in which learning and teaching will take place.

Custodial care: care provided with an aim for simply keeping children safe.

Developmentally Appropriate Practices (DAP): the concept that equipment, activities, and guidance are carefully tailored to the developmental characteristics and needs of each group.

Deviation analysis: an analysis to determine the difference between budgeted amount and actual amount earned and/or spent

Directing: the part of a job that involves providing leadership for a program and influencing others to successfully meet their responsibilities.

Drop-in care: care provided on an occasional basis for children whose parents may need child care to take care of intermittent or personal business

Early childhood programs: according to NAEYC, programs for children from ages birth through eight years.

Employment at-will: no reason is needed for the employee or the employer to terminate employment of a non-contract employee.

Encumbered funds: money for which a commitment has been made, but may not have been spent yet.

Enrollment: process that occurs when the program has an opening and a child's parent(s) or guardian(s) make a commitment that the child will attend.

Fiscal year: a period of time during which a particular budget or source of money is in effect. This may or may not coincide with the calendar year.

Fixed expenses: expenses to which a program is committed and that recur on a regular basis/expenses that remain the same no matter how many children are present (e.g. rent, building insurance)

For-profit program: a program that operates to make a profit for the owners or investors.

Fringe benefits: financial benefits included in compensation in addition to salary (e.g. annual leave, insurance, memberships)

Full Time Equivalent (FTE): a common standard of measure in education that compares the actual enrollment to possible enrollment.

Goals: the desired results you hope to accomplish through the mission of the center or program. Goals define what you are trying to achieve through your work. Goals may be short term like "increasing facility's curb appeal," or long-term, such as "children developing a sense of independence."

Grievance procedure: a procedure that specifies the process by which employees can complain if they feel they have been unfairly treated.

Home-based care: care that is provided in a home setting

Inclusion: refers to a set of practices and beliefs that all children should be educated, regardless of disability, in their neighborhood school, and in age appropriate general education settings with appropriate supports and services.

Independent consultant: recognized expert in a field who can be hired to provide additional knowledge or expertise.

In-kind support: items or services provided without a fee attached.

In-service training: training provided by an employer for its employees.

Job descriptions: documents that spell out the required qualifications, experience, and duties for each job.

Journal a daily record of written reflections on events, activities, and learning.

Laboratory schools: programs that exist for the purpose of training future teachers and studying children. Usually these schools are affiliated with colleges and universities or technical schools and high schools.

Liabilities: Money the center owes others (e.g. payroll, loans)

Line of credit: a short-term loan. As it is paid, the amount becomes available to borrow again.

Mandated reporter: individual who is legally obligated to report suspicion of child abuse or neglect to proper authorities.

Mentor: a person who serves as an advisor, a role model, or friend.

Mission statement: a clear and simple statement that describes what your organization exists to do. It is a description of the overall purpose of your business or organization, communicating the essence of your organization to stakeholders and the public in just a few sentences

Networking: Creating and maintaining lines of communication with people who have similar interests, jobs, or goals and can provide information and support.

Net Worth: a statement of the difference between assets and liabilities.

Not-for-profit program: a program legally organized to operate without making a profit.

Objectives: the things you need to accomplish in order to achieve your goals. They are usually thought of as being observable and measurable.

Organizational chart: a graphic representation of board, administrative, and staff positions showing their relationships and authority.

Partnership: a business that is owned by two or more people, or partners.

Parent cooperative/coop: program usually owned and operated by a group of parents who volunteer services and time to reduce the cost of care.

Parent handbook: written communication to which parents can refer regarding rules, policies and procedures

Personnel policies: policies that spell out the nature of the agreement between your organization and its employees.

Positive guidance: guidance that helps children learn what behaviors are acceptable.

Proposal: document explaining what you want to do, why there is a need to do it, why think you can do it, and what kind of help you need

Quorum: the number of board members who must be present in order to conduct legal business

Resource and referral (R and R): an agency with a primary purpose of providing services designed to support child care programs of all sorts. These are sometimes organized around specific regions of a state.

Resume: a summary that includes pertinent information about an individual seeking employment.

Request for Proposal (RFP): a formal request from an organization or agency willing to contract with other organizations or agencies to fill its needs.

Sole proprietorship: a business that is owned by a single person. The proprietor or owner employs individuals to work at the center and operates the center like any other business.

Staffing: recruiting, hiring, scheduling and retaining of skilled individuals needed to operate a program.

Start-up-costs: expenses incurred before you receive income from a program.

Subsidized care: care provided for a reduced fee for families who meet specified guidelines.

Target population: the individuals who will be helped by your service

Technical assistance: help available through a variety of agencies, organizations, consultants, and institutions. Technical assistance takes many forms and may include services such as training or consulting, telephone support, or lending libraries.

Theory: a logical explanation or model based on observation, facts, hypotheses, experimentation, and reasoning that attempts to explain a range of natural phenomena

Time line: a graphic display of time elements of a project.

Validators: professionals in the early childhood field who have received special training in the validation process.

Variable expenses: expenses that vary depending on the number of children cared for/costs that are paid on a regular basis, but the amount may vary.

Windows of Opportunity: a concept regarding the optimum times for learning and brain wiring.

Sources

Abbey, Osborne, Jr. "Early Childhood Education's Role in Providing a Foundation for Success in the Work Force." Presented at the International Conference on Education: Redesigning Pedagogy – Research, Policy, & Practice, Singapore, 2005.

Arwood, E. & Young, E. *The language of respect: the right of each student to participate in an environment of communicative thoughtfulness.* Nashville, Tennessee: Lightning Print, Inc., 2000.

Assessment Technology, Inc. 5099 East Grant Road, Suite 331, Tucson, AZ 85712 ,800-367-4762 http://63.172.114.196/galileoPreschool/overview/index.htm

Barnet, A. B., & Barnet, R. J. *The youngest minds: Parenting and genes in the development of intellect and emotion.* New York: Simon & Schuster, 1998

Berk, Laura E. and Winsler, Adam. Scaffolding Children's Learning: Vygotsky and Early Childhood Education. NAEYC, Washington D.C. 1995.

Bloom, Paula Jorde-Bloom, Sheerer, M. Britz, J., & Richard N., *Blueprint for Action: Achieving Center-Based Change Through Staff Development*, New Horizons, Lake Forest, IL, 1991.

Bowman, Barbara and Moore, Evelyn K. School Readiness and Social-Emotional Development: Perspectives on Cultural Diversity. National Black Child Development Institute, Inc., 2006

Brooks, Julie K. and Stevens, Barry A., *How to Write a Successful Business Plan*, ANACOM, New York, NY, 1987.

Brualdi, A. (1996). Multiple intelligences: Gardner's theory. Practical Assessment, Research & Evaluation, 5(10). Retrieved , March 27, 2007 http://PAREonline.net/getvn.asp?v=5&n=10

Bruner, Charles. "Seven Things Policy Makers Need to Know about School Readiness". Des Moines, IA:

State Early Childhood Policy Technical Assistance Network, January 2005.

Cannie, Joan Koob, *Keeping Customers for Life*, American Management Association, New York, New York, 1991.

Carter, R. (1998). *Mapping the mind.* Los Angeles, CA: University of California Press.

College of Education and Human Development, University of Minnesota, 215 Pattee Hall, 150 Pillsbury Drive SE, Minneapolis, MN 55455. 612-625-2898, 734-485-2000, ext. 218. http://ggg.umn.edu

Conyers, M. & Wilson, D. (2005). *BrainSMART 60 Strategies for boosting test scores.* Orlando, Florida: BrainSMART Inc.

Conner, D. (1998). *Leading at the Edge of Chaos.* Wiley and Sons, Inc: New York.

Copple, Carol and Bredekamp, Sue. Developmentally Appropriate Practice in Early Childhood Programs. NAEYC, Washington D.C. 2009.

Covey, S. (1996). *Performance Agreements.* Covey Leadership Center.

Covey, S. (1996). *Synergy: Creating Unstoppable People, Teams, and Organizations.* Covey Leadership Center.

Creative Curriculum, Teaching Strategies, Inc. P.O. Box 42243, Washington, DC 20015, 800-637-3652 or 202-362-7543 http://www.teachingstrategies.com

Crisp, Michael (Ed.). *Rate Your Skills as a Manager*, Crisp Publications, Inc., Menlo Park, California, 1991.

De Bellis, M. D., Bum, A. S., Birmaher, B., Keshavan, M. S., Eccard, C. H., Boring, A. M., Jenkins, F. J., & Ryan, N. D. (1999). Developmental traumatology. Part 1: Biological stress systems. *Biological Psychiatry, 45,* 1259-1270.

De Bellis, M. D., Keshaven, M. S., Clark, D. B., Caseey, B. J., Giedd, J. B., Boring, A. M., Frustaci, K., & Ryan, N. D. (1999). Developmental traumatology. Part 2: Brain development. *Biological Psychiatry, 45,* 1271-1284

DeVries, R and Kohlberg, L. (1987). Constructivist Early Education: Overview and Comparison with Other Programs. Washington, D.C.: National Association for the Education of Young Children

Diamond, Marion, and Janet Hopsen. Magic Trees of the Mind: How to Nurture Your Child's Intelligence, Creativity, and Healthy Emotions from Birth through Adolescence. Penguin Group: 1999.

Education Week. Quality Counts 2007: From Cradle to Career, Connecting American Education From Birth to Adulthood. Education Week, 4 January 2007.

Edwards, C., Gandini, L., & Forman G, (1993) *The Hundred Languages of Children: the Reggio Emilia Approach to Early Childhood Education.* Greenwich, Connecticut: Ablex Publishing.

Epstein, Ann S. *Me, You, Us Social-Emotional Learning in Preschool.* High Scope Press, Ypsilanti, Michigan 2009.

Epstein, Ann S. *The Intentional Teacher: Choosing the Best Strategies for Young Children's Learning.* NAEYC, Washington, D.C. 2007.

Feuerstein, R., Feuerstein, R., & Gross, S. (1997). "The learning potential assessment device". In D. Flanagan, J. Genshaft, & P. Harrison (Eds.), *Contemporary intellectual assessment.* New York: Guilford Press.

Field, T. M. (1995). "Psychologically depressed parents". In M. H. Bornstein (Ed.), *Handbook of parenting: Vol. 4. Applied practical parenting* (pp. 85-107). Mahwah, NJ: Lawrence Erlbaum Associates, Inc.

Fletcher, K. E. (1996). "Childhood posttraumatic stress disorder". In E. H. Mash & R. A. Barkley (Eds.), *Child Psychopathology* (pp. 242-276). New York: Guildford Publications, Inc.

Gestwicki, Carol. Developmentally Appropriate Practice: Curriculum and Development in Early Education. Delmar Publishers, Albany NY, 1999.

Goldstein, Anne, Joan Lombardi, and Rachel Schumacher. "Birth to 5 and Beyond: A Growing Movement in Early Education." Zero to Three Journal. June 2006.

Gonzalez-Mena, Janet, Diversity in Earl Care and Education. McGraw Hill 2008.

Gopnik, A., Meltzoff, A. N., & Kuhl, P. K. *The Scientist in the Crib: Minds, Brains, and How Children Learn.* New York: Morrow 1999.

Haberman, M. *STAR Teachers of Children in Poverty.* West Lafayette, Indiana: Kappa Delta Pi, an International Honor Society in Education, 1995.

Haggern, Paul, *Your Attitude is Showing*, American Business Communications, Inc., Overland Park, Kansas, 1991.

Harris, I. B. *Children in Jeopardy: Can We Break the Cycle of Poverty?* New Haven, CT: Yale Child Study Center, 1996.

Hart, B., & Risley, T. R. (1995). *Meaningful Differences in the Everyday Experience of Young American Children.* Baltimore: Brookes Publishing.

Hauken, Paul, *Growing A Business*, Simon and Schuster, Inc., New York, New York, 1987.

Helburn, Suzane W. "The Cost, Quality and Child Care Outcomes Study". *Cost, Quality, and Child Care Outcomes in Child Care Centers.* Denver: University of Colorado at Denver, Economics Department, 1995.

Helburn, Suzanne W., and Barbara R. Bergmann. America's Childcare Problem. New York: Palgrave, 2002.

High/Scope Foundation, 600 North River Street, Ypsilanti, MI 4819 Center for Early Education Development http://www.highscope.org/Assessment/cor.htm

Hills, Tynette W. "Reaching Potentials Through Appropriate Assessment," *Reaching Potentials: Appropriate Curriculum and Assessment for Young Children, Vol.1,* Bredekamp and Rosegrant, Editors, Washington D.C., NAEYC 1992.

Huttenlocher, J., Haight, W., Bryk, A., Seltzer, M., & Lyons, T. (1991). "Early Vocabulary Growth: Relation to Language Input and Gender." *Developmental Psychology, 27,* 236-248.

Huttenlocher, P. R., & Dabholkar, A. S. (1997). "Regional Differences in Synaptogenesis in the Human Cerebral Cortex." *Journal of Comparative Neurology, 387,* 167-178.

Hyson, Marilou. *Enthusiastic and Engaged Learners; Approaches to Learning in the Early Childhood Classroom.* Teachers College Press, NY, NY 2008.

Jablon, Judy R., Dombro, Amy Laura, and Dichtelmiller, Margo L. *The Power of Observation.* Teaching Strategies, Inc., Washington D. C. 2007.

Jensen, E. *Teaching with the brain in mind.* Alexandria, Virginia: Association for Supervision and Curriculum Development, 1998.

Johnson, Kay, and Jane Knitzer. *Spending Smarter: A Funding Guide for Policymakers and Advocates to Promote Social and Emotional Health and School Readiness.* Washington, D.C. National Center for Children in Poverty, November 2005.

Kagen, S. and Bowman, B (eds.). (1997). *Leadership in Early Care and Education.* NAEYC: Washington DC

Kagan, Sharon L., and Nancy E. Cohen. *Not By Chance.* New Haven, CT: The Bush Center in Child Development and Social Policy, 1997.

Kahn, D. (ed.). (1995). *What is Montessori Preschool?* Cleveland, Ohio: North American Montessori Teachers' Association.

Kaufman, J., & Charney, D. S. (1999). Neurobiological correlates of child abuse. *Biological Psychiatry, 45,* 1235-1236.

Kotulak, R. *Inside the Brain.* Kansas City: Andrews and McMeel., 1996.

LeBoeuf, Michael, *Working Smart,* Warner Books, New York, New York, 1979.

Lemert, Martha M. "Fostering Positive Employee Relations." Published presentation to The National Child Care Association Southeastern Leadership Seminar, Orlando, Florida March 2009.

Lemert, Martha M. *Handeling I-9's*. Published presentation to The National Child Care Association Southeastern Leadership Seminar, Orlando, Florida, March 2009.

Lemert, Martha M. "Hiring & Firing: Doing It Right." Published presentation to The National Child Care Association Southeastern Leadership Seminar, Orlando, Florida, March 2009.

Lemert, Martha M. "Pay Now or Pay Later: Wage and Hour for Child Care Agencies." Published presentation to The National Child Care Association Southeastern Leadership Seminar, Orlando, Florida, March 2009.

Lieberman, A. F., & Zeanah, H. (1995). "Disorders of Attachment in Infancy." *Infant Psychiatry*, *4*, 571-587.

Lundy, James, *Lead, Follow or Get Out Of The Way*, Pfeiffer & Company, San Diego, California, 1993.

Luther, William M., *How to Develop a Business Plan in 15 Days*, ANACOM, New York, NY, 1987.

MacMillan, H. L., MacMillan, J. H., Offord, D. R., Griffith, L., & MacMillan, A. (1994). "Primary Prevention of Child Physical Abuse and Neglect: A Critical Review. Part I." *Journal of Child Psychology and Psychiatry and Allied Disciplines*, *35*, 835-856.

MAPS For Life, P.O. Box 667, Perrysburg, OH 43552. 419-661-1945, http://www.marazon.com/default.htm

Marzano, R. *Classroom Management That Works Research-based Strategies for Every Teacher*. Alexandria, Virginia: Association for Supervision and Curriculum Development, 2003.

Marzano, R., Pickering, D., Pollock, J. *Classroom Instruction That Works Research-based Strategies for Increasing Student Achievement*. Alexandria, Virginia: Association for Supervision and Curriculum Development, 2001.

Margerison, Charles, *How to Assess Your Managerial Style*, AMACOM, New York, 1979.

Martin, Don, *Team Think*, Penguin Books, New York, New York, 1993.

McKeever, Mike P., *How to Write a Business Plan*, Nolo Press, Berkeley, CA, 1992.

McWilliams, John-Roger and Peter, *Life 101*, Prelude Press, Los Angeles, California, 1991.

Mead, Sara. "Open the Preschool Door, Close the Preparation Gap." Washington, D.C.: Progressive Policy Institute, 8 September 2004.

Meier, D. *The accelerated learning handbook: a creative guide to designing and delivering faster, more effective training programs.* New York: Mcgraw-Hill, 2000.

Miller, James B., *The Corporate Coach*, St. Martin's Press, New York, New York, 1993.

Muchnick, Bruce. "What Would You Do If....? Published presentation to The National Child Care Association Annual Leadership Conference, Long Beach, California, March, 2008.

National Association for the Education of Young Children, Developmentally Appropriate Practice in Early Childhood Programs Serving Children from Birth through Age 8., A position statement of the National Association for the Education of Young Children. NAEYC, 1997.

National Center for Early Development and Learning. (1999). *The Children of the Cost, Quality and Outcomes Study Go to School.* Chapel Hill, NC: Frank Porter Graham Child Development Center.

Olds, D. L., Henderson, C. R. Jr., Phelps, C., Kitzman, H., & Hanks, C. (1993). "Effect of Prenatal and Infancy Nurse Home Visitation on Government Spending." *Medical Care, 31*(2) 155-174.

National Center on Education and the Economy. "Tough Choices or Tough Times." Washington, D.C.: Jossey-Bass, 2007.

National Child Care Association. The National Economic Impacts of the Child Care Sector. Conyers, GA: National Child Care Association, 2002.

National Reporting System: Information Brief from the Associate Commissioner (April 2003), http://www.acf.hhs.gov/programs/hsb/pdf/NRS.pdf.

Nelson, Bob, *1001 Ways to Reward Employees*, Workman Publishing Company, New York, New York, 1994.

Neugebauer, Roger. "Listening to America's Families." *Child Care Bulletin*, No. 22 (2000).

Nimmo, John. Emergent Curriculum. NAEYC, Washington, DC 1994.

Pearson Early Learning, P.O. Box 2500, 135 South Mt. Zion Road, Lebanon, IN 46052, 800-552-2259. http://www.pearsonearlylearning.com/

Pinson, Linda and Jimett, Jerry, *Anatomy of a Business Plan*, Fullerton, CA, 1989.

Phelps, Pamela. "Supporting Children's School Success: Addressing All Seven Domains of Development." Power Point presentation for Creative Center for Childhood Research and Trainings, Inc.

Ramey, C., & Ramey, S. "Early Intervention and Early Experience." *American Psychologist*, 53, 109-120, 1998.

Ramey, C., Campbell, F., & Blair, C. (1998). "Enhancing the Life Course for High-risk Children." In J. Crane (Ed.), *Social programs that work* (pp. 184-199). New York: Russell Sage Foundation. Additional statistics cited on the Abecedarian Project's Web site at http://www.fpg.unc.edu/verity/

Ramey, Craig T. and Sharon L. Ramey. *Right from Birth: Building Your Child's Foundation for Life*. New York: Goddard Press, 1999.

Rebus, Inc. P.O. Box 4479, Ann Arbor, MI 48106-4479, 800-435-3085, http://www.pearsonearlylearning.com/index2.html

Riley, Dave, San Juan, Robert R., Klinkner, Joan, and Ramminger, Ann. *Social & Emotional Development*. Red Leaf Press, St. Paul, Minnesota 2008.

Schiller, Pam. "Setting Priorities One Step at a Time." Power Point presentation to the Colorado Child Care Association, Denver, February 10, 2006.

Schuller, Robert, *Power Thoughts*, Harper Collins Publishers, New York, New York, 1993.

Schweinhart, L. J., J. Montie, Z. Xichg, W. S. Barnett, C. R. Belfield, M. Nores. *Lifetime Effects: The High/Scope Perry Preschool Study Through Age 40*. Ypsilanti, Michigan: High/Scope Press, 2005.

Seidman, A. Changing the System with Professional Development and Implementation. June 8, 2008. Fischler School of Education and Human Services. Nova Southeastern University, Fort Lauderdale, Florida, 2008.

Shaywitz, S. *Overcoming Dyslexia a New and Complete Science-based Program for Reading Problems at any Level*. New York, New York: Random House, Inc., 2003.

Shore, R. *Rethinking the Brain*. New York: Families and Work Institute, 1997

Seligman, M. (1990). *Learned Optimism*. Simon and Schuster: New York.

Selye, Hans, *Stress Without Distress*, New American Library, New York, New York, 1974.

"Survival Skills for Center Directors: Best of Exchange Reprint Collection #1." *Child Care Information Exchange*, Redmond, Washington.

"Stepping Up – Financing Early Care and Education in the 21st Century." Vol. I. Ewing Marion Kauffman Foundation. March, 1999. This publication consists of four papers presented at a working meeting held in Santa Cruz, California.

Swift, Madelyn and Victoria Mathies, *Teach Your Children Well: A Parent's Guide to Encouraging Character and Integrity*, Southlake, Texas: Childright, 2004.

"Taking Stock - Tools for Teacher, Director and Center Evaluation: Best of Exchange Reprint Collection #8." *Child Care Information Exchange*, Redmond, Washington.

Thompson, Donna, Hudson, Susan D., and Olsen, Heather M., S.A.F.E. Play Areas. Human, Kinetics, Champaign Illinois 2007.

Tomlinson, C. (1999). *The Differentiated Classroom: Responding to the Needs of all Learners*. Alexandria, VA: Association for Supervision and Curriculum Development.

Tyre, Peg. "The New First Grade: Too Much Too Soon?" *Newsweek*. 11 September 2006.

Wallis, Claudia and Sonja Steptoe. "How to Bring All Schools Out of the 20th Century." *Time*, 18 December 2006.

Viscott, David, <u>Risking</u>, Pocket Books, New York, New York, 1977.

Von Oech, Roger, *A Whack on the Side of the Head*, Warner Books, New York, New York, 1983.

Werner, E. E., & Smith, R. S. (1992). *Overcoming the Odds: High Risk Children from Birth to Adulthood*. Ithaca, NY: Cornell University Press

Wien, Carol Anne, *Emergent Curriculum in the Primary Classroom: Interpreting the Reggio Emilia Approach in Schools*. Teachers College Press, NY, NY 2008.

Wilson, D. & Conyers, M. (2005), *Courageous Learners: Unleashing the Brain Power of Students from At-risk Situations*. Orlando, FL: BrainSMART Publishing.

Wilson, D. & Conyers, M. (2006). *Thinking for Results Safer Schools and Higher Student Achievement*. Orlando, Florida: BrainSMART Inc.

Wingert, Pat and Martha Brant. "Reading Your Baby's Mind." *Newsweek*, 15 August 2005.

Yip, R., Binkin, N. J., Fleshood, L, & Trowbridge, F. L. (1987). "Declining Prevalence of Anemia Among Low-income Children in the United States. *Journal of the American Medical Association, 258*(12), 1619-1623.

ZERO TO THREE. (1992). *Heart Start: The Emotional Foundations of School Readiness*. Washington, DC: Zero to Three.

Contributors

Over the years, the NAC has received text contributions from a number of individuals. We wish to acknowledge and thank everyone who has been involved. Listed below are those who are known to have contributed significantly to the development and completion of this text:

Connie Craft has been an educator and children's advocate for more than 35 years. She has a B.S. Ed. Degree from the University of Georgia and a masters in early childhood education from West Georgia College. She began her career as a public school teacher and later became co-owner and president of Learning Tree of America, Inc. She does training and consulting and has been active in numerous state and national organizations.

Sandra Duncan has more than 40 years experience in the early childhood field. She has been the national advertising director for Scholastic's Early Childhood Today and publishing and editorial director for *Early Childhood News*. She has been involved in developing on-site child care centers and involved in the Indiana AEYC where she received the Lakeporte Association for the Education of Young Children Distinguished Service Award in recognition of exceptional leadership and devoted service.

Ira Dury received his B.A. in Government & Politics from University of Maryland and his M.A. in Business Organization from Duke University. He is a business professional who counts among his successes the start up and development of four companies; three child care service related entities providing early childhood and after-school educational programs and one management consulting company which provided support to healthcare companies on a national basis. He has held the position of vice president in two university based teaching hospitals and received a Fellowship in the American College of Health Care Executives. Often he has been called on to serve the early childhood profession on state and national committees.

Jim Loving has held various management positions in both the public and private sectors. He has more than 35 years experience working in human service programs including programs for incarcerated juveniles, hospital-based psychiatric services, and residential programs for people with developmental disabilities. Mr. Loving has worked as Director of Government Relations for ARAMARK Educational Resources and served both as assistant director and director of the Minnesota Department of Human Services in Regulatory Reform. He is past president of the National Child Care Association, has served on the Early Care and Education Consortium, and currently serves on many state and national boards.

Joan Nichol is a graduate of the University of Utah and is the owner of three early care and education centers in Utah. She has more than 30 years experience in early childhood education and is co-founder of a training organization for educators and leaders in early childhood education.

Roger Neugebauer holds a masters degree in day care administration and publishes the *Child Care Information Exchange,* a management magazine for directors of early childhood programs. *Exchange* is published every two months and daily on the internet. Mr. Neugebauer has served on the governing board of the National Child Care and Resource and Referral Agencies and on national advisory panels including the National Early Childhood Policy Study of the National Association of State Boards of Education and the National Study on the Costs and Quality of Early Childhood Care and Education. He volunteers as a board member for several schools in the Seattle area.

Eric Perkerson has been a member of the State Bar of Georgia since 1987. He has served as guardian ad litem for the Juvenile Court of Gwinnett County, representing abused children and representing children of divorcing parents. He is a member of the Family Law Criminal Law and Fiduciary Law Sections of the state bar. Mr. Perkerson speaks frequently at continuing legal education seminars on topics concerning juvenile justice.

Paul Reilly is a consultant and former President of Magic Years Child Care and Learning Centers. He has extensive background in corporately-sponsored child care as well as community based centers operations.

Andre Ransom-Sampson has a B.A. in political science from Xavier University in Chicago and a master of urban affairs degree from the University of Colorado. She has been the owner and founder of three business related to the early childhood education field serving children ages zero to 16, and pioneered before and after school care in Colorado. She was a founding member and past president of the Early Childhood Education Association of Colorado and has been appointed by two different governors to serve on state commissions. She currently does start up and management consulting in the early childhood education field, legislative liaison work, presents at national conferences and participates in various local, state, and national boards concerned with early childhood education, urban redevelopment, and micro enterprise including the National Child Care Association.

Mark Walsh owns a child care consulting firm which assists clients in child care center acquisitions, sales center marketing, and general services relating to the industry. Mr. Walsh is the former president and CEO of Apple-A-Daycare Centers located in upstate New York. He has served as president of the New York Child Care Association and on the board of directors of the New York Governor's Advisory Committee on Child Care. Mr. Walsh has also served on the board of the National Child Care Association and presenter at conferences on management concerns.

We also wish to acknowledge the following persons for contribution to the first text: **The Georgia Child Care Council** for financial support, **Joe Pereault** focus group facilitator and manuscript reviewer, **Dr. Ken Scheiderman** former President of California Health and Sciences for format assistance, **Marsha Gates** Georgia Department of Human Resources, Child Care Licensing, **Michelle Cook**, Policy Associate with United Cerebral Palsy

Associations for review of the American With Disabilities Act information, **Michael Daley** for review of portions of the legal section, **Suzanne Grace** for editing, and **The Georgia Child Care Leadership Forum** for fully developing the course and tes.

Made in the USA
Middletown, DE
20 November 2024

64951334R00183